P9-DVJ-371

Strategic Choices for the Academy

Daniel James Rowley

Herman D. Lujan

Michael G. Dolence

Foreword by Robert H. Atwell

⧟ Strategic Choices for the Academy

How Demand for Lifelong Learning Will Re-Create Higher Education

Jossey-Bass Publishers
San Francisco

Copyright © 1998 by Jossey-Bass Inc., Publishers, 350 Sansome Street, San Francisco, California 94104.

All rights reserved. No part of this publication may be reproduced, stored in a retrieval system, or transmitted, in any form or by any means, electronic, mechanical, photocopying, recording, or otherwise, without the prior written permission of the publisher.

Substantial discounts on bulk quantities of Jossey-Bass books are available to corporations, professional associations, and other organizations. For details and discount information, contact the special sales department at Jossey-Bass Inc., Publishers (415) 433–1740; fax (800) 605–2665.

For sales outside the United States, please contact your local Simon & Schuster International Office.

Jossey-Bass Web address: http://www.josseybass.com

Manufactured in the United States of America using Lyons Falls D'Anthology paper, which is a special blend of non-tree fibers and totally chlorine-free wood pulp.

Library of Congress Cataloging-in-Publication Data

Rowley, Daniel James
    Strategic choices for the academy : how demand for lifelong
learning will re-create higher education / Daniel James Rowley,
Herman D. Lujan, Michael G. Dolence.—1st ed.
      p.   cm.—(The Jossey-Bass higher and adult education series)
    Includes bibliographical references (p.) and index.
    ISBN 0-7879-4067-4 (hardcover : alk. paper)
    1. Education, Higher—Aims and objectives—United States.
2. Continuing education—United States.   I. Lujan, Herman D.
II. Dolence, Michael G.   III. Title.   IV. Series.
LA227.4.R69   1998
378.73—dc21   97-44074

FIRST EDITION
HB Printing 10 9 8 7 6 5 4 3 2 1

The Jossey-Bass
Higher and Adult Education Series

Contents

—⁓— Foreword

One hears and reads contradictory voices about American higher education. On the one hand, we are told that our colleges and universities are the envy of the world and, on the other hand, that they are stodgy and resistant to necessary changes. To some extent, perhaps both assertions are true. The reality is that almost anything one wishes to say in praise or in denunciation of these remarkably diverse institutions is true of some places on some days. It is the diversity that makes generalizations so difficult, and yet the necessity to offer the crucial nuances makes it almost impossible to say anything useful about the enterprise as a whole.

Compounding the problem is that we are plagued with a single model of excellence in higher education, that being the major national research university. There are no more than fifty of these national treasures in the United States, yet too many other institutions are inappropriately striving to emulate them. Instead, we in the academy need multiple models of excellence, reflecting quite different but equally worthy missions and accomplishments. Many years of working with institutions so divergent from each other as to render value judgments meaningless have convinced me that a comprehension of the range of institutional purposes is central to an understanding and truer appreciation of American higher education.

The authors of this book have performed an immense service for higher education in a reasoned documentation of the forces pushing for radical change in the delivery of educational opportunities. The book examines the steps being taken by a range of institutions to effectuate change. With years of experience as administrators and faculty members, the authors combine the theoretical with the practical. Particularly useful are the myriad illustrations of the changing face of American higher education.

Indeed, this book is a testimonial to the resilience of the enterprise. At the same time, it recognizes that there is a long road ahead if we are to become a less producer-centered and more learner-centered enterprise.

ROBERT H. ATWELL
President Emeritus
American Council of Education

⟁⟋ Preface

The dawning of the twenty-first century has been called the Information Age, the Knowledge Age, and the Age of Learning. The terms may be different, but the intent of all of them is clear. They signal a radical shift in the mental model of the new millennium.

There is a much more basic indicator of this shift, however, one that is more personal, more compelling, even more profound. It is the answer to this simple question: If you want to learn something, *when* do you want to learn it, and *how* do you want to learn it? We have asked this question to over fifteen thousand educators over the past year in interviews, workshops, keynotes, and plenary speeches throughout the world. The thunderous response is always: *right now,* and as conveniently as possible! We believe that these responses define the primary design criteria for education as we move into the twenty-first century.

In this new era, time is the master. Everyone not only needs access to information but also needs to keep up with the ever-changing nature of the knowledge bases. Although many learners will continue to expect their colleges and universities to provide them with the type of education their parents received in the last half of the twentieth century, many more will expect their colleges and universities to be more responsive to their increasing knowledge needs. Many learners who need college educations will want alternatives to the traditional models, alternatives that will provide them with learning opportunities when and where they want them. In the new age, such opportunities will be available. Indeed, even in this period of transition, many of these opportunities are available already. As we enter a new millennium and into the new economies of the emerging information age, these demands will certainly increase and will pose several fundamental and imposing strategic questions to the academy.

How should today's colleges and universities respond to this change in demand? What are the needs of today's learners, and more important, tomorrow's learners? Can the academy continue to lead the creation of knowledge, or is it in danger of losing its franchise? What forms should education take, and how should it cultivate an ability to deliver new knowledge effectively throughout our shrinking world? How should the professorate prepare for the learning and research demands of the new age? What will happen to the traditional campus? How will technology aid the growth of the academy? Will it kill those institutions that refuse to meet the needs and demands of the emerging world economies? What comes after the Internet, and how will that impact colleges and universities of the twenty-second and twenty-third centuries?

These questions, and many others like them, represent a call to action that, happily, has not gone unanswered by educators from around the world. As we write, there are over ten thousand courses already indexed on the World Wide Web and over fifty virtual universities either on-line or in design. Clearly, faculty get it. Even more clearly, they are acting on their insights. The new academy is emerging, an academy that is more diverse, more streamlined, and characterized by more innovation and risk taking. It is moving from being provider-centered to being more learner-centered to meet the needs of the rapidly growing worldwide knowledge society.

SCOPE OF THIS BOOK

Clearly, we are living in a time when all of the economies of the world are undergoing a dramatic and intensely threatening series of changes. These changes are the result of a major paradigm shift, which is occurring as the industrial age comes to a close and the information age emerges to take its place. No one is exempt from the impact of these changes. As technology, communication, and travel continue to shrink our world, and as organizations of all types struggle to keep pace with a dizzying level of emerging challenges and opportunities, the economy is shifting, and the implications of those shifts are as yet unclear and for many, they are frightening. The academy is part of this change process and must take a position of leadership as the new age defines itself.

Yet, not all colleges and universities are participants in the development of this new era of knowledge generation and knowledge transference. Many hold to the concept that they have a right to exist just as they are and that they should be the only determiners of what the knowledge base of the world's society should be. This is unfortunate. The rest of the world no longer shares this view. As we discussed in our previous book, *Strategic Change in Colleges and Universities* (1997), those campuses that refuse to change with the changes in their environments risk losing everything. Today, we see that across the country (and across the world), exactly such an outcome is occurring already.

On the other hand, there are many colleges and universities that are seeing pathways of change that make sense for their missions of teaching, research, and service. They are starting to pave the way to the educational activities of the future. And that future *will* be different. For example, Pascarella and Terenzini tell us, "Considerable evidence exists to suggest that certain individualized instructional approaches or systems that emphasize small, modularized units of content, mastery of one unit before moving to the next, immediate and frequent feedback, . . . active student involvement in the learning process are consistently effective in enhancing subject matter learning over more traditional instructional formats such as lecture and recitation" (1991, p. 109). Responding to such evidence, many colleges and universities are starting today to reshape themselves and their directions into the future. New learners are more sophisticated and demanding than their predecessors, and entire new forms of education are starting to emerge to provide more effective responses.

From the growing presence of the virtual universities to the radical changes in traditional classrooms, where challenges to seat time and economically-based course structures are making way for new and exciting ways of learning, change is on its way. It is exciting and it is challenging. But this change is also a determinant of success. For each campus, the opportunities and threats associated with this changing external environment provide the basis for creating a strategic plan that will help that campus better achieve an effective fit within those environments. On some campuses, the resulting changes may seem minuscule, as those particular colleges or universities are already well along their way toward achieving a good strategic fit. For others, the changes will be dramatic and wrenching, as they find that in order to survive in the exciting yet unforgiving environments of the information age, fundamental shifts in philosophy and style will be necessary.

We have written this book to bring more clarity to the issues surrounding the emergence of the information age as it affects the academy. Building on the strategic planning model we presented in our earlier book (Rowley, Lujan, and Dolence, 1997), we look at the external environment of higher education and try to elucidate the complex challenges that come with the paradigm shift from the industrial society to the knowledge society. We also look at the internal environments of colleges and universities as they seek to define their purposes anew, align their capabilities with their sparse resource bases, and find a niche in the new age of higher education.

WHO SHOULD READ THIS BOOK?

We believe that *Strategic Choices for the Academy* should be read by the leaders in higher education, both academic and administrative. We attempt to identify the strategic options that all such leaders will need to consider as they view both their academic and their administrative programs of the future. Presidents, chancellors, vice presidents, vice-chancellors, deans, department chairs, and faculty governance leaders need to be directly involved with the changes that are coming their way as the academy shifts to meet the demands of the new world. Governing boards, classroom educators, and campus researchers should also consider the issues discussed here as they map out both the methods and the means of their responsibilities in the future, a future that will be different from the protected academic world so many enjoy today. Policymakers, governmental decision makers, and funding agencies should also pay attention to the issues discussed here, because of the close partnerships that exist between them and the college and university campuses for which they are responsible. Finally, anyone interested in learning more about the direction that higher education needs to take in a worldwide economy that is redefining itself to meet the demands of a new age will benefit from examining the issues discussed here.

ORGANIZATION OF THIS BOOK

The book is organized into three parts. Part One looks at the several bases of change and how they affect the academy. Colleges and universities cannot resist the forces for change, though many try. In Part One, we examine the forces that have propelled change on society as a whole and on the academy in particular. These are powerful forces, and the speed and relentlessness with which they have entered the picture demand a considered response. We also examine several of the sectors both on and off the campus that seek to resist these forces and how campus leadership can work to overcome the negative effects of these sectors. Most important, we identify the nature of the new knowledge society and the needs of the new learner, who is an integral part of that new society.

Part Two looks at the many trends and emerging models that are already in place, both in the United States and around the world. The information age is not just an American event, it is a worldwide event. Even though the United States continues to lead the world in the development of educational bases and methods, it is important to see the different approaches to establishing more effective educational interchanges that are emerging, regardless of the sources of those new models. We look at the growing importance of technology as a medium for providing education to a larger and larger number of information age learners. We look at a variety of applications, some already in place, some in development. There are also other models, which are being developed outside the traditional academy. They are being developed in the proprietary and corporate universities, which are growing and gaining a foothold in the traditional niches that the academy has dominated for centuries. We also look at many innovations that several of today's colleges and universities are developing and are finding successful, as they seek to provide better access to and transference of their growing knowledge bases to the knowledge society.

Part Three sketches the future as seen through the eyes of the authors of this book. The trends, the applications, the shifting nature of the learner, and the new methods that are emerging and will continue to emerge, all of these present the backdrop for a series of models that we develop for the academy (as we believe it will be) of the future. We believe that the future will hold a series of models, not a single monolithic standard of higher education that can be superimposed, cookie-cutter style, from one campus onto the next. Individuality, innovation, and creativity will all be the hallmarks of the models that each campus will evaluate and adapt, as it determines its most appropriate strategic direction for the future.

The future is both a threatening and an exciting place. We believe that strategic planning is the only effective means of building a bridge between the place where many colleges and universities find themselves today and the place where they will all need to go in the future. By developing a more comprehensive understanding of the complex environments of the emerging information age and the knowledge society and preparing to cope with the changes that will come, we can move to the future of higher education, a future that can prove to be exciting and prosperous. The keys are all there. The decision to aim for success, as well as the decision not even to try, are also there. By gaining a greater knowledge about what the future holds and by employing a proficient strategic planning system, every college and university can effectively map out a future for itself that will help it survive and prosper.

Greeley, Colorado	DANIEL JAMES ROWLEY
Evans, Colorado	HERMAN D. LUJAN
Claremont, California	MICHAEL G. DOLENCE

January 1998

───ᴡᴡ─── The Authors

Daniel James Rowley is currently a professor of management in the College of Business Administration at the University of Northern Colorado (UNC). Between the years 1992 and 1995, he took a leave of absence from teaching and joined the president's office to head the development of a strategic planning process at UNC. During this time, he also served the university as chief of staff and secretary to UNC's board of trustees. In his capacity as the strategic planner, he oversaw the development of strategic planning at the university, division, college, and unit levels. He worked directly with the UNC board of trustees in developing and approving strategic management policy for the university. He also helped formulate strategic priorities, which helped guide the development of UNC's budgets during this time.

In 1995, he returned to the classroom to resume his teaching, writing, and consulting activities. He is currently working with other universities, school districts, and nonprofit organizations in their strategic planning efforts. He is cofounder and past president of the Institute of Behavioral and Applied Management, a national, academic professional organization for management professors, students, and practitioners. He is sole author or lead author of several journal articles on the subjects of business management and strategic planning. He has also given several national presentations on these subjects. Working with UNC's president, Herman D. Lujan, and Michael G. Dolence of Michael G. Dolence and Associates, Rowley was lead author for a chapter on strategic enrollment management in a scholarly casebook for the American Association of Collegiate Registrars and Admissions Officers. Going beyond his experience in business strategic planning, his efforts at UNC have helped to design a unique system that fits the needs and characteristics of public higher education. This has resulted in growing national interest. Rowley received his bachelor's degree at the University of Colorado at Boulder in political science. He earned a master's degree in public administration at the University of Denver and a doctorate in organizational management and strategic management at the University of Colorado at Boulder. He and his wife Barbara are the parents of one daughter, Rebecca.

Herman D. Lujan is president emeritus and distinguished professor of business and public policy at the University of Northern Colorado. In his tenure as president from 1991 to 1996, he established UNC as a teaching university whose first priority is to serve Colorado with high-quality undergraduate programs. In addition, he brought new energy and direction to the university in its role as one of twenty-nine Doctoral I universities in the country. In 1992, he initiated a campuswide strategic planning process designed to identify and better focus campus resources to help the university build on its strengths and develop a stronger fit with the needs of Colorado and the Rocky Mountain region. In addition, he launched a series of programs to help increase and improve the diversity of UNC's faculty, staff, and student body.

Lujan's career in higher education began at the University of Kansas, where he was a faculty member in political science and an administrator for thirteen years. He was the director of the university's Institute for Social and Environmental Studies from 1972–1979. He took a one-year leave in 1974–1975 to serve as director of the Division of State Planning and Research in the Kansas governor's office. Immediately prior to coming to UNC, Lujan served as vice provost at the University of Washington. In all, he spent thirteen years at the University of Washington as a faculty member and administrator. He served as vice president for minority affairs before becoming vice provost in 1988. He has worked on more than thirty research grant projects and has published numerous scholarly articles and books. He serves in several civic, educational, and charitable organizations nationwide. He is active in the American Council of Education, the American Association of State Colleges and Universities, and the National Association of State Universities and Land Grant Colleges.

Lujan is a native of Hawaii and holds a bachelor's degree in political science from St. Mary's College in California, a master's degree, also in political science, from the University of California at Berkeley, and a doctorate in political science from the University of Idaho. He and his wife Carla are the parents of three children and the grandparents of six.

Michael G. Dolence is president of Michael G. Dolence and Associates. He consults with higher education institutions, systems, associations, and vendors nationally. He is a specialist in organizational transformation; strategic positioning; institutional strategic planning; strategic enrollment management; information technology planning; and management processes that link planning to budgeting, academic transformation, public advocacy, and public relations. He is a nationally acclaimed keynote speaker on these subjects.

Dolence has served as strategic planning administrator for the California State University at Los Angeles; director of research, planning, and policy analysis for the Commission on Independent Colleges and Universities; founding director of the New York State Public Opinion Poll; and founding director of the Science, Engineering, and Research Campus Hook-up.

As a consultant, Dolence has worked with numerous institutions of higher education nationally to develop campuswide strategic planning processes and strategic enrollment management programs with a special emphasis on crisis avoidance and crisis intervention. He consults on strategies to respond to state and federal initiatives as well as to reposition institutions to enhance their competitiveness. He has also worked with information system vendors in the development of state-of-the-art strategic enrollment and instructional management systems.

During the time he served as strategic planning administrator at California State University at Los Angeles, Dolence had the opportunity to implement a campuswide strategic planning process as well as to guide the development of an integrated planning and budgeting system. In addition, he has had extensive experience in developing the tactical plans necessary to implement a strategic management system in a university of twenty-two thousand students.

Dolence has authored numerous publications and has made many presentations before such national audiences as the Society for College and University Planning, the American Association of Collegiate Registrars and Admissions Officers, the American Association for Higher Education, CAUSE, and EDUCOM. He is a member of Who's Who Worldwide, Who's Who in American Education, and is listed in the Who's Who Registry of Global Business Leaders. He and his wife, Maryann, have a son, Michael, and a daughter, Katie.

Strategic Choices for the Academy

PART ONE

The Bases for Change

CHAPTER ONE

Pressures on Higher Education in the Information Age

A s the twentieth century draws to a close, the world we live in is evolving rapidly. An explosion in communications and transportation has shrunk the world, changing it from a collection of autonomous and semi-independent states into a consortium of inter-acting and interdependent neighbors. As communication and trans-portation have shrunk our world, technology, because of its growing importance and use, has contributed to a general paradigm shift from what we have known as the "industrial age" to a new "information age." This change is marked by a shift in the world economy from the production of goods and related services to the generation of ideas and information processes (Rost, 1993). Ideas and information drive the new global economy.

THE NEW AGE

This shift is basic and endemic. It is changing the economic, political, and social structures that historically have controlled the ways in which populations have lived, worked, traded, and interacted with each other. Satellites, e-mail, CD-ROM, and the Internet have revolutionized how we communicate, move goods and services, and create new knowledge as we go (Kearsley, 1985). This shift is bringing about changes at an ever increased tempo. In business, some companies now make their own products obsolete to maintain the leading edge in their competitive niche.

To survive this shift, many business organizations have moved rapidly not only to adapt to the rate and substance of today's changes but also to create benchmarks that set the pace for others. The road maps and road signs in this race to set the pace are being rewritten almost daily. Microsoft, Intel, Netscape, and Yahoo are examples of major innovative companies that are leading the rest of the world into a future where change will be ongoing. In this new world, one thing is certain: enterprises will atrophy if they do not move beyond the comfort of the traditional niches they have forged for themselves in the industrial age to a point where they can fashion new ideas and forms of competition for the information age (London, 1987). Again, one can find several interesting examples in business. Apple Computer's ongoing battle with Microsoft, IBM's sluggish shift to the personal computer, and Wang's misadventures in the chaotic field of personal computers are prime examples of companies that appear sometimes to be faltering as they seek ways to survive in this complexifying world. As Leslie and Fretwell (1996) have suggested, colleges and universities are not immune to these changes. In-house customized computer programming has been the approach taken by many universities. Most of these systems have been displaced by desktop software. Automated human resource and student information systems also abound. Electronic classrooms exist that use e-mail and chat spaces for on-line learning.

In the face of this paradigm shift, some organizations are choosing to ignore these new forces. They cling to the hope that autonomy will buffer them or that successful management practices of the past will also serve the needs of the present and the future (Williams, 1995). As the world has shrunk, however, the door of competition has opened wider. Now, all types of organizations—business, service, for profit, not for profit, and government—are all being thrust into an environment where change is more than a periodic aggravation necessary for catching up. Change and adaptation are a constant—for in a world full of information, old news is no news.

Again, it appears that companies like Microsoft, Intel, and Netscape are recognizing these irreversible shifts and are helping shape them.

These companies understand the importance of providing new and better ways of creating, collecting, and organizing information from every corner of the globe. They do so in ways that permit information users to learn both more quickly and more efficiently. Consequently, a new competitiveness is emerging. It is based on being innovative, informed, and ahead of the pack in any given industry, including the knowledge industry and higher education (Peterson and Dill, 1997).

Although it makes us uneasy to refer to higher education as an industry and to compare universities to businesses so directly, we think it is necessary to view them that way because of two elements that concern us. The first is that in the information age, there will be winners and losers. Those who try to shape change and its effects on them will likely be the winners, and those who resist adapting will likely be among the losers. Both groups will have to contend with the organized anarchy and loose confederation of elements that increasingly characterize higher education (Peterson and Dill, 1997). Second, we firmly believe that no one and no organization can be exempt from the demand for new knowledge or the speed with which responses to the demand must occur. In this frenzy for information, it worries us that quality reflective reasoning, thoughtful assessment, and critical analyses—all of which are at the core of higher education— run the risk of being smothered by the sheer volume of information. As one of history's primary creators of knowledge, the institution of higher education has a special challenge to retain its leadership in generating knowledge and to subject that knowledge to the scrutiny of mind and method that sorts fad from fact and the trivial from the true.

IMPACT ON HIGHER EDUCATION

This shift from reflection to rapidity and from finite data to volumes of specific information poses challenges to how we learn. Whereas a survey course used to require four or five major sources, today the range and volume of relevant information is geometrically larger. Education is reflective learning, a process we use to sift through facts and theories, posing questions that help us distinguish truth and explanation from the appearance of truth and explanation. This fosters comprehension. As Fosnot (1989) notes, learning consists of interpreting information, not just storing it. This interpretation is at the core of learning and scholarship and is the fundamental reason for higher education. Understanding the reflective nature of learning also helps clarify how learners learn, how they act on the information they receive and, stimulated by teaching and research, give it interpretation that can be scrutinized by others. Reflection such as this takes time, and time is a luxury in the information age. The consequence is the need to stretch learning from a discrete into a continual activity, thus the growing importance of lifelong learning and the need for colleges and universities to forge those links as a necessary element of a proper and enabling education (Harasim, 1990).

Quick and decisive action is often required in order to ensure a competitive advantage and organizational success. For colleges and universities, competition is on the rise; some are taking too much time to recognize the paradigm shifts, formulate competitive responses, and implement change. This may mean a significant loss not only in the service base of these colleges and universities but also in the ability of some to survive at all.

The call for appropriate and effective action and response is occurring everywhere, including at the highest levels of government. In his second presidential inaugural address on January 20, 1997, Bill Clinton made the following argument: "At the dawn of the twenty-first century, a free people must choose to shape the forces of the information age and the global society, to unleash the limitless potential of all our people." He also stated, "In this new land, education will be every citizen's most prized possession. Our schools will have the highest standards in the world, igniting the spark of possibility in the eyes of every girl and every boy. And the doors of higher education will be open to all. The knowledge and power of the information age will be within reach not just to the few, but of every classroom, every library, every child." These statements focus on the challenge to extend knowledge through education to everyone, in ways that make access and competency a routine part of how citizens deal with information.

This book explores the learning needs of a society that approaches information differently, the opportunities and constraints posed by rapidly changing technology, and ways that higher education is responding to these forces. We focus on how planning strategically and practically can assist colleges and universities in shaping the future. As we address these matters, we offer scenarios and sketches of what the universities and colleges of the future may look like, underscoring our view that higher education will respond individually to its varying constituencies, resulting in a variety of institutions better able to meet the wider range of learning needs among lifelong learners.

FORCES OF CHANGE

Things *are* changing. Demographically, the United States will change dramatically over the next several years, according to demographics expert Harold Hodgkinson (1992). Among other things, he predicts that by 2010, 30 to 40 percent of all U.S. jobs will require a college education and will be well paying. But 30 percent of the jobs will continue to be held by the working poor. He also predicts that by 2010, people we currently refer to as minorities will account for over 50 percent of the population, shifting the meaning of the term *minority* for the first time in U.S. history. Much of what we consider today to be issues of race may well become issues of class in the future.

The same changes will affect any manager, whether in a business or in a college or university (such as an academic department chair). The changes that accompany the information age will confront the academy with choices, not all of which will be readily apparent. Because these changes are emergent, the unknown plays a big part in them. This means that choices may sometimes have to be made without complete information. The shift from the industrial age model of production, in which relative certainty was essential for mass production, to an information age model, in which intuition, creativity, and reasoned approximation may displace that certainty, is profoundly challenging. The shift will complicate strategic thinking and challenge colleges and universities to overcome the reticence to risk that characterizes fear of the unknown.

Changing Role of Higher Education

As we have pointed out before (Rowley, Lujan, and Dolence, 1997), colleges and universities have been around for centuries and have been crucial in the development of knowledge, the education of millions, and the improvement of the overall standard of living. In the industrial age, they experienced rapid growth, as society found that it needed to have a more highly skilled and educated workforce to help guide the development of industrialization around the world (Dolence and Norris, 1995). An educated workforce was also required to provide appropriate management and other expertise to help the industrial economy prosper. The growth of liberal arts colleges, land grant colleges and universities, comprehensive colleges and universities, and research universities meant that higher education became available to more and more people, who then became leaders in industry, education, government, and all other sectors of society.

Society rewarded the service of higher education (educating people to serve industrial age roles), and support for colleges and universities was easily forthcoming and very generous. Carnevale (1991) tells us that the standards for the industrial age included quality, customization, convenience, customer service, and timeliness. As long as colleges and universities provided their services along these lines, they prospered. Up through the 1970s, the worth of a college education was without question, and growth in higher education continued at a pace above many other sectors of the economy, particularly in the United States.

Although an often-stated goal of American education was to achieve 100 percent literacy, this was never a goal that consciously included higher education. As a society, the United States has not yet reached that literacy goal, and emerging literacy remains a national effort (Davidson, 1988). At the same time, only about 10 percent of the population have ever received any form of higher education. Higher education has not viewed this modest percent as a failure, however. For one thing, to provide economic leadership, only a small percentage of the population of the industrial age was required to achieve the advanced skills and knowledge that come from a college or university education. The academy met those requirements. The balance of the population, those without college degrees, served as the workers of the industrial age and raised the families that produced those workers. Reserving college for the best, the brightest, and the few worked both economically and socially. However, this is one of the basic changes that the information age is making, and the implications of this change are significant for higher education.

The 1980s and the 1990s signaled the beginning of this change as the general regard for the academy diminished. The Western Interstate Commission for Higher Education (WICHE) states that 1991 was the first year that thirty states appropriated less than they had in the previous year (1992a). This trend has continued through the 1990s. It is not uncommon for states to spend more on prisons than they do on higher education. As the politics of the developed world has become more conservative, more and more taxpayers and the government officials they have elected seriously question the resources they have traditionally allocated to higher education in all forms. Some have even begun to question the quality of the graduates and other academic results of a college education.

As Davies (1997) points out, public colleges and universities are coming more and more under attack from the political environment as the prioritization of state funding is such that higher education is now ranked below prisons, health care, and K–12 education. Worse, Davies tells us that several states, such as Virginia, are actively discouraging students from going on to higher education both as a way of saving money and as a reflection of the political movement that denies the current generation the same educational privileges that the older generation enjoyed. Davies sees that the impact of these movements will be the severe undercutting of the power and influence of publicly funded colleges and universities and the elimination of the "cartels" that higher education systems had been able to create over the past few decades (p. A68).

In a previous book (Rowley, Lujan, and Dolence, 1997), we discuss many of these issues. We suggest candid and careful strategic planning as a way to help institutions of higher education better fit the changing needs of society and address the desires of their constituents and stakeholders. In this book, we extend that discussion by suggesting that there are forces in the environment of the information age that equate survival with the need for a better and more broadly educated population. In addition to providing this population with proper training and up-to-date skills, an information age education must now cultivate an ability to abstract, analyze complexly, and extend present knowledge to new levels. In an age when knowledge and information predominate, those societies that are most broadly and best educated will thrive and lead this new age. Because information is so central, education will be far more critical than it has been in the industrial age. Providing information, knowledge, and the capacity to critique and generate new knowledge as we go is the challenge. Our future turns on how well we rise to the occasion and how effectively individual colleges and universities plan strategically to provide the necessary educational leadership.

It is important also to note that the information revolution began in the world of business, not in academia. Bill Gates left Harvard without his undergraduate degree to build Microsoft. An information age learner, he could not find what he needed in the curriculum. Unlike in the industrial age, when higher education was easily transformed to provide educated people to serve its needs, learners in the information age find the academy inadequate and slow to make the changes required in curriculum and pedagogy to serve their needs.

New Learning Needs

Carnevale (1991) tells us that one of the major hallmarks of the new age is that today's market is driven by a new consumer-like learner, one that demands high-quality, customized products and services, timely response, and convenience. Further, Thurow (1992) has suggested that competitors have been able to capture large segments of the market when they have adopted superior production technologies, improved the speed of production and quality control, and developed ways to keep costs as low as possible. As these two observers note, the needs of the information age are different from the needs of the industrial age, and this dramatically affects how colleges and universities do the work they do. WICHE (1992b) has suggested that as quantum changes occur in the workplace, the demand for higher-level skills increases for all workers. The information worker, whom we call the "knowledge worker," is therefore faced with workplace realities that the industrial worker was not faced with and new learning approaches and expectations that the traditional college student did not require. First, knowledge workers need to be highly educated to interface effectively with the technical and international components of their jobs. Second, knowledge workers interact with a wider variety of people and situations than their industrial age counterparts. This means that the education they receive should be more general and analytical than specialized and rote. Third, they require educational updating on a periodic basis, a basis that is itself becoming less and less periodic and more constant. This results in the necessity to learn continually and become a lifelong learner. Fourth, knowledge workers must be able to access updating and additional training on demand and in a variety of educational formats and methodologies. For example, an engineer and a scientist putting a space experiment together and facing a firm time line cannot wait for the definitive answer. They will have to scan present knowledge, consult, and improvise a solution. Fifth, knowledge workers need to develop their flexibility, so that as the dimensions of their jobs change, they can change right along with them. This maintains their value to their employers.

These needs of the knowledge worker present several challenges to today's colleges and universities. There are challenges to traditional degree-granting systems, as students move between work and the classroom and cross several disciplines. There are challenges to the classroom as the primary method for knowledge transfer. Chodorow (1996) tells us how students now take advantage of powerful computers and Internet facilities that allow them to learn at their own pace. He also laments that the traditional academy is responding slowly to this new avenue for learning. The new learners have major concerns and expectations regarding the curriculum and its relevance, including the link to the workplace, the call by employers for critical thinking and analysis, the interest in transdisciplinary learning, and the interest in a shorter time to degree.

Knowledge workers as learners pose an array of concerns, which center around how they connect with the campus. New learners find themselves characterized as part-time, full-time, traditional, nontraditional, lifelong, electronic, and global. There are students who are residents, students seeking distance education, students seeking degrees, students seeking continuing education. The meaning of these categories is not the issue. The inadequacy of these categories to characterize these students in terms of their learning needs is the issue.

New learners and their needs are discussed at length in Chapter Five. The point we wish to make here is that understanding their needs, describing them accurately, revising what colleges and universities offer in the curriculum, as well as how education is delivered, are strategic essentials for an adapting institution. In addition, any strategic response to these needs should distinguish between what is essentially job training and what is education as a process that develops the ability to recognize, parse, and critically analyze information and phenomena.

Alternatives to the Academy

None of these are easy matters to resolve. Since the Renaissance, the academy has been the major repository of human learning. Its truths and wisdom have been painstakingly built over the centuries. Its changes have not come easily. The battles involving the Inquisition, Galileo, Copernicus, Columbus, Einstein, and the atom were all raspy and clamorous. But the result has been the steady and comprehensive growth of human understanding. It is no wonder that the academy can be a doubting Thomas at times, wanting proofs before it adapts. It is not obstinacy of dogma but rather the measured skepticism—wariness of fads and quick conclusions—that is essential to protect the core of human knowledge.

The problem becomes more complicated as we begin to discover that business is not waiting for traditional higher education to catch up. Many businesses, such as IBM, Intel, Motorola, and even McDonald's have created their own "universities" to provide remedial education and training for their own people in order to serve corporate needs better. Such proprietary training is a controlled response focused on specific job skills. Are these a threat to the academy? Maybe yes, maybe no. They are a threat in that they take away certain learners from colleges and universities, based on the supposition that these learners cannot get the information they need from an academic institution. They are not a threat in that these programs concentrate more on training, which is not a primary goal of the academy, and they seldom engage in academic research. Regardless, these company "universities" represent a new player on the block, a player who could become more and more of a challenge in the future.

Further, some less traditional institutions of higher education are entering direct competition with the traditional core of colleges and universities and are offering alternatives to knowledge workers for both gaining a college education and extending that education. The University of Phoenix is a fascinating example of a nontraditional member of the academy addressing these matters. It is moving rapidly to fill an ever expanding void for knowledge workers who cannot get into a traditional college or university, because they may be deemed unqualified, or they may not have the necessary time to attend a traditional campus program. Phoenix also serves the knowledge worker who needs to update his or her knowledge or just take one or two particular courses without getting involved in a full degree program. Its willingness to offer training and skills, as distinct from an in-depth education, makes it more responsive to the short-term needs of new learners.

Another nontraditional alternative is the virtual university. Currently, several college and university initiatives worldwide are developing and implementing virtual learning through the Internet and the World Wide Web. For example, the Western Governors Association (WGA) in 1996 proposed a virtual university in twenty-one western U.S. states (Western Interstate Commission for Higher Education,

1996). Even though the proposal has been scaled back, as of April 1997, the Western Governors University now includes fourteen participating states (Alaska, Arizona, Colorado, Hawaii, Idaho, Montana, Nebraska, Nevada, New Mexico, North Dakota, Oregon, Utah, Washington, and Wyoming), and the Territory of Guam, with the governors of Colorado and Utah taking the lead. Each of those states has now put up at least $100,000 to begin implementing the project with the cooperation of some twenty-one initial colleges and universities within their borders. The WGA Virtual University has so far picked up some strong corporate sponsors, including Sun Computers, AT&T, and the William and Flora Hewlett Foundation, which add strength to the project and will help raise the $25 million the project will need to fund its first eight to nine years of operation (Western Interstate Commission for Higher Education, 1997).

Jones University, a corporate university, is part of a communications firm that has decided not to rely on traditional institutions but rather to become creator and supplier of information tools and to provide a degree-seeking program for knowledge workers and other new learners. In June 1997, it graduated its first student.

SOME RESPONSES FROM THE ACADEMY

Some traditional institutions are also responding. The National Association of State Universities and Land Grant Colleges (NASULGC) is focusing on lifelong learning as a key element in its reformation of undergraduate education and the land grant mission. The Mid-Atlantic Consortium of ten higher education institutions is a collaborative partnership designed to address the educational needs of new stakeholders in higher education. The Kellogg Commission on the Future of State and Land Grant Universities is looking specifically at ways to address the needs of new learners and the evolving link between universities and their constituents.

To put the situation more succinctly, the information age is spawning its own educational system with and without the participation of the members of the traditional academy. There are some colleges and universities that realize this and are looking into the requirements of the information age and developing impressive techniques for dealing with them. For example, the University of Pittsburgh is designing a unique technological architecture system throughout the campus, which will integrate the entire campus—academics, student affairs, and campus administration—into an enterprise-wide information architectural system (Laudato and DeSantis, 1996). Likewise, the University of Rochester is developing a data management system that will have campuswide usage and have implications for an integrated system no longer dependent on the campus mainframe (Stewart, 1996). The University of California at Los Angeles (UCLA), recognizing the possibilities that the new technologies offer, is beginning a major program to use computer technology not only to link various parts of the campus together in an integrated system but also to develop programs that will significantly improve teaching and learning without being confined to the classroom (Wilson, 1996).

These examples make the important point that innovative initiatives are occurring in colleges and universities. As Ravenche (1996) has suggested, today's colleges and universities are uniquely positioned to develop crucial partnerships with external industrial partners, because these business enterprises have the capacity to train, to identify strong business practices, to use technology effectively, and to help in developing effective marketing methods. Cohen (1994) calls attention to the emergence of a network of scholars, government researchers, and private sector specialists who come together to deal with issues of common interest such as global warming. They cross disciplines and sectors to learn about and address the issue of concern. These interest groups form "web nests," where valuable new information resides and is readily available. Activities like this reflect the great potential for scholars to stimulate and shape knowledge in the new era. Both Cohen and Ravenche underscore how the information age creates the impetus to break down the barriers of specialization and cross boundaries to create new knowledge. Individual colleges and universities participate in these knowledge-generating activities primarily through their faculty and new learners.

Global Learning

Certainly, one of the areas in which colleges and universities are taking initiative is in internationalizing the educational experience to improve literacy about the entire world in which we live. NASULGC has long had ongoing mechanisms in its organization to focus on international education. Many colleges and universities are engaged in the expansion of their curriculum into a more international endeavor, using a number of different strategies (Cohen, 1997). First is the standard and longstanding strategy of international student exchanges. Students from campuses in different countries switch with their counterparts on campuses in other countries and study abroad as members of those campuses for a set period of time, usually a year. The participating campuses have agreements about the transferability of course credits earned during the international exchange, and most students can apply this experience toward their degree programs without adding additional time to their degree pursuits.

A more recent strategy is international recruiting. Here, campuses actively recruit in other countries for students to come to the host country for their entire student experience.

Another strategy involves establishing international campuses. Tufts University in Cambridge, Massachusetts, not only maintains its U.S. campus but has already established a second campus in France and as of this writing was busy establishing another campus in Asia. This strategy works with the students on all of its campuses, who can interchange their studies seamlessly as they move among the campuses.

An additional and growing strategy relates to international campus alliances. In this arrangement, two campuses in two different countries agree on a long-term relationship and create programs that take advantage of the particular strengths of each. For example, the University of Northern Colorado allies with Kaoshiung Municipal University in Taiwan so that students from Colorado can learn Chinese in Kaoshiung, and Taiwanese students from Kaoshiung can study special education and other sought-after majors at Colorado. Both students and faculty are part of the agreement. The programs of the two campuses are continual and relatively seamless for degree purposes.

There are other forms of establishing international relationships in the academy. The capacity to broaden the curriculum and the worthwhile experiences of the students and faculty who participate in these programs is impressive. For example, British Council members of the former commonwealth, such as Australia, have their governments vigorously promote their higher education institutions to foreign governments, not only for short-term revenue but also for seeding future alliances. As business continues to expand internationally, it is likely that this form of international academic programming will also expand.

At the core of global learning is best use of infrastructure. As we argue in this book, the key to shaping the future strategically is to build on distinction. In international scholarship and learning, this means that colleges and universities worldwide seek linkages and alliances that build on strengths and complement weaknesses so that balanced partnerships evolve and endure.

Facing a Shift in Leadership

The academy is not used to following societal development (Rothblatt, 1995). It is accustomed to leading it. Over the past hundred years, colleges and universities, particularly those in the United States, have been the center for the study and development of methods to better the human condition and add to the growing body of knowledge.

The information age has changed that to a significant degree. The internationalization of business, transportation, and communications has opened up new knowledge bases that mechanisms such as the Internet are exploiting as quickly as they are discovered. In order to support the demands of the rapidly increasing global economy, these knowledge bases are generally being moved into the intellectual mainstream *without* going through the academy (Dill and Sporn, 1995). For example, much of what business has developed and discovered in terms of multinational manufacturing and assembly has not been the subject of major study or development on college or university campuses. So far, the impacts of new developments on the economy, implications for national integrity, and influences on the modification of political institutions have occurred prior to study and interpretation by the academy.

The rapid changes emerging from the information age have had the effect of moving the impetus for developing new knowledge, especially in technology, away from the academy and into the world of commerce. The software explosion exemplifies this. For the first time since church and state split and education became secular, a major center for developing knowledge is rising outside the academy. This has occurred because the commercial sector needed to understand the new paradigms of the information age and would not wait for academia to do so. The result is that, especially in technology, a substantial body of current knowledge is being generated outside college and university campuses (Peterson, Dill, Mets, and Associates, 1997). This outside knowledge base is growing much more rapidly and pervasively than it would at an academic tempo, and in some areas, the academy is starting to fall behind.

The impact on the information age learner is profound. Those knowledge workers who need to update themselves on the nuances and methods of emerging work typologies are experiencing a variety of barriers to getting what they need from the academy. Many are experiencing difficulty finding programs or courses available on college or university campuses. If such programs are available, they may not be scheduled conveniently. In addition, many college and universities continue to raise the entry barriers to campus programs. The notable exceptions are adult education and continuing education programs, which generally do not provide full access to on-campus courses or faculty. Finally, many campuses require admission to a degree program in order to take advantage of certain learning experiences. These obstacles and conditions are leading new learners to start looking elsewhere (Gast, 1991).

Rethinking Access

We have already suggested that there are certain colleges and universities that are changing the traditional rules. But across the United States, Europe, Asia, and Australia, some colleges and universities are making it more difficult for potential students to enter their programs or even to take a course or two outside a degree program without satisfying prerequisite requirements. The academy must look again at this access issue. The American Association of State Colleges and Universities has focused on this matter for some time. Their concern is that the knowledge worker demands lifelong learning and expects the traditional seats of learning to accommodate these needs adequately. In the absence of meaningful access reform, the rapidly growing nontraditional sources of knowledge will continue to expand and establish their legitimacy. This is a source of competition the academy has never faced before, particularly on the scale that the information age will create. And in any competitive environment, the stiffer the competition becomes, the more likely it is that weak players in the game will not be able to survive intact.

Digital Learning Environment

Competition in the form of virtual universities and Internet access are already in place, and they are growing exponentially. As of this writing, a variety of professors from around the world have already created well over ten thousand different courses available through the Internet. Although they are currently disorganized (as is true of the Internet in general), nonstandardized, unregulated, unpredictable, unrelated in many instances to degree or certification programs, and of varying degrees of quality, the number of these courses will grow, their quality will improve, they will get organized, and they will become a powerful competitive reality. Today's smorgasbord education may be tomorrow's accepted degree—if the academy stands pat and does not engage this issue.

The proliferation of new educational opportunities is also worldwide. With the ease of access to the Internet, the courses available not only are created by a global professorate but also are viewed and taken by a worldwide audience (Gast, 1991). The professors who are creating and running these programs have seen the opportunities afforded to them by the Internet, and their success can be measured by the proliferation of courses and the growing interest of those who take them. This is an important resource for the knowledge worker. As the market mechanism kicks in, these learners will find it easier and easier to locate the knowledge bases they seek and will also discover ways of requesting customized training or learning opportunities (Mason and Kaye, 1989). They will eventually be able to have such opportunities created for them—on their own terms, in their own time, and from a growing list of high-quality educational providers, including some of the most prestigious professors from the most prestigious colleges and universities around the world.

Avoiding Exclusion

Another problem is the social threat technology poses. It could broaden the division between the haves and the have-nots around the world. It is not at all clear at this point whether or not the undereducated classes of the world will have access to the technological wonders of the information age, due to prohibitive costs and a lack of foundational education. Major strides would be required of government, the academy, and hardware and software manufacturers around the world to provide access to and training in the new technology.

So far, the information age is color blind, religion blind, politics blind, ethnicity blind, sexual orientation blind, physical capacity blind, and status blind. It is driven by business competition and is preoccupied with maximizing outcomes. It is moving with dizzying speed and waits for no particular individual. To date, it has not demonstrated significant social consciousness. It is up to those educational and social institutions that have traditionally been concerned with the general well-being of the human condition to ensure that no person, no class of people, and no geographical population is denied access to the information age. The gulf between the academy and the general society must not grow wider, but both must seek ways of cooperation so that both will benefit (Ewell, 1995). The explosion of opportunities presented by the information age underscores the possibility that there need be no large underclass. Technology can include rather than exclude—if education is extended to all. Otherwise, the information age could create a knowledge-based super class. We firmly believe that both government and the academy can address this problem of access to technology through education.

REVISITING THE CARNEGIE REPORT

Forecasting the future of higher education is a tricky business. As we engage in some prognostication, we recall a major study that was conducted and published in the seventies and early eighties. The Carnegie Report looked at education up to the end of the century and attempted to predict key trends in higher education, particularly in the United States. Some predictions proved to be insightful, whereas others did not. But there are lessons in the report and value in extending the good work of the Carnegie Commission as an encouragement to academic decision makers to be aware of the world into which we are headed.

The Carnegie Commission peppered the seventies with benchmark works on the condition of higher education in the United States. (Carnegie Council on Policy Studies in Higher Education, 1975; Carnegie Commission on Higher Education, 1973). The data reported in these studies evoked a sense of crisis and transformation in American higher education. Most of the findings proved to be accurate in some way about some aspect of the changes that have taken place since then. They were certainly instructive about the issues and forces that shape and accompany change.

The focusing work came from the Carnegie Report (Carnegie Council on Policy Studies in Higher Education, 1980). It outlined the hopes and fears colleges and universities experienced as they faced the 1980s and 1990s (fears that would eventually prompt change). They were fearful of such things as dropping enrollments, reduced resources, competition for students, rigid and defensive faculty reactions, diminishing standards related to access, intrusion by public authorities on the internal life of institutions, rising costs, the challenge of technology, tenure, and presidents caught between resisting faculty and micromanaging boards. These fears reflected a campus culture torn apart by special interests on the inside, which on the outside looked like chaos.

However, these fears were mitigated by hopes, including enrollments holding their own; tuition counterbalancing rising costs; per capita income rising, thereby offsetting tuition increases (keeping higher education's piece of the budgetary pie stable); emphasis shifting from expansion to quality; accreditation being used to sustain quality; research and teaching being rebundled; and tenure being balanced with a steady flow of new scholars. While all of this was taking place, the 1980 report concluded that faculties would develop realistic expectations and place the welfare of the institution first, that students would become more intelligent consumers demanding quality, that public authorities would resist urges for intrusion and micromanagement, and that the internal academic culture would restore collegiality, as institutions reshaped themselves for the challenges of the twenty-first century (Carnegie Council on Policy Studies in Higher Education, 1980, pp. 4–5).

When the report card of the nineties is superimposed over these hopes and fears of the early eighties, instructive results emerge. Enrollments declined initially but rose once again at mid-decade. Tuition compensated for most of the drop in public funding. Higher education saw its share of the budget drop significantly at the state level, with the state share of university budgets dropping from 46 percent in 1980–81 to 37 percent in 1991–92 (National Association of State Universities and Land Grant Colleges, 1996a, p. 5). Quality and accreditation remained a controversial national issue, which led to a reorganized accreditation process and the establishment of the Council for Higher Education Accreditation. Some faculties resisted change; others led it. Institutions grew new and very talented junior faculty by offering early retirement to more senior faculty and by reorganizing academic units to create openings (Finnegan, 1993). Tenure came under fire in Minnesota (Magner, 1996, p. A13). Two new institutions, Florida Gulf Coast University and Arizona International Campus of the University of Arizona, began operations without having a tenure system in place

(Trombley, 1996a, 1996b). Presidential turnover rose, with key leaders stepping down, including Chancellors Tien at the University of California at Berkeley, Young at the University of California at Los Angeles, and Presidents Duderstadt at the University of Michigan and Gerberding at the University of Washington in Seattle. Some trustees have come to favor managers of decline over innovators as presidents. Others have limited the authority of presidents and chancellors, as in the New York system and the regents of the University of California. So far, higher education has survived these actions, but at the price of rising public disenchantment about tuition, quality, and the competency of graduates. These issues have gotten the attention of legislatures, governors, and governing boards who seek ways to fix these problems.

Perhaps Altbach has captured the current challenge facing American campuses best. He writes, "There is a kind of struggle going on for the soul of the university in the United States. Although there is no flash point of political crisis, as was the case in the 1960s, the American university is profoundly divided" (1993, p. 219).

SOME BASIC CHANGES ALREADY UNDER WAY IN THE ACADEMY

As was true of the Carnegie Report, most predictions can be based on demonstrated trends. As we turn our attention to the new millennium, the needs and demands of the information age are already suggesting certain changes that the academy should seriously consider as it shapes the nature of its role in the new era.

Learning as the Key Requirement of the Twenty-First Century

A key change is how we view the person receiving the education. A *student* is taught by others, has little control over what he or she will be taught, and must fulfill institutional requirements. A student is often involved in passive learning, reacting to the stimulus of the instructor and confined to the road map of the syllabus. By contrast, a *learner* is an active participant in individual education. The learner interacts more assertively with the materials, other learners, and the instructor. The difference is akin to the difference between the lecture class and the seminar. Put simply, the student is more a reactive object and the learner is an active subject. By viewing individuals who come to a campus (in person, through the mail, or through the Internet) as learners instead of students, one's perspective changes. Enrollment managers begin to understand that they are in a competitive environment. Instructional delivery systems begin to reflect what the learner needs as opposed to what the campus traditionally may offer. The instructor can become more interested in fulfilling the knowledge needs of the individual learner, rather than treating everyone the same in a rote practicum. And, the knowledge base for learning can be constantly updated through research and application of what is learned in a joint process involving the instructor and the learner. Processes like these are among the strategies campuses may choose to pace and shape the rapid changes of the information age.

Market-Driven Versus Provider-Driven Education

One reaction we have seen in some academic circles when they have discussed instituting a more consumer-driven rather than provider-driven system of higher education is concern over trading academic excellence and quality for crass consumerism. Some feel that learners do not necessarily know what they really need to learn and, if you simply give learners what they want, quality and rigor suffer. We agree with that concern and believe it should contribute to how colleges and universities address the learning demands brought on by technology, the information explosion, and global economic competition. There is a genuine resistance to change within the academy among those who believe they are caretakers of the storehouse of human knowledge and the guardians of quality. But that proper reluctance is sometimes a shield against developing new forms of knowledge. In this form, it is more static than homeostatic and impedes the extension of scholarship to new things and new ideas driven by technology and the new age. We have often been told that technical schools train, colleges and universities educate. That is a useful distinction. But we do differ with the view that the content of the information explosion can be reduced simply to skills training. Ideas, projections, new facts, new theories, and massive new data do not reduce so simply. If anything, the volume and rapidity of their emergence require the very analytical perspective attributed to education—if order, reason, and meaning are to emerge from the melange of information bombarding us.

Perhaps their making this distinction represents a deep-seated fear that letting the educational customer (learner) dictate the subject matter will corrupt the very foundation of what has made the academy great. Throughout its long and distinguished history, the academy has discovered and passed along knowledge that has contributed substantially to the improvement of the general human condition. Determining what others should learn has always been its prerogative. Providing the tools to make an individual assessment that meets a reasonable standard of proof has always been its obligation.

As we noted earlier, the academy now finds itself in the position of not being the generator of a good deal of the knowledge spawned by the information age. Here, the need to know is often generated by emerging events and activities, which the scholarship of the academy has not created and about which it may be unaware. The challenge is to merge the academy's abilities for knowledge generation and knowledge transfer with what emerges from the technology and tempo of the information age and to accomplish this in part by considering the genuine educational needs of new learners.

University as a Learning Organization

To do this, the academy must become a learning organization, not an organization of learners. It must also be a knowledge-generating organization. A learning organization transforms as it scans, evaluates, and uses information. A useful metaphor is the space probe of the sort that landed on Mars or the space capsule whose physical structure changes as it goes from launchpad to recovery. Although some may think this a bit faddish, it makes the point we wish to make: most organizations are static and organizational change is slow. The new age with its rapid generation of ideas, information, and processes requires an intelligent flexibility not found in standard organizations. This flexibility, coupled with the capacity to use what you learn as you are learning it, is especially useful to sort through technology and what it produces. It also allows institutions to couple and uncouple, forming constructive partnerships without damaging basic competencies in any way. This will encourage finding ways to sort appropriately and to use knowledge, education, and training to benefit all those involved. Because change rather than constancy is the fuel, fear of change will no longer stand in the way of progress. If education is to be the engine of the information age, it will require these attributes.

EARLY PROGNOSIS

We end this chapter with some initial ideas about how colleges and universities will fare in the new age. Through reading, research, consulting, and years of experience as faculty and administrators, each of us has sought a reasonable understanding of where the academy is now, where it needs to go, and how it will get there over the next several years. As society continues to transform itself, members of the academy, all of us, have a choice—to move with or to move against the tides of change.

Not every college or university is going to survive the transition. The colleges and universities that endure will do so because they have been able to develop a focus for themselves that fits an important niche in the society and economy of the information age and that blends with their character and distinctive attributes. Certain high-quality liberal arts colleges and small, mostly private, universities will move into the information age relatively intact. There will always be a core of individuals who want to have the classic college experience and will agree to pay for it, as long as institutions modify their academic offerings to ensure that the college education of their students will lead to the first job. But everyone will not be able to rely on this approach.

The top research schools should also survive, some with minimal change. Their research will drive the information age, and because their research obviously benefits society as a whole, those research universities that can continually demonstrate this value and quality will enjoy ongoing external and even international support. But some research schools will face severe challenges. Already, medical schools are under siege as federal health funding has changed. The cost of teaching hospitals has skyrocketed, just when there is an oversupply of physicians, and the nature of medical practice is changing. Stanford and the University of California Medical School are merging to cut costs. In other fields, law schools are turning out a glut of graduates. The cost of big science programs limits having topflight science programs in many places. Traditional history and English majors struggle for a livelihood. And some argue there are too many Ph.D.'s. If all of this is minimal change, how severe will major change be in this new age?

Most comprehensive schools will act on what they have long known, that they will need to become more consumer oriented. With governmental entities, particularly in the United States, calling for more accountability and relevance, these important players in higher education will have little choice but to become more involved in a focused role and to devise a related marketing concept. These institutions may find themselves becoming what Kerr has called the "polytechnic university" (Munitz, 1995). As comprehensive colleges and universities, they are designed to mix a general education with professional or focused master's level studies. Traditionally serving regions, they are going to need to find new ways of interfacing with a more localized version of the information age worker and to offer ongoing, lifelong learning linked to the workplace. Distance learning, use of technology, and a shift from courses to learning modules may characterize the efforts of these institutions to serve their regions more effectively. Otherwise, these schools may find their funding bases eroding further and their future increasingly uncertain.

The smaller, under-resourced, and nonspecialized colleges and universities are at greatest risk. In particular, if they have faculties or administrative staffs that doggedly hold onto the traditions and practices of the past, they will find the competitive environment brutal, and some will simply not survive as we know them today. Others will be merged into more dynamic state or even regional systems, as change is forced on them. Minnesota's merging of state and community colleges is an example of this consolidation. Still others will simply close up and be sold.

All else notwithstanding, we find some reason for optimism in facing the changes before the academy. The opportunities outweigh the threats. The real issue lies in the capacity of individual campuses to recognize the fundamental changes required in the information age, to design effective roles for themselves within those change opportunities, and to innovate how they reach out to new and lifelong learners. Partnerships with business, government, and the professions will be especially important in these outreach activities.

Our goal here is to prompt people who are interested in the future of higher education to consider the nature of present and future changes brought about by technology and the information explosion and to develop constructive ways of making a successful transition from the industrial age to the information age.

CHAPTER TWO

Strategic Change in the Wake of Controversy

A̲s the information age matures, colleges and universities are facing the reality of change. They are also sensing the responsibility to identify which changes will affect a campus most beneficially. Based on that, they must determine how to incorporate the changes into the existing lifestyle of the campus. They must develop and choose among options to design a campus of the future, and they must implement the innovations that they select to effectuate a strategic transformation. The strategic planning process we introduced in our earlier book (Rowley, Lujan, and Dolence, 1997) provides a framework for a comprehensive look at how a campus can shape its own future. This chapter looks at environmental analysis, a key first element in strategic planning. It describes how institutions can use that analysis to design a better fit between a campus and its setting.

EXTERNAL ANALYSIS— THE WAKE OF CONTROVERSY

In the twilight of the twentieth century, American higher education is the world-class leader. More foreign students come to study in the

United States than Americans go abroad to attend college (Dessruis-seaux, 1996). American Nobel laureates are many. In spite of criticisms about how poorly American students score in science (National Center for Education Statistics, 1996a, 1996b), American academic scientists are always among the world leaders in scientific research. In the current transition to the information age, American leadership in knowledge creation and technology is undisputed.

However, even with this preeminence, public criticisms about American education persist. In some quarters, these critics have become shrill and urgent. After looking at the titles of some recent publications, we have concluded that it appears that demise is right around the corner. These titles include "Where Universities Have Gone Wrong" (Piederit, 1996), "Higher Education Governance in Despair" (Atwell, 1996a), *Killing the Spirit* (Smith, 1990), and *The Moral Collapse of the University* (Wilshire, 1990). Words like *wrong, despair, killing,* and *collapse* announce that a breakdown within the academy is imminent. Furthermore, these publications intimate that the breakdown is seeping into the fabric of American society. For example, Atwell argues that "the governance of colleges and universities is broken by external interventions, fiscal realities, and self-serving constituencies" (1996a, p. 1). Elsewhere he concludes that "we are a badly fractured and gridlocked society. Fractured because we are the lowest consensus society of any of the major democracies. . . . We have lost both the capacity for compromise and the possibility of consensus when we desperately need both" (1996b, p. 2).

Rising from the church seminary to the modern university, higher education thrived from secularization and the protection of academic freedom. The public university has benefited from this separation and has been especially wary of overt political intervention. Protected by lay boards largely appointed for their business acumen and political connections, in the battle between acumen and politics, acumen prevailed. Boards often buffered the public university from the backwash of politics. But today's boards are different. The University of California regents have directly intervened in the detail of admissions even in the face of resistance from campus chancellors and many students (Scott, 1996). The Minnesota regents attacked the tenure code, focusing on the law school and seeking ways to lay off faculty as funding diminishes (Magner, 1996). In Virginia and New York, major turnovers in board membership after gubernatorial elections have been controversial. In all of these policy shifts, partisan politics appear on the rise and leave a wake of controversy in the environment of higher education.

The wake of controversy is most evident in the criticism of research by outsiders. Perkins, former president of Cornell, argued that the very research that would vault American science and the economy to sustained world leadership would also be seen as an academic Trojan horse, bringing discovery at the expense of teaching. He worried that this trade-off could cost the academy its university soul. Jaspar believed a university was "the corporate realization of man's basic determination to know" (Perkins, 1965, p. 5). If that were true, then as Perkins observed, the discussion of the university would come to "the point where theory and doctrine must encounter the practical problems of management and direction" (p. 5). Kerr's metaphor of "constructive chaos" addresses the paradox of internal excellence and external criticism that Perkins poses (p. 27).

In its postindustrial age structure, the university can be seen by outsiders as rigid, parochial, inward looking, and reflective on past glories—and for good reason, as universities have helped create and preserve the things that have made us a great society. Rigidity is not necessarily negative, unless it stifles creativity. Creativity needs openness and is fed by constructive chaos and controversy. Although campuses may look chaotic from the outside, internally, they are seedbeds of discovery. As Perkins points out, the advancement of the university boils down to two things: "The first has to do with the external relations of the university—that it may lose its identity. The second has to do with the internal cohesion of the university—that it may lose its capacity to manage its own affairs" (p. 7).

CHANGING THE CAMPUS CONSENSUS

In spite of the value of constructive chaos, every organization needs a working consensus. As Perkins wisely argues, "Those who make the consensus are not likely to produce the revolution to upset it" (p. 80). What they are likely to do is refine the consensus they helped contrive. A good example of this was the rush by many comprehensive universities to clone the research university in the years since the sixties. The faculty and administrators who led this move had come by and large out of research universities. For them, the urge to turn a college into a university was logical, irresistible, and served a purpose. Clark makes an interesting point: "A strong state college was never far from a weak university in the first place. It took only the addition of a few Ph.D.'s to the faculty and a little more inching into graduate work in order to say: Why not us?" (1995, p. 374).

Apart from the internal-external environmental dichotomy, two additional forces are at work in any college or university—the force to resolve the dilemmas of cost, competency, and productivity and the force to be excellent. The former is external and leads us to turn to the external world of corporate management for models of efficiency. The latter is internal to higher education and seeks excellence by replicating the basic research university curriculum and embellishing it with electives and touches of the liberal arts. Clark is insightful on these matters. He argues, "Perhaps the rule is: organizational species that are markedly different can live side by side in a symbiotic relation; species that are similar, with heavily overlapping functions, are likely to conflict, with accommodation then often taking the form of convergence on a single type" (1995, p. 374).

Does this convergence on a single type always occur? What happens if the organizations are not side by side? What have other nations learned about the form and structure of higher education? What is the external-internal relationship elsewhere?

Many European countries, like Italy and France, use a ministry to manage higher education. The central bureaucracy of the ministry determines national funding, a national curriculum, and a national personnel system. This bureaucracy has not handled financial issues any better than the U.S. model, and their institutions by and large are not very competitive with the extensive record of scholarship in the United States. In Europe, with power centralized in the bureaucracy, faculty often elect chairs, deans, and chancellors. The result is a weak middle, with leaders caught between the authority of the bureaucracy and the political power of the faculty.

The problem with this strong top, strong bottom, weak middle is that the command structure cannot respond in a timely manner. Rigid processes intervene, often placing rules ahead of substance. Responsiveness can be held hostage as process works its will. Frustrated by this, Europe is now decentralizing its universities.

National standards also pose a concern. Domination by any single form of organization coupled with a monopoly of power will breed dogma and homogenized knowledge rather than the frothy, dynamic learning that arises from difference, pluralism, and the tolerance for variation. As Clark (1995) observes, institutional differentiation is the key. Instead of cores and tight standards, variety and a marketplace of ideas shape change and evolution. Equated systems are lockstep, shaped by narrow benchmarks and less likely to breed new forms of knowledge or approaches to learning. Pluralist systems are open and encourage both variety and differentiation, both of which breed distinction.

Democracies need pluralism and openness. They thrive on tolerance for the ideas and rights of others, seeing these as wellsprings from which freedom rises. With or without freedom, every system needs its font and its tributary. In Europe, the conflict over openness has led to early selection and tracking in precollegiate education. A closed system results. In the information age, in which broad access to knowledge is at the base of knowledge competency, early exclusion can undermine the need for broad access to both knowledge and competency. When you add the intense technological competition driving information, educating all elements of the population becomes critical—both for knowledge creation and for its effective use. As Thurow argues, "In the end the skills of the bottom half of the population affect the wages of the top half. If the bottom half can't effectively staff the processes that have to be operated, the management and professional jobs that go with these approaches will disappear" (1992, p. 7).

The experiences in Europe can also offer some interesting insights into the opposite of the tracked and tightly controlled approach to education. Because of a closed system in traditional universities, demand for postsecondary education has grown substantially in Paris, Rome, and London. Each has its own open university. In Rome, there are 150,000 students, in Paris nearly 200,000, and in London 218,000. In each case, advanced study is being offered at a level sufficient to attract sustained and sizeable enrollments. The faculty involved and delivery systems used are not always traditional. In reality, these have become Europe's alternative universities, offering a pathway around early tracking. And what has worked in Europe is working elsewhere. For example, the former members of the British Commonwealth began the Commonwealth of Learning in 1987 to network university resources and faculty worldwide and to share expertise (Lundin, 1988). In Thailand, the open university serves over 250,000 learners (Shane, 1989).

Changing the consensus within a university is a theme in the work of Barry Munitz, who served as chancellor of the California State University System. Munitz argues that the old consensus is gone, and for the first time in the American experience, we will have to create educational change without significant new resources. He uses the "triage concept" (pp. 1–2) as the new metaphor for shaping change. This antidote to the characterizations of *wrong, despair, killing,* and *collapse* is graphic, but its content is more constructive. Munitz asserts that when you do not have enough resources and are faced with events of catastrophic magnitude, you devise a sequence in which help or resolution will be provided. In a world of global change, *triage* means to take the healing strategies for change that will shape the future and use them to transform higher education through some reasonable sequence into a better and more responsive contributor to quality and to competent solutions for humanity's pressing problems. This requires linking knowledge to real-world needs. He believes funding must be tied to societal needs, and the need for the 1990s and beyond is the polytechnic model of applied research, technology transfer, and faculty involvement with undergraduates, providing skills for the workplace. If Munitz's conclusions are right, and we think they are, this move from ivory tower to polytechnic will require a new consensus about the university and its environment.

Munitz's own effort at consensus began with assessing the California State University system's needs and the attitudes and concerns of the California public and its legislators. He struck a political agreement with public leadership and the governor and, in exchange for stable funding over the short term, began a systemwide long-term analysis of problems and proposed solutions using the rubric of Cornerstones Principles, which will be discussed in more detail later. The Munitz perspective is definitive. Adapting to information age changes is not a choice. Working with academic and public leaders is a prerequisite. A strategic assessment of Strengths, Weaknesses, Opportunities, and Threats (SWOT) is a strategic requirement for building a new consensus.

There are important lessons observed in Munitz's approach to change that match our ideas about strategic change. Begin with a clear and uncomplicated assessment of the external environment, isolate the opportunities and threats found in that environment, and build a set of responses based on strengths and areas of distinction.

BUILDING A NEW CONSENSUS BASED ON NEW FACTS

In building a strategic model for campus rebirth, campus leaders should realize that the facts driving a new consensus vary somewhat from the opinions fueling the criticism of higher education. Critics opine that higher education takes more and offers less (Will, 1996). But what are the facts? Hartle (1996) has noted that state spending per student in higher education, when adjusted for inflation, is lower than in 1984. He also suggests that state spending on higher education (historically in the 15 to 20 percent range) dropped from 14 percent of state budgets in 1990 to 12.5 percent in 1994. It is not uncommon to find that the state pays less than 20 percent of the budget of research universities. Rather than state universities, these are increasingly becoming state-seeded institutions. As a University of Florida report notes, "At no public universities do the required tuition and fees paid by the student equal the cost of the education received" (University of Florida, 1996, p. 1). College is still a good buy.

Between 1980 and 1994, tuition, room, and board at public institutions increased from 10 percent to 14 percent of median family income for families with children six to seventeen years old (National Center for Education Statistics, 1996b). The increase is modest. In addition, the benefits to the states are not trivial. Although the percentage of university budgets funded by the states has dropped from 46 percent in 1980–81 to 37 percent in 1992–93, every state dollar invested in higher education raised another $2.50 to $3.50 in the states of California, Colorado, Indiana, and Ohio (National Association of State Universities and Land Grant Colleges, 1996a). It is estimated that the University of Washington generated statewide economic activity of $2.8 billion, more than ten times the state's net investment in the university (National Association of State Universities and Land Grant Colleges, 1996a).

In the information age, there are individual benefits to a college degree. Those with bachelor's degrees will earn $600,000 more per lifetime than high school graduates will. A master's graduate will earn an additional $800,000 over a lifetime. Professional school graduates will earn an added $1.3 million (Hartle, 1996). In terms of median earnings, in 1994, males with high school diplomas earned $14,584; those with bachelor's degrees earned $38,709; and those with master's degrees earned $46,635. The comparables for women are $7,618, $23,405, and $38,701 (National Alliance of Business, 1996). As of summer

1996, public university students paid less than $3,000 per year in tuition and fees (National Association of State Universities and Land Grant Colleges, 1996b). For students who pay less than one-third of the cost of their college undergraduate education, this is an extraordinary bargain and a very wise investment.

What about the quality of American students? In 1997, they are doing well in reading literacy but still lag in math and science. Student-teacher ratios are among the lowest in the industrialized nations. More students complete high school and earn college degrees in the United States than in any other nation (National Alliance of Business, 1996).

Why review these facts you wonder, facts that many educators already know? It is because facts, not anecdotes and impressions, must drive strategic planning to build a realistic, practical, and fitting internal consensus for change. Hearsay may do just fine for public opinion, but it is inadequate for strategic thinking.

STRATEGICALLY SCULPTING CHANGE

Understanding the new facts, Munitz (1995) sets the parameters for sculpting change in the transition period between centuries. He argues that this is the first time in U.S. history when profound educational change must occur in the face of both shrinking resources and public support. In the 1930s, government infused education with funding support while dealing with the Great Depression. Today, government cuts education in the face of economic restructuring and new prosperity. In Munitz's view, the economy, even as it recovers, will not help, because large numbers of new students will be driven by the requirements of the information age to seek lifelong learning. Munitz underscores how the student profile will change with Caucasians diminishing from three-fourths to one-fourth of the student population. Students will generally be older. Rising prices will raise questions about affordability and access at a time when society will have to educate all of its citizens to compete in the new age. In this, Munitz argues, the priorities of the academy are not aligned with those of the paying public. To the extent that the campus reward system stresses research, it is at odds with the public desire for teaching and service.

Within the faculty, teaching, research, and service are practiced, with varying emphases depending on the type of campus. Educated to be creators and discoverers, many faculty teach in institutions where research is overshadowed by teaching and service. All faculty, regardless of the mix, see tenure as an appropriate protection against the threat of external intrusion into the development and transmission of knowledge. No society would be well served if its scholars could not investigate the unthinkable or the unpopular. But to outsiders, tenure is simply a job guarantee—something they do not have, therefore, something that others should not have.

Within this context of contradictions, there are some known drivers of change. Enrollments will grow. An estimated twenty million full-time-equivalent students will seek education by the early years of the next century. They will require 672 new campuses able to enroll thirty thousand students each. At $350 million per campus, the cost to build them would be $235 billion, and it would take $217 billion per year to run them (Dolence and Norris, 1995). One-half of the faculty now in place and one-half of current buildings and equipment will need replacement. Technology will have to be current and considered an ongoing expense. Graduate education will need reshaping to advance knowledge and to develop the skills to teach and convey the knowledge base of the information age (Atwell, 1996c). Lifelong learners will link school to work. The classroom will cease being the one and only centerpiece of learning.

At the same time, the business world will redefine both its educational linkages and its providers. In 1995, corporate training budgets totaled $52 billion, an increase of 15 percent from 1990. Over one thousand corporate universities are already in place. Total payroll for professionals and managers have tripled from 1991 to 1994 (National Alliance of Business, 1996). Businesses need to keep these people competent and current with changes in technology and information. If universities do not adapt to forces of this magnitude, businesses will not wait. They will initiate their own remedies, and the cost to the academy could be very great.

The problem here is not simply the one facing a person needing lifelong learning. The problem goes further in this way: when individuals and organizations realize that particular colleges and universities are uneven in how they provide substantive learning (learning that allows the individual to develop competencies and a broad base of knowledge, as well as lifelong learning—learning that supplements basic knowledge over the working lifetime of an individual), both learners and the organizations that employ them will seek other settings that meet their needs. On one end, employers will develop their own institutions to handle both basic and lifelong aspects of education. This is already happening with organizations such as IBM and Motorola (discussed later in this book). At another end, learners may form their own institutions, a possibility already evident at the elementary and secondary levels with charter schools. The real problem facing colleges and universities is competition, and in a competitive environment, the strong adapt and survive. Colleges and universities are not used to zero sum competition, and when the competitive field is expanded to include not only peer institutions but also proprietary and business universities with the strength and motivation to compete, the traditional campuses may face a serious challenge.

The commercial capacity to use and handle technology raises issues about who best can transfer information. Transfer of information is at the foundation of the traditional college or university. Lower-division education is preoccupied with it, using the tools of introductory and survey courses. These are the primary means for transferring information. When commercial technology can provide this service in a timely and cost-effective manner, the question arises as to what will happen to lower-division education in both two- and four-year institutions. What will this imply for secondary education? The nature and types of linkages between levels of education are clearly challenged by this simple change in how we store, retrieve, and transfer information. If Bill Gates can digitize the art collections of the world for his own pleasure, it is not a large step to think of making these collections generally available to the public. What can portage the finest art of the world can surely carry much of the basic knowledge of present disciplines.

Another question involves the nature of employment. What will employment become in a university that is technologically able to respond to sophisticated professionals who want to advance their knowledge? If an inquisitive student has a choice between a Nobel laureate's presentation of a subject and unknown professor X on the same subject, what is the likely choice? Through technology, people and their knowledge are mobile. What will keep professors from turning to free agency as athletes have done? What will keep professors for whom there is a demand from "teaching through technology" at several institutions simultaneously? Linked locally by e-mail, video services, and visits planned at intervals timely for the courses involved, professors can teach and become resources without dependency on a single campus. Though this seems a bit futuristic, it may be closer to reality than we wish to admit.

PRESENT PRACTICES POINTING THE WAY

Considering the backdrop of the conditions and trends just discussed, what elements currently in place are most likely to change? Obviously, the analytical skills needed to handle and create new information will have to adapt and evolve. The increased dependence on technology and professionalization in the business world is already under way. Some of this is driven by cross-disciplinary knowledge in fields like molecular biotechnology. Other changes come from overcrowded professions like law and medicine. Further changes follow from fields that are rapidly changing, as evidenced by the occupations emerging in the allied health sciences and engineering. We see the following areas of change:

Areas in Which Change Is Most Likely

The Changing Economy

- Globalization of the curriculum
- Market share of private universities
- Labor costs
- Increased proprietary instruction

Needed Education

- Analytical skills to parse, recombine, and create information
- Professional education
- Technology and how it links to learning
- Graduate education

Campus Capacity to Respond

- Linkages between levels of education
- Indicators of quality

These elements place demands not only on the economy, labor skills, and the capacity of particular campuses to respond. They also affect current courses of study and create expectations for new fields of study and professions that cross traditional lines. The short and rapid cycles of technology design and usage serve as a constant catalyst for innovation. The emerging global society and its highly competitive marketplace regularly spawn new techniques and subjects of information. Labor costs are clearly affected—lowered in most cases—

thereby generating financial flexibility for institutions with operating budgets in which 80 to 90 percent of cost involves labor. Responding to diminishing public support will also be essential, especially for the public college or university. As noted earlier, addressing proprietary business universities, private institutions, and for-profit institutions will place a greater burden of proof on public higher education. This is particularly the case if higher education is to serve as the primary conduit of educational skills and knowledge in rapidly changing times.

What is worth keeping from today's university in tomorrow's world? We suggest the following attributes:

Academic Traditions That Must Be Maintained

The Changing Economy

• Access

• Cost of education subsidized

Needed Education

• American primacy in graduate education

• Necessary research to further knowledge

Campus Capacity to Respond

• Tenure clearly linked to responsibility for active scholarship

• Linkages reinforced with K–12 and improved basic education

• Healthy and competitive private and independent universities

• Collegial culture and shared governance focused on the whole institution

Among forces driven by the changing economy, access is central because the information age calls for educating and not just training the whole society in order to be competitive. Access has been broadened through student financial aid and affirmative efforts to enhance educational and cultural diversity, especially involving the economic and ethnic excluded classes. But these innovations are now under challenge. Creative ways to continue aid and access will have to emerge, perhaps learning from the approach to aid used in the 1960s, as the country responded to the challenge of Sputnik. A National Defense Education Act was passed to infuse support for advanced study that was designed to regain the competitive edge in science gained by the Russians. Lacking war (or even cold war) as a motivator, the needs of a new global competition could drive innovative forms of aid as an investment in a competitive edge for the human infrastructure of the new age.

At the base of the campus capacity to respond is tenure. We believe that tenure will be kept to ensure the academic freedom essential for the generation of ideas that drive the information age. However, the right to tenure will be balanced by the responsibility for active scholarship, and its relation with job security will be redefined. In an age in which new ideas emerge rapidly and dramatically, the guarantee that unpopular ideas will not be expunged or punished will be a necessary precondition for creative inquiry and scholarship.

Closely related to tenure are the very substantive issues of collegiality (among faculty and between faculty and administration) and campus governance. Tenure without a collegial framework can deteriorate into a sort of combative entrepreneurship, in which those with resources have power and advance at the expense of those without such means. Over time, this can lead to homogeneity and orthodoxy, the very forces that undermine creative thinking and the risk-taking scholarship that is required for bold thinking and discovery.

As for needed education, academic research will be the engine of change in the information age. Both public and private sectors must support it more directly than is currently the case and must do so over the long term for the self-interested purpose of survival in the intense competition over information. Research in the pursuit of knowledge for its own sake is especially fitting in the information age. In the American case, both basic and applied research are the basis for the primacy of American education. Foreign students come to study in the United States in part because of the quality of research and research-based learning. This attribute is an essential ingredient in the future of American higher education. What we believe will become more prominent is research that addresses some of the essential problems of the time. In the new era, research that serves will be as valuable as research that stimulates.

One area of great importance is the linkage between levels of education. America's K–12 schools are in decline. For some time, higher education has seen this as K–12's problem. But the reality that teachers in K–12 are college graduates is dawning. As a result, U.S. colleges and universities increasingly recognize the need to renew partnerships with the common schools. At the same time, the community college is increasingly an avenue of first choice for entry to higher education.

Community college graduates do respectably in college, a condition not widely valued under the old consensus.

Other innovative forces pointing the way to change (Pelton, 1990) include the digital library; instructional software; simulations and technologically innovative lab experiences; the cultural needs of the global society including language, social practices, and legal and political relations; environmental constraints of a global nature; responsible exploration of space; quantum increases in knowledge about the human mind and body; ethics and its role in shaping change; the proper handling of intellectual property made prominent by the information explosion; understanding and managing the rapid, flexible organizations of the future; and redefining the relationships within and governing of the kinetic university of the future.

Robert T. Jones of the National Alliance of Business (NAB) argues the issue in this way: "It is important to remember that the workplace, not Washington, is driving these changes. The swirling pace of economic change cannot be legislated away. We must develop a comprehensive investment and educational system that is directly tied to the needs of employers. The most important message is that we must work with, rather than against, market forces" (1996, p. 3). This credo is comfortable for those outside the academy, but unsettling for those in it. There is good reason for this. Education cannot become simply the handmaiden of the economy. Although education must be tied to the workplace, that tie cannot be exclusive. For one thing, knowledge for knowledge's sake helps spawn the very ideas and questions that generate information in this new age.

Basic research has always driven new knowledge, because it pursues questions whether or not they are current or applicable. The danger in responding only to the needs of the new age is that the speed of change can mire researchers in the issues of the present, simply because of their sheer volume. Although responding to current matters is important, some must get out in front of the curve and grapple with what lies ahead. Such long-term knowledge must compete for resources that inevitably respond more to the current marketplace of ideas and things.

Richardson (1996a) points the way with the observation that in 1996, colleges and universities seemed like veterans who had not adapted to a new purpose in peacetime. Although current practices can mark the trail of change to some extent, Dolence and Norris (1995) make the important argument that one cannot simply lay information age tools atop a system of values, functions, and structures of the industrial age factory model of education. Old tricks will not work. As discussed earlier, the academy can and should reshape itself genuinely to serve the information age learner. This means networking resources to educate individual learners who are active in their own education and seeking both knowledge competency and personal-best achievements. In this, the university becomes a kind of developer or general contractor. This shift from being the producer of education to being the synthesizer and sponsor of education (which includes being responsive to the needs of the students) has important consequences, especially if it must also advance human knowledge.

An important consequence of these changes is that they require strategic reorganization (Peterson, Dill, Mets, and Associates, 1997). As already noted, the factory model with its tight sequence of survey and advanced courses, its rigid major, and its credit units will likely give way to modules that can be pieced together to meet the varying needs and appropriate competencies of the student. This more flexible approach will mean different units of delivery, different means of acquiring expertise, and different methods of pricing. The configuration of labor will also change (Kanter, 1995; Finnegan, 1993). Instead of resident faculty turning out graduates based on common units and majors, faculty will become guides and masters in the process of modularizing the education of individual learners. Networks of faculty, regardless of location, actively involved in these modules, will displace those resident faculty isolated in their specialties. In the new consensus, where faculty are located will be less important than their expertise and how that expertise is accessible.

The corporation-like structure of many colleges and universities is normally characterized by vertical authority from trustees to president to faculty to students. It is hierarchical in its internal organization, from president to vice presidents to deans to departments and their faculties and students. It is designed for certainty, with graduates having to complete a known number of credits. This certainty of credits will probably give way to a form of certification that fits with a particular student's approved study plan. There will be more flexibility in terms of human judgment about content and semantics, elements that impart meaning and value to the spawn of information turned loose by technology. Data and information also will be readily obtainable and easy to recombine throughout the campus, largely due to updated technology (Pelton, 1990). In such a world, the university will be able to shed its vertically integrated and corporate structure for the more horizontal and flexible structure that is suitable for a learning organization. As expressed in Chapter One, the new model, the learning organization, will be more space capsule than conveyor belt, exploiting the capacity of an organization to diffract and analyze, shed its parts, and design new structures as it adapts to an ever-changing environment with ever-changing requirements. We underscore the importance of this shift from a rigid and rule-bound model of certainty to an adaptive, flexible one of fit and constant reinvention.

STRATEGICALLY CASTING THE FUTURE

In thinking about the future and sketching innovation, some forces are already determined (Carnegie Council on Policy Studies, 1980). We know that enrollments will increase; half of the faculty will retire; half of the buildings will need replacement; and new technology will change the way we teach and the college classroom. Thus, trade-offs will occur between space and technology, probably turning the aging of buildings into a disguise for new capital investment and technology design. Knowledge will become cross-disciplinary for the simple reason that the questions of the marketplace of ideas and of the economy do not always fit the straitjackets of traditional disciplines and professions. Already, at the State University of New York at Potsdam, a renowned music program is teaching its music majors about the business end of music.

As stated earlier, students, like the fields they study, will be different. There will be more women than men, as many over twenty-one years of age as under it, and minorities will grow significantly in numbers and proportion. Paying a larger percentage of the cost of their education, students will be a greater force in governance and the curriculum. By voting with their feet and notebooks, students will lead some disciplines to atrophy and others, many of which are currently unknown, to thrive. Several career changes will characterize life after college for these students, and changing skill requirements will prompt lifelong learning.

There is a litany of new forces that also will influence change in the coming decade or two. The following list outlines what we believe these forces will be. They sort into the three major categories discussed earlier—the changing economy, needed education, and the capacity of campuses to respond to change. When all of the category elements are combined, five summary descriptors emerge—access, how we learn, what we learn, the ethics of using knowledge, and the need for social as well as individual responsibility in sustaining a learning community. These descriptors translate into five forces of consequence for the future university—access, pedagogy, knowledge, ethics, and responsibility.

Forces Influencing Change in the Academy

The Changing Economy
- Size of enrollment growth
- Education kept accessible to all
- Rapid evolution of technology

Needed Education
- Lifelong learning
- Choice and flexibility in learning
- Communication skills for the global economy
- Thinking and working in groups
- Responsible use of knowledge

Campus Capacity to Respond
- Atomism of learning alone
- Protection of intellectual property
- Ethical issues of new discoveries
- Tolerance of risk-taking leadership
- Collegiality and its rights and responsibilities redefined

HOW LEADERS SEE THE FUTURE

After conducting interviews with numerous leaders in higher education, we broadened this core of forces. James Appleberry, president of the American Association of State Colleges and Universities, suggested several areas in which he believes changes will influence higher education in the next several years, outlined in the following list. He pondered especially over the atomizing effects of technology-driven learning and the intense acquisitiveness of a highly competitive global economy. Where, he wondered, would the sense of the common good needed for social cohesion come from? He thinks this is especially problematic if the emphasis in business competition and computer-driven learning is on the individual and one's own gain. These thoughts underscore the fact that the future of education is linked not just to the magnet of knowledge but also to the incubation of social freedoms and responsibilities that underpin the human community. Of the five forces of change, Appleberry was most concerned with ethics and responsibility (James Appleberry, interview with authors, October 1996). His concerns are as follows:

Appleberry's List of Changes That Will Influence the Academy

The Changing Economy
- Shift to a user pay system
- Explosion of available information
- Impact on technology

Needed Education
- Preparation for multiple careers
- Coping with the global marketplace

Campus Capacity to Respond
- Atomizing effects of technology-driven learning

Likewise, Peter Magrath, president of the National Association of State Universities and Land Grant Colleges (NASULGC), is among those already looking into these questions in an effort to reshape the role of the land grant institution. There are several areas that worry Magrath regarding societal needs that will affect education:

Magrath's List of Societal Forces That Will Change the Academy

The Changing Economy
- Access

Needed Education
- Improvement of the undergraduate experience
- Promotion of a learning society

Campus Capacity to Respond
- The campus culture and reward system changing
- Universities in a global age linked internationally

Magrath argues, "In my view, universities will survive. I do not have much doubt about that; but they will be marginalized," presumably unless they build bridges of support to the public by implementing Magrath's calls for action on these issues (Peter Magrath, interview with authors, October 1996). NASULGC is working with the Kellogg Foundation in a major effort to address these concerns. As the Kellogg Commission on the Future notes, "In refocusing public higher education, how can we reform what needs to be changed while preserving what is best about our institutions?" (Kellogg Commission on the Future of State and Land Grant Universities, 1996, p. 4). To Magrath, the past is the cornerstone for change and not the architect for the future.

Robert Atwell, president emeritus of the American Council of Education (interview with authors, 1996), speaks of these and other issues:

Atwell's List of Forces That Affect the Academy

The Changing Economy
- Inadequate resources to meet demand
- Accredited learning outside the university setting

Needed Education
- Education for civil discourse

Campus Capacity to Respond
- Graduate students cloned at the research universities
- Technology redefined by teaching
- Broken internal and external governing bodies
- Fate of the less selective liberal arts colleges
- Academic alliances and partnerships
- Restored concern for the good of the institution

Atwell has long focused on the internal environment of the university and its capacity to respond. He opines (Atwell, 1996c) that research universities prepare Ph.D.'s for research universities, although most of them work at comprehensive or private universities. Teaching suffers as a consequence, and the reward system reflects this incongruity. Like Munitz, he sees inadequate resources as a long-term problem, challenging Americans to change with less. Broken governance systems are a major worry. With turmoil at the top, campuses have great difficulty constructively adapting to major changes. Special interests and a hardening of lines between campus constituencies corrupt the dialogue necessary for the good of the university and undermine the civility required for learning. Traditions get in the way of adapting to the challenges of for-profit universities, a more seamless educational system, linking teaching with technology, and addressing the fate of the liberal arts.

UNIVERSITIES AS ORGANIZATIONS OF THE FUTURE

These themes inform the analysis that follows. The ideas they trigger come under the lens of what organizations of the future will require (Magsaysay, 1997). In futurist looks at the economy, the attributes of the successful twenty-first century organization include discontinuous change, flexibility, shared information, constant reinvention of advantage, and a more horizontal–less authoritative structure. Some of this is recast by William Richardson of the Kellogg Foundation:

> University leadership—administration and faculty—must articulate a multifaceted mission that is balanced and forward looking. Within this context, faculty appointments, among other things, may be viewed as licenses that enable faculty to pursue their own work, but in a way that puts revenue in the university's accounts. Faculty activities include teaching at a level that generates enough credits to support oneself and the work or a mix of these. The same logic applies for faculty who are engaged in clinical practice. This strategy reflects a clear correlation between the organizational setting that the university is providing and the work that it wishes accomplished—its mission. Such an approach promotes flexibility within the university. . . . As taxpayers increasingly expect higher education to become engaged with society, we'll need this flexible, mixed model orientation to respond effectively. [Richardson, 1996a, p. 4]

For Richardson, like Magsaysay, flexible is the watchword for change.

Dolence and Norris (1995) add another template to flexibility. It is the template of fundamental change in the underlying model for higher education. To reiterate an important point:

> In reality the basic patterns and cadences of academic life predate even the Industrial Revolution. But the processes and organizations

perfected during the 1960s and 1980s are classic late Industrial Age design. Referring to these as a "factory model" in an intentionally hyperbolic manner dramatizes the contradiction of laying Information Age tools atop a basic system of values, functions and structures that remain unchanged. Three simple questions must be answered by political leaders, educational leaders, faculty, students, and other stakeholders contemplating the future of higher education. First, "Is today's Industrial Age educational model appropriate to the learning needs of the Information Age—for either traditional learners or learners in the workplace?" Second, "Is society willing to pay for a 20th Century 'Industrial Age' model in the 21st Century 'Information Age'?" And third, "Can academe afford to miss the opportunity of reshaping itself to serve the emerging needs of the Information Age learner?" [p. 7]

Happily, these questions can be answered. But these answers are contained within the internal environment of the university, which we will discuss. We close by reiterating the essential building blocks of strategic change. Effective strategies and the management practices they imply begin with a frank, practical, fact-informed analysis of the external environment of the university. This consists of an inventory of opportunities and threats to the institution and its stakeholders from contextual forces in the environment. From that inventory, the most salient opportunities and threatening weaknesses can be identified through a participative process, ideally assisted by an objective means for culling these into a manageable set. We encourage the use of Decision Support Laboratories where they exist. (See Dolence, Rowley, and Lujan, 1997).

CHAPTER THREE

Cultivating Internal Readiness for Change

In the previous chapter, we considered many of the issues colleges and universities should weigh when they assess their external environment. This environment is dramatically changing, under pressure from technology, demography, and the global economy. This chapter looks at several of the issues that academic leaders (presidents, chancellors, governing boards, academic leaders, and faculty members) should appraise as they prepare their campuses internally for new learners and the knowledge requisites of the next several decades. The internal university environment is critical, for no matter how skilled and perceptive the external review of opportunities and threats, without internal agreement on strengths and areas of distinction, the consensus for change will wither. We start with an analogy.

The cave and the campus have some things in common. Ehrmann, Renwick, and Hebenstreit (1994) in their study of educational technology in Europe describe this comparison with a delightful tale. It seems that the first user of educational technology was a cave dweller named Thok. Thok was a survivor, so his neighboring cave dwellers came to his cave to observe the secrets of Thok's survival, bringing him goods and gifts in return. They talked in groups, as Plato and his students would do while sitting in a grove in a time yet to come. Thok was a good teacher, so he learned as much as he taught. But whereas Thok only taught, his students had to hunt and gather in addition to study. Time did not wear so well on them, so they would pass away while Thok would just get older. Finally, Thok got so old that his voice began to fail. He could not be easily heard. To resolve that, Thok came up with the idea of rolling a banana leaf into a cone and using the cone to project his voice. In this way, Thok's "distance learners" could continue to learn. Word got around of this thing Thok called a "megaphone" and cave dwellers came from far and near. His teachings were now heard by both those at his feet and those outside the cave.

But there were some skeptics about this new "megaphonology." To test it, they took banana leaves and placed them on their heads. As they left the cave, they could not go very far before Thok's voice disappeared. Learning nothing, these first of all evaluators concluded that megaphonology was a useless tool.

Campuses are as scattered as caves. For a long time, such learning resources as people and their ideas were physically scattered, and one had to get into each cave to learn. As demand grew and techniques for delivering knowledge improved, caves gave way to cloistered libraries, and Plato's grove turned into the lecture hall. Soon these clusters became campuses, which found ever more creative ways to get the word out. Thok's banana leaf evolved into hieroglyphics, manuscripts, the printed book, the lecture hall, and the Internet. Campuses became the new caves of learning, bringing select scholars, students, and books together in one place. Ehrmann, Renwick, and Hebenstreit (1994) argue that these small, protected oases of human and material resources are like Thok's voice, becoming less accessible at a time when both society and the economy need skills for the arriving information age. Some, like the critics of megaphonology who wore the banana leaves on their heads, discount new techniques and stick to the old ways. But campus oases are nevertheless transforming via e-mail, computer networks, digital libraries, and CD-ROMs. The printed book, which displaced the genealogist as the repository and oracle of learning, is itself being displaced by this range of digital devices. In each case, from the mythical banana leaf to the hieroglyphic, the scribe's manuscript, Gutenberg's book, and the CD-ROM, all have had the common effect of taking the knowledge of the teacher to more and more students and reducing the student-teacher ratio along the way.

CHALLENGES TO THE
INTERNAL ENVIRONMENT

Why the elaborate analogy? It makes the point that educators must be at the leading edge shaping change and cannot just react to external forces. The challenge the external environment places on the internal university is to transform place-bound campus-based learning into accessible, high-quality, and low-cost education. Ehrmann, Renwick, and Hebenstreit (1994) help us pose three questions that shape our internal assessment: How do we educate, as distinct from train, the full range of adult learners essential for the information age? How do we improve the chances for learning of lifelong learners? Where do we find the resources necessary to keep costs within the range of the vast majority of citizen learners? Ehrmann, Renwick, and Hebenstreit also argue the important point that learning is crucial to the information age, for without the brain of education, the information explosion may not be harnessed to advance knowledge in the new age.

How we educate is an issue framed by leadership. Kerr, a beacon in these arguments over the future of higher education, observes astutely, "Never before have so many been engaged in fighting so many and prospectively for so long, nor has there been so much endemic guerilla warfare. . . . Leadership is under great pressure. The new divide among presidents is between those who are proactive to the new set of problems and those who are reactive—so far the great majority are on the reactive side of that divide. Will it change? Who, if anyone, will take charge?" (Altbach, 1993, pp. 12–13).

A quick scan of higher education in the twilight of the twentieth century gives some indications about who is "in charge." Many presidents are stepping down, even from the leading universities. The average tenure of presidents is now four to five years, down from terms of eight to ten years in previous generations. Turnover is also high on boards. Significant changes in boards have occurred in Minnesota, New York, Virginia, Colorado, and Missouri. Concern for presidential leadership has led to a major Association of Governing Boards study and report, *Renewing the Academic Presidency* (Commission on the Presidency, 1996). Its conclusions call for risk-taking change-agent presidents, supportive governing boards, faculty committed to the institution and willing to work with presidents and state leaders, and trustees based on merit. But the lesson for strategic efforts is that unstable leadership undermines stable and thoughtful approaches to educational reform that help us educate new learners.

Rothblatt adds some common sense to this: "The university today is part of an extraordinary intricate set of linked substructures, many of which are the result of historic transformations" (Dill and Sporn, 1995, p. 21). Academic specialization leads to a loose confederation of units in which the parts are often greater than the whole. Faculty loyalty is historically and understandably to the discipline. In search of support, the public university strikes a social contract with society to exchange knowledge for support. The barter holds so long as the knowledge involved is valued. But when access is a sore point and college graduates are not seen as competent or possessed of the skills needed for social and economic survival, the bargain sours. If costs rise as the bargain sours, and the attitude of the public becomes that universities are not accessible, the quality of what they do is suspect and they cost too much.

NEW SOCIAL BARGAIN

How we educate is also tied to striking a new social bargain of public expectations. Of all the metaphors and descriptors used, the idea of *eutrophy* is apt for higher education and the problems it must overcome to strike a new bargain. Eutrophy is a condition of a pond or other living ecosystem that is rich in nutrients. So rich, in fact, that there is excessive plant growth killing off forms of life by depriving them of oxygen. The modern university is rich in a sprawl of structures and programs, loosely held together to grow freely—constructive chaos, so to speak. But in their growth and the pursuit of their separate interests, these flourishing programs sometimes strangle the larger institution, making it unable to provide what society expects from its educational bargain. The question is how to make a coherent whole out of a decentralized entrepreneurial enterprise.

Dolence and Norris (1995) set a framework for internal coherence and address the questions of how we improve learning and provide the requisite resources. If you look at the university as a *learning franchise,* two things become obvious. The first is that no one really owns the franchise. States may claim ownership, but they typically pay for far less than what an owner would to exercise ownership in the free market. Boards come and go and are too limited by their political ties to act as responsible owners. They are transients anyway, and transients cannot exercise ownership rights over the long term. Faculty reside the longest in the university, but their sense of ownership is vested in the discipline or profession rather than in the institution. Students are the most transient of constituents, and their fiscal ownership—in the form of tuition—is rising far more rapidly than their involvement in governance. What we have is a public utility without the sustained control of a commission to guide policy over the long term.

Ownership and leadership matter because they can create a stable context for change. But the important internal relationship for the learning franchise of the future is *network learning.* Network learning eliminates barriers to access and progress, providing opportunities for learning agents and their facilitators. Using technology as a communications backbone, a learning franchise is a web of the networked records, services, modules of study, faculty to guide mastery, resources to provide information, and a study plan from entry to exit—one that can be adjusted as knowledge and skills accumulate.

Dolence and Norris (1995) describe how it works. The scenario goes something like this: a university automates its records system. Its smart application process receives a contact from a prospective student. This contact comes from its home page sites on the Internet, in community colleges, high school libraries, counseling centers, personnel offices of businesses who hire from the institution, and at branch sites where university extension and other distance programs serve as franchise centers. The application process kicks in, asking the applicant to convey her educational needs, using prompts and other descriptors that are on-line in the process. Her digitally stored transcript is read and evaluated electronically. After she has been admitted, she is invited to begin her studies by transferring her on-line record and supporting information to the academic management system (AMS).

The system adds her name to the e-mail account, to automated accounting, and to the rosters of learning spaces available. AMS scans her application, her inventory of specific interests, and her competencies. These are forwarded simultaneously to a faculty mentor coordinating each learning space. For each interest area, she immediately receives online syllabi, texts, and other information for downloading on CD-ROM and diskette. She also gets access to on-line tutorials for use throughout her plan of study. She is sent software for her science simulation laboratory work. She is immediately linked by e-mail to each faculty-led learning model. Throughout, she is connected via her personal computer phone center with the facilitator at the university. Before she chooses her elective learning models, but after she has looked over the mandatory modules, she is assigned a major professor who will be her adviser and mentor. With the mentor's concurrence, she sets time lines for the learning modules and signs up for face-to-face discussion groups and e-mail group sessions designed to aid learning and to prepare for tests, projects, essays, and other assignments and projects that are part of her record of mastery and skills certification. Her study plan is authorized and she begins learning.

As she learns, she is put in touch with likely employers or with institutions for advanced study. She interns in one of two areas—as an employee-intern if her route is professional or as a research aide and observer in the equivalent of semester or summer abroad programs of study. The program, however, is part of an early screen for advanced study and a capstone experience for her present study plan.

These innovations are available in present technology. Much of this will come to pass as a new social bargain is cast between the internal university and its external environment.

COMPLICATION OF AN OFFLOADING STATE

The complication in all of this is the role change among interested parties, especially the state. Employers want competent graduates schooled in practicalities and problem solving. Students want flexible curricula that allow them the chance to mix and match subjects for both basic and applied knowledge. Faculty want to keep control over the curriculum and stay focused on their disciplines and professions. Boards expect rapid change from a deliberate university community. Presidents are cautious middle persons sometimes caught between tradition-oriented faculty and strong-willed trustees. In the case of the public university, all of these role expectations are confounded by the offloading state.

In Europe, in Australia, and in the United States, central governments are cost cutting. This is often accomplished by passing programs without funds to lower levels of government. In the United States, state responsibility for higher education is longstanding. But as the federal government passes programs including law enforcement, welfare, and health care to the states, these programs compete with higher education for state dollars. In Europe, the offloading state passes responsibility down to regions and local governments (Dill and Sporn, 1995). In Spain and France, for example, a fiscal sleight of hand takes place as the central government passes down responsibility for raising taxes to fund universities along with what the governments call decentralization. Such fiscal maneuvers are often accompanied by a political shell game. The central government defuses political conflict at its level by decentralizing without accompanying funding. This shifts the conflict and strife among competing interests to the local or regional governments. Often, this decentralization includes latitude at the institution level to move resources around internally. Together, these moves prevent the build-up of conflict over community expectations at the national level.

This baiting and switching does little to build the courage needed for maximizing a society's capacity to compete effectively and provide the knowledge requirements of the information age. One expression frames the issue this way: it is easier to build the young than to repair adults. As learning will be lifelong and the competition over new knowledge and information will be intense, the society that steps up to educational change, especially for the young and those in their productive years, will likely prevail in the coming decades.

ACCEPTING RESPONSIBILITY

Political sleights of hand serve one useful purpose. They make it clear that higher education can and should accept responsibility and step up to these issues, because government really should not and probably will not. There are too many precedents in history of what comes from direct government intervention. Because of the many layers of special interests in universities, Levine describes the resulting problem: "All in all, our actions are akin to a boat's hitting an iceberg and the captain's announcing that his highest priority, as the boat sinks, is saving the crew. The next priority is avoiding any inconvenience by continuing all activities—the midnight buffet, the bingo game, the shuffleboard tournament. The third priority is repairing the boat. And the fourth and final one, should time permit, is saving the passengers" (1997, p. A48). The parody may be broad, but the message is clear. Higher education and government need both the will and the processes to make educational changes and to fund them adequately.

CHANGING THE CYCLE

Procedure legitimizes and legitimate change characterizes the academy. But the available processes are part of things gone wrong. They are unlikely to induce forward-looking change. Levine argues that "the usual mechanism to accomplish this has been the creation of an 87-member strategic-planning committee, which, after two years of weekly meetings, manages to select one program for cuts—which has not had a student in three years. The panel's recommendation triggers a faculty no-confidence vote in the president. A new president is hired, who says, 'We can get out of this situation by raising more money.' And the cycle starts again" (1997, p. A48). Though this description may seem overstated, it is to make a point: the recourse is to break the cycle.

But how? The sliding support for higher education has been under way since the 1980s. Most believe that this has been the result of the declining economy and the lack of tax revenues. This decline has been accompanied by a shift in government priorities, especially at the state level. As we have already argued, higher education must compete with prisons, welfare, and health care. Levine offers a plausible alternative. He suggests that American higher education has become a mature industry. Mature industries have characteristics and strategies for coping with their condition. Governments provide tax breaks and other assistance to the business world to attract growth industries. But mature industries succumb to increased regulation, as they are being left to find efficiencies and opportunities through internal belt-tightening and increased productivity. Doing more with less is the motto for these industries.

The health care industry is Levine's example of breaking the cycle. Government has turned to regulation via a managed-care policy. The cost of services is a focal point for government scrutiny. So is the efficiency and productivity of doctors, nurses, hospitals, and for-profit health providers. In the case of education, overall cost is scrutinized, tuition and fees are a concern, and student aid is shifting from grants to loans. Faculty productivity and accountability for the use of state dollars are policy issues in many states. As noted, harried higher education's typical strategy has been first to seek more money and then to cut costs the easy way—by across-the-board reductions, hiring freezes, and deferred maintenance (Levine, 1997). If these strategies do not suffice, the next step is to cut the nonacademic budgets. Meanwhile, most academic programs persist, even the bloated ones.

This cyclical strategy suggests that administrative leadership turns to processes that are safe when the pressure for change is great. Political scientist Earl Latham may have put it best when he wrote: "Administrative absurdity increases directly with the square of the distance between context and process" (Corson, 1960, p. 18). Tongue in cheek perhaps, but the argument is that leadership responds to the context of constituents and their special interests through procedures that avoid upsetting those groups and their interests. Absurd maybe, but apt.

LEARNING BY LOOKING AHEAD

The antidote is to look ahead. There are too many war stories of the past about administration versus faculty fights, of intrusive regents, or of boorish governors and pushy legislatures to find any tools for turning things around. Levine is probably right. Higher education is a mature institution and like all adult entities must leave the past and learn to fend for itself. Avoiding change fails. What works is at the heart of strategic planning: assess the shifting external environment of relevant forces, look for available external opportunities and internal strengths, and set a course to use them as resources for shaping change. This means strategically and candidly assessing what is to be taught in order to respond to these resources. How are universities to reorganize and nurture innovation and also keep the strengths of past excellence? How can campus conflicts be curbed for the common good? It is essential to answer both of these questions to determine the best way to attract and educate learners.

Part of looking ahead is sketching instructive strategic scenarios about future forms. What can the mature university become both intellectually and socially? Can the transformed university nourish quality as it cultivates social mobility and addresses society's needs? What will its character be, and how will it provide intellectual and moral leadership—moral in the sense of good citizenship and a shaping of the common good. Gibbons (Dill and Sporn, 1995) offers some insights. He describes current universities as academic and rooted in basic research, discipline and profession based, homogeneous and institutionally specialized, academically accountable, and quality controlled by peers. He then sketches an approach to knowledge and learning for the new age, whereby learning is knowledge produced in the context of application. It is transdisciplinary, heterogeneous and institutionally diverse, socially accountable, and quality controlled via intellectual acceptance and the durability of the solution.

The contrasting images these two sets of attributes portray are instructive. The first list describes characteristics of the current academy, while the second list describes characteristics that could be the embryonic elements for sketches of future universities. In the new age, students will engage in what we call *appositive learning;* that is, they will learn from knowledge derived from addressing real-world problems. By *appositive learning* we mean knowledge generated in the context of application. We imply by this that such learning gives rise to new cognitive and social norms which broaden the definition of good practice in inquiry and address problems that extend beyond the narrower interests of the academy. The relevant difference is between problem solving currently based on and confined to the theories and conceptual frameworks of disciplines, and problem solving based on a particular application so that results are widely diffused. This diffusion triggers new applications which lead to additional iterations of knowledge. Students will be guided by codes of practice that are continually negotiated intersubjectively as they draw on useful ideas, theories, and metaphors that explain a phenomenon or solve a problem. Then, the explanation or solution they select must weather the test of application and durability—how well it endures both practically and in the marketplace of ideas and products.

Whereas today's storehouses of knowledge are disciplines and professions, tomorrow's will be transdisciplinary in this sense: rather than developing theory first and then applying it, new learning will be driven by creativity, will be inquisitive, and will be prone to adding and refining ideas in the crucible of application. The theoretical consensus that evolves will not be easily reduced to disciplinary parts (Dill and Sporn, 1995).

Whereas current knowledge grows in homogeneous departments, labs, clinics, and other specialized sites, new age knowledge "yeasts" and "morphs" among groups of networked inquirers with varied backgrounds, each bringing insight and concepts to the problem at hand. Interactions face-to-face, by e-mail, by fax, and by on-line communication bring competing ideas and negotiated syntheses to creating new knowledge. Knowledge derived in this way is larger in scope than the many specialized perspectives brought by learners to bear on the problem of concern.

Today's students and scholars are assessed by experts and peers. In the new age, knowledge, products, manuscripts, equations, and other explanations and solutions will have been derived heterogeneously, and no set of homogeneous peers will be able solely to judge quality or relevance. In this world, broad social accountability will play a role as people, regardless of specialty, deal with that piece of the morphed and negotiated solution they comprehend.

Quality, like accountability, will not be determined solely by discipline-based specialty or intellectual content. In the new age, quality not only will face scrutiny as to intellectual content, but it also will have to survive the appositive test of addressing real issues. The symbiotic interplay between knowledge in the abstract and real-world consequences—as equal partners—will distinguish new learning. The argument is not that knowledge for knowledge's sake has no place in the world of the future. That will be the minimum standard of knowledge in the new age, not the maximum standard. The maximum will call for demonstrably and appositively helping advance human understanding and the quality of human life. This important change in how we learn will require processes and structures that induce these attributes in the internal environment of the new university.

POLYTECHNIC AS ONE NEW FORM

To answer the questions of how do we educate, improve learning, and identify resources, Kerr puts forth the idea of the polytechnic as one sketch of what the future university might look like: "In general I believe that the greatest single trend in the reorientation of program efforts within American higher education, as already in Western Europe, will (and should) be toward more emphasis on training polytechnic type skills and toward more polytechnic type applied research and technology transfer. This is where the competitive battles will focus increased attention" (Munitz, 1995, p. 1). Kerr's polytechnic is an early form of appositive learning. The polytechnic is where real-world issues are being addressed in Europe, especially in England. In this country, polytechnics conjure up images of engineers and techies busily engrossed in mundane matters. In reality, much of technology has come from these efforts. Their use in business, health care, and space exploration speaks aptly to the mix of the intellectual and the practical that emerges from the polytechnic experience.

Kerr's former colleague Munitz (1995) builds on this theme. He states that regardless of what you call it, the pressure for change is irreversible, and the competition will primarily be among the comprehensive universities to bridge the worlds of theory and applicability. As discussed in Chapter Two, this competition will occur without new resources and amidst diminished public support. Universities are now facing the fact that they appear to cost too much, sometimes spend carelessly, are believed to teach poorly, plan myopically, act defensively, and change slowly. Those who shift from defending against these criticisms to revitalizing teaching, stressing higher-order thinking and critical analysis, doing applied research, and developing problem-solving skills separate themselves from the pack. They will also fashion niches of excellence, thereby enhancing themselves in the intense competition for enrollments and funding.

The California Sate University system has sketched its own version of the polytechnic. Systemwide teams came together to consider five themes—being student centered, achieving demonstrable results, effectuating lifelong learning, achieving institutional effectiveness, and financing quality (Cornerstones Principles, 1997). They describe their major guiding principles—demonstrated learning as the basis for a degree, students as the center of the effort, outreach and retention as keys to undergraduate education, reinvestment in a faculty core essential for a teaching-centered university, students as active partners in learning, assessment of student learning, graduate and continuing education as equal partners, allowing local flexibility, bridging the resource gap, and maintaining quality and access.

Four task forces used these cornerstone themes and principles as they focused on: providing learning for the twenty-first century; meeting the enrollment and resources challenge; striving for institutional integrity, performance, and accountability; and providing quality postbaccalaureate and continuing education. These task forces developed principles to shape change in each of these topical areas. For learning, they focused on demonstrated learning, students as the center of academics, students as active partners in learning, and retention and outreach as central strategies in undergraduate education. For enrollment and resources, they included students paying a reasonable and predictable tuition, no differential undergraduate fees, a state-funded core, costs connected to financial aid, and graduates paying more of their own way. For performance and accountability, they focused on assessing student outcomes, assessing the learning environment, evaluating personnel through best-practices methods, including accreditation in shaping change, conducting program reviews to focus on quality, and linking to stakeholders. For postbaccalaureate and continuing education, the key ideas concerned making graduate education a full partner with undergraduate education, finding resources for expanded applied and professional education, committing to lifelong learning, developing a seamless postbaccalaureate education system, collaborating with sister institutions, instituting flexible pricing and increased self-financing of graduate programs, and fast-tracking approval for programs. This list of principles illustrates strategic thinking that uses an environmental scan as a basis for internal changes in the California State University system and its campuses. It is an example of effective strategic thinking. Its emphasis is to shape an internal environment that is student centered, responsive to external concerns, and enhances the performance of students and the quality of their education. The Cornerstones Principles also reflect the five forces of strategic change discussed in Chapter Two—access, pedagogy, knowledge, ethics, and responsibility.

FACULTY AS IMPORTANT RESOURCES

Faculty work hard. Allen finds that the 885,796 faculty in higher education work from fifty-two to fifty-four hours per week (Wechsler, 1996). Interestingly enough, research university faculty work the longest hours. In most universities, faculty spend twice as much time teaching as doing research. In research universities, faculty balance their research and teaching, spending about the same time on both. Among disciplines, humanities faculty spend nearly two-thirds (64 percent) of their time teaching, followed by faculty in education (57 percent), and fine arts (54 percent). On the lower end, faculty in agriculture and the health sciences spend from 34 to 39 percent of their time in the classroom. In these areas, laboratory, experimental, and other types of activities that involve direct contact with students are an important part of a faculty member's professional life. On balance, faculty publish about one article every two years. Research faculty publish four articles over the same time period. In addition to publication, faculty use research time to keep up in their fields. Allen concludes, "Faculty members work hard—due mainly to intrinsic motivations rather than external incentives or popular appeal—and most are actually more productive in this era of scarce resources" (Wechsler, 1996, p. 30).

Intrinsic motivation is one way that faculty productivity varies from simple notions of labor productivity. Simple notions of productivity assume that productivity is a divisible, individualized output. That is not the case. There is another complicating factor. Factory workers manipulate invariant materials when producing a commodity. But social commodities vary widely. Their motivations and forms of participation vary. Professors work with materials—students—that can answer back, ignore instruction, vary in their attention, differ in their abilities, and control their own responses. Shaping such a commodity is profoundly complex. For these reasons, faculty productivity is not likely to be gauged well by simple measures such as course loads, student contact hours, and number of publications.

At the same time, policy leaders are not ogres whose sole purpose is to torment the academy and thwart its need for resources, support, and the freedom to discover and teach. Public officials and parents are not uninformed hayseeds with no understanding of what the academy is and needs. Many of them are our college graduates. If they are critical of alma mater, alma mater would do well to listen.

Ewell (1995) offers a clue. He suggests that "the academic management trick may lie less in 'redefining' faculty work than in creating a fiscal and structural environment within which the strongly cooperative and entrepreneurial tendencies already nascent in faculty culture can be more effectively channeled" (pp. 6–7). Though "channeled" may be a bit strong, "encouraged" and "enabled" are apt descriptors of the kinds of strategies that recognize faculty as a strategic resource.

Take the issue of balancing research and teaching. Politicians, business leaders, administrators, and alumni believe the imbalance between research and teaching must be redressed. Faculty believe (and facts show) that the two are not out of balance. Critics call for redesigning the curriculum to be more responsive to the economic needs of changing times. Faculty appropriately argue that an education is more than just preparing people for jobs. Education involves critical thinking and a course of study beyond mere professional requirements. Critics say increase quality and productivity. Educators such as Kenneth Ashworth reply that universities already do that. They argue that educational excellence spurs the new economy because "most of the engines that drive the American economy had their origins in universities. The hybrid plants that sparked the agricultural revolution, the computers that do the work of the information processing industry, the genetic engineering that made the U.S. the world leader in biotechnology, the innovative materials on which the world's foremost aerospace industry depends are all the products of a society that had the foresight to link education and research" (Commission for Educational Quality, 1994, p. 10). External leaders say universities need to respond more directly to job market challenges. Educators respond that there are three-year accounting degrees as at the University of Northern Colorado; the University of Miami School of Architecture provided assistance to South Dade County in rebuilding after Hurricane Andrew; and the University of Illinois at Chicago provides emerging businesses with resources to advance their enterprise (Office of Policy Development and Research, 1996). Critics seek strengthened linkages between colleges, schools, and the workplace. Faculties reply that they have such connections, as in the case of the University of Southern Colorado's long-term project with School District Sixty, in which the university provides assistance to the schools as it trains future teachers in a truly joint venture. Then there is the Maine degree-granting, interactive, technologically based educational delivery system. And most institutions have internships in business, the health sciences, and other professional fields of study.

ADDRESSING POLICY CONCERNS

Addressing policy concerns begins with a common way of counting, identifying, and analyzing the issues. The lack of a common ruler is evident in a survey of California leaders by the California Higher Education Policy Center (Immerwahr and Boese, 1995). The public worries about the price of a college education. Leaders fret over the cost of higher education. Higher education focuses on the needed revenue. No wonder the chasm. No wonder all are pessimistic that a solution can be found.

Were there areas of consensus in this study? There were. They include the following:

- Higher education issues are serious and a priority.
- The state needs an effective process for dealing with these issues.
- Major changes are needed in higher education (restructuring).
- Better thinking is needed about the purposes of higher education.

This list could apply anywhere. It also shows that when people focus on the problem rather than on who is to blame for it, agreements can be reached that begin to bridge the chasm.

In the California case, some consensus recommendations did emerge:

- Better use of existing facilities
- Better ways of paying pegged to income
- Better use of technology
- Increased focus on select high-quality graduate and professional programs
- Increased review of teaching loads

None of these are earthshaking recommendations. These are common sense items that are at the core of concern over the future of higher education. Cynics might say that the devil is in the details of these general recommendations. But the devils that may exist in items derived from consensus have a far better chance of being found and overcome than the devils cloaked in the differences of conflict.

Among the remaining controversies are three-year bachelor degrees for some programs; variable fees, especially for professional schools; and a greater role for private institutions.

The near-routine nature of these California issues resurfaces in a national survey by the American Association of State Colleges and Universities. Their survey of policy issues uncovered several items of concern—accountability, duplication, and administrative costs. Nothing insurmountable here either. Once more, differences occur less over the substance of the issues than from the context of distrust that turns ordinary issues into extraordinary obstacles.

The National Association of State Universities and Land Grant Colleges (NASULGC), in concert with the Kellogg Commission, has embarked on bridging the gap between public issues and university practices. With a focus on linking member institutions with important public issues, NASULGC projects are providing models for change. Ohio State University (OSU) campuses have developed Project Reinvent, which uses communication and marketing to create a more effective way to share discoveries and changes developed on the OSU campuses in the areas of food, agriculture, and the environment. Iowa State University is collaborating with fifteen community colleges to fund innovative projects in agriculture. These partnerships show what can be done without major new resources or battles over principle and jurisdiction. And there is always room for negotiation, which suggests that steps of negotiated success bridge gaps.

But some gaps are not quite so routine or modest. Appleberry (1995) offers some landmark observations about the future of higher education. He finds that people everywhere are rethinking their relationships, that information expands with unprecedented rapidity, that technology enhances information expansion, and that the nature of work changes worldwide. These conditions put higher education through a virtual tectonic shift, because fundamentally reshaping the environment of learning is to the world of education what tectonic shifts are to the world of geology. These shifts take learning beyond the classroom to the workplace and elsewhere. As a consequence, universities have lost their monopoly over information and expertise. These four aspects of change that Appleberry described are already having significant effects on higher education, including the following:

- The competition for economic dominance is matched by the competition for intellectual dominance.
- The structures that hold us together, such as families, communities, and governments, are being displaced by the increased atomism technology brings about.
- Information available to humankind will double every seventy-three days.
- Virtual offices and learning places will enable students to learn from where they are via lectures on CD-ROM, progressing at their own pace, taking classes as they fit life and work schedules.
- A cafeteria approach will characterize learning.
- Subject matter will be modularized with assessed specific learning outcomes.
- People will study to understand other cultures.
- Students will learn to function in group problem-solving situations.
- Just-in-time instruction will permit unprecedented learning in application.
- Students will be partners with faculty in learning.

• Mission differentiation will be required of colleges and
universities.

Each of these factors is more complex and difficult than the issues
faced in California or those discussed above. Bridging them with
higher education practice will require building from present practice
one step at a time, beginning with innovations reflective of the
strengths of current practice. Smart change builds on quality. Effective change begins with engaging issues in a tough but fair-minded
discussion of what changes are needed and why. Then, required negotiation takes place in a jointly set framework for discussion and completion. This change process hinges on well-designed SWOT analyses
and brainstorming the results and their cross-impacts. (See Dolence,
Rowley, and Lujan, 1997.) As needed changes become clearer, their
required trade-offs will also become evident, setting the stage for further negotiation and advancement. This levering of change requires a
strategic perspective and sensitivity for campus politics.

SHAPING POLICY RESPONSES

Leaving resolution to those in positions of power vests change in the
hands of politicians, governors, legislators, trustees, and other influ-
entials largely outside the academy. This is a game the academy is sure
to lose, for its strength has traditionally been in the use of reason to
create knowledge and resolve conflict.

So how is the mantle of power to be reclaimed by those who prefer the route of reason? Breneman (1997) offers some insight. Reductions in state support have led colleges and universities to scramble
for substitute resources. The result is the increased privatization of the
university, and campuses have gone from being state supported in
their early years, to state assisted in their years of growth, to state
located in the face of current reductions in state funding. This has
prompted some to look seriously at becoming private. In Michigan,
state support amounts to only 10 percent of total revenues. In Virginia, the comparable amount is 13 percent, and state support has
dropped from 32.7 percent of its budget in 1990–91 to 20.7 percent
in 1995–96. A vestige of power could be reclaimed in the short run by
privatization. But in Virginia's case, assuming a 5 percent annual pay-
out, it would take a $2.4 billion base to generate the $120 million now

provided annually by the state. If this route is unwise, it would take a 130 percent increase in tuition to compensate for state support.

The reality is that colleges and universities are really state-seeded institutions. There is benefit to retaining at least this relationship, especially if state policymakers would deregulate the institutions, allowing flexibility within budgets to move resources around in response to program priorities that reflect, at least in part, negotiated public priorities. To be beneficial, this would also require that the state not deduct from its contribution the resources saved by careful and opportunity-seizing management of university resources. Such flexibility would also allow privatization in certain parts of an institution, including such obvious functions as real estate, auxiliary services, purchasing, technology, and research. In Breneman's words, "Each of the steps I've cited moves the university a bit closer to independent status, but always within a framework of negotiation and the slow-but-steady development of trust between state and university officials" (1997, pp. B4–B5). To repeat a point made earlier: strategic steps of negotiated success bridge policy gaps and reduce policy conflict. They also remove harmful roadblocks carelessly placed that block the path to innovation and strategic change as well as help uncover internal strengths and strategies that will begin and cement change.

CHAPTER FOUR

Analyzing Global Responses to New Learning Needs

T his chapter looks at some of the issues that face education worldwide. Even though we realize that many readers are much more interested in what is happening in the United States, the information age is not an American phenomenon. It is international, and education around the world is significant to how the age will evolve. Many nations of the world look to the United States, as the world's educational leader, to provide the models that they may use. However, there are interesting models taking shape beyond U.S. borders that provide valuable examples and insights of alternatives that can be instructive to any campus, regardless of where it is located.

FACING THE NEW REALITIES AT HOME

Higher education must face the new realities or risk becoming academic Jurassic Parks, quaint historic places where time stops as the world goes by. Richardson argues that higher education has a new calling: "a commitment to make a difference in the lives of people where they live," to "play a central role in finding their own solutions," and "to impact public policy that creates economic and social opportunities for people to improve their quality of life" (1996b, p. 1). Not only should this calling affect people where they live, the information age requires that it affect them where they work. If there is any theme central to change, it is linking education to the workplace. The workplace will help generate problems for appositive learning—the generation of knowledge informed by application in the real world. This will lead not only to the application of knowledge, but also as Donald Schön argues, "for its generation. We should ask not only how practitioners can better apply the results of academic research, but what kinds of knowing are already embedded in competent practice" (Richardson, 1996b, p. 2).

We have been doing some of this in the academy for some time. The space program is an example of solving real problems while advancing human knowledge. The Johns Hopkins effort to launch the Hubble Telescope is a case in point. It linked the university to the workplace through research, long the engine that powers the conversion of basic knowledge to practical application. The advances in medicine from the kidney shunt to the heart transplant reflect this. The university hospital, partner to the quality medical school, has been such a linking mechanism. As Richardson notes (1996b), so too are the historic efforts of agricultural extension, university extension, agricultural experiment stations, large science laboratories, continuing education, branch campuses, midcareer graduate and professional programs, and distance learning. The problem has not been the quality or effectiveness of these programs but the distances at which these enterprises have been kept by the traditional core of the academy. The problem is not that universities have not reached out to new learners; it is that universities have not valued what these learners have done.

Lifelong learning has become necessary because knowledge is so perishable (Richardson, 1996b). Before Hubble, we learned that there were ten billion galaxies. Post-Hubble, we have discovered forty billion new ones. We used to think of cloning as science fiction. Today, we clone sheep and other mammals. Yesterday's truth is today's untruth (and vice versa). The paradigms in use are not as durable as they used to be. Counter paradigms displace them at a dizzying rate, generating both new problems and new solutions at a pace unknown in human history.

FACING CHANGE ABROAD

What is happening in the United States is also happening abroad. Each case has its own twist, but the old three r's of education are being replaced by a plethora of new r's. Italy is "rightsizing." Italy's higher education system is the most crowded in Western Europe (Bollag, 1997). Universities have become "exam factories" (p. A45), where contact with faculty is minimal, promotion is controlled by national discipline-based commissions, governance is centralized in the Ministry of Public Education, and admissions are centrally approved. Swollen from twenty to sixty-six institutions since World War II, these universities suffer from inadequate libraries and laboratories as well as classrooms. The University of Rome has 180,000 students. The faculty of law have 40,000 students. Things are so crowded, people who arrive late stand, or go home. The rector of the University of Rome has a simple solution: "We need more buildings, professors, and money" (Bollag, 1997, p. A46)—a familiar refrain to American ears. There is also talk of breaking up the feudal kingdom of the university. The rector resists. The need to rightsize persists. The resolution will be a question of political power, not educational policy.

In London, Cambridge expects enrollments to increase 25 percent by 2020 (Walker, 1997). Cambridge's solution is relocation and doubling its physical size. The older buildings in the center of Cambridge will be vacated and likely sold, as science and technology are relocated at a 150-acre site west of the city. A casualty of the move will be the Cavendish Laboratory, where the first atom was split. A gain from the move will be up-to-date world-class teaching and research facilities. Plans to finance the relocation are vague, and there is no current estimate of cost.

For the rest of England, the issue is reputation. Started twelve years ago to evaluate the quality of research, a panel of experts named by the Higher Education Financing Council for England, the government's funding agency, performs assessments every four years (Tugend, 1997). Each faculty and department must chronicle its accomplishments and aspirations. Institutions are rated and the rating affects funding for research. Though Oxford edged past Cambridge, the rest were accepting of their rankings, seeing it all as worth more than reputation. Rankings also bring money and public relations, both of which help in the competition over faculty and top students. With public funding increasingly flat and scarce, reputation aids in the competition over scarce resources.

Both France and Australia cope with reforms. In France, financial aid grows in importance. New reforms have been proposed by the minister of education, but funds have not been provided for the changes. These changes link aid to need. Open access continues as the policy, but without funded aid, only those with the means can attend (Giudice, 1997). The course of study is also under reform. The intent is to move from an annual term to a semester system for the first two years of study. This would give flexibility for students to change planned fields of study and ideally would reduce the time to completion. It now takes an average 2.7 years to complete the first two years' course work. Internships are being encouraged along with academic credit for work. The concern is the same as in the United States—linking learning to work and providing graduates who are skilled and competent to face the rapidly changing world of work.

Australia suffers not from a wealth of interested students but from enrollment declines. This is the result of a major governmental policy change in which free college and university tuition has gone by the board, and students now pay tuition (Alan Tilley, interview with authors, July 1997). Major tuition increases designed to cover costs in engineering, science, and technology resulted in dropping enrollments. The prime minister cut budgets, leading to an 80 percent increase in fees for these areas. This has jeopardized funding as enrollments faded, leading to the lowering of admissions criteria to meet federal enrollment quotas. Some, like the University of South Australia, have about five hundred unfilled seats. The State of Victoria is undertaking its own study of the fall-off and is also scrutinizing the future of higher education, doing so ahead of a national study just now under way for the same purpose (Maslen, 1997). The national panel has raised hackles among academics. The quarrel is over the head of the panel, a private school headmaster, and the panel consultant, a former Cambridge vice-chancellor. Opinion is that the latter's involvement reinforces Australia's "colonial origin" (p. A47). At issue for the academy is the panel's charge, which is to assess the ability of the universities to meet the nation's social, economic, scientific, and cultural needs over the next twenty years; the options for financing that include private funds; the nature and degree of demand for graduates and for research; and teaching and course content. This government-led inquiry has educational leaders on edge, because it is an external process that will shape future educational policy.

The Netherlands has retrenched (Acherman, 1988). The first retrenchment occurred in 1982 and the second in 1986. In the first case, it occurred from within the academy. Facing a budget cut of 8 percent over four years, university leaders from thirteen institutions took the initiative to manage the reduction largely on their own. The second cut was externally imposed. It was masked by the slogan, "selective retrenchment and growth" (p. 43). The idea was that retrenchment (cuts) would be balanced by a fund for innovative projects. Imposed as it was, resistance to it was strong and determined. Compromise emerged for the long run. Every ten years, institutions must undertake a reconnaissance of their programs, submit a report, and respond to issues in their biennial budgets. They must assess teaching every five years. This staged retrenchment is designed to encourage adaptation from within the academy and provide a means for program reduction as budgets level off or decline.

By contrast, Canada is revitalizing. Classically European and therefore centralized and homogeneous, higher education in Canada has been chafing as resources have varied (Lewington, 1997). Proud that its universities are all very much alike, both in cost and quality, the government has been looking for a way out as the demand for new resources builds. A new and more conservative government has looked at options that include deregulation of fees and privatizing of some services in universities within Ontario's seventeen universities and twenty-five colleges. These institutions enroll 542,000 students, 40 percent of all students in Canada. A panel has reviewed the situation and urges restoring financial support to levels comparable with the United States and the rest of Canada, letting institutions set their own tuition and fees, introducing a student loan program that ties repayment to earnings after graduation, giving tax incentives to encourage saving for college, establishing an advisory body to assess performance and quality, eliminating geographic restrictions on recruiting, and developing a provincial rather than institutional diploma. The effect of these changes would be more flexibility and variety among Ontario's colleges and universities than is currently the case. But the colleges would probably suffer, because their students come from working-class backgrounds in which cost is a major obstacle and because they would have to compete for students. Losers in this competition would have to cut programs. This, of course, is a dilemma that America's comprehensive colleges and universities currently face.

Costa Rica, one of the world's small enduring democracies, is quietly reflecting on the changes going on elsewhere. Jose Andres Masis Bermudez, director of the National Council of Rectors, observed that countries like his "have to weigh and consider change in a global context" (interview with authors, November 1996). Higher education in Costa Rica has been influenced by France, Germany, other Latin countries, and the United States. What emerges comes slowly and reflectively. Among the conflicts are the French influence on the abstract and theoretical versus the American influence on tying theory to experience. The debate goes on less in words and more in the ideas that define curricula, shape requirements, and define degrees. The University of Costa Rica is comparable to America's larger universities, although there teaching rather than research is emphasized. The research effort is growing, but funding is limited. The country is struggling economically and its infrastructure is deteriorating. Here, the concern is how to remain educationally competitive with limited resources internally and the pressure of rapid global change externally. Costa Rica's solution will likely be eclectic and practical. Costa Ricans will sustain universities at the level they can afford while persisting to sustain the requisites of quality. As universities seek global partners and become networked technologically, universities like those in Costa Rica can become part of a larger educational resource. Already, Costa Rica has a respected distance learning effort in place. In this way, a richer educational experience than is currently available can be introduced and serve as a bridge to the information age (Jose Andres Masis Bermudez, interview with authors, November 1996).

Taiwan poses a real contrast. Economically vibrant, it enjoys double-digit growth. It invests heavily in education. Since 1989, educational expenditures have exceeded the percent increase in gross national product (Bureau of Statistics, 1996). Education has been a high national priority. Taiwan's President Lee Teng-hui is a Cornell University graduate with interests in science and agriculture. He has supported this rise in investment, in both elementary and higher education, and sees this investment as essential for the continued competitiveness of Taiwan in the global marketplace (Lee Teng-hui, interview with authors, October 1994). His chief aide, Secretary General Huang Kun-huei, is a former minister of education and university president. Huang is a steadfast supporter of higher education, especially teacher education (Huang Kun-huei, interview with authors, January 1997). This high-level interest in education, along with the view that education is an investment rather than a cost, stands in strong contrast to the political dialogue in the United States.

With this level of support, Taiwan is reinvesting, especially in teacher education. In 1994, the Teacher Education Law was amended to broaden access to teacher education beyond the teachers colleges to all colleges. In addition, Hwang Chen-ku, President of National Kaohsiung Normal University in Taiwan, has talked about the plans for an additional twenty-two colleges, raising the number from fifty-eight to eighty during the transition to the twenty-first century. Teacher education is almost fully subsidized by the government, along with aid for special needs. This effort to broaden access to teacher preparation is a reflection of the priority given to education and teacher preparation. Secondary teacher education is also under scrutiny, and the normal universities now provide leadership in secondary teacher education. Hwang has undertaken strategic planning to address this matter and the general quality of university study: "We need to approach change strategically, so that quality is enhanced at the same time that skills are improved. Education is the foundation and prime force behind progress" (Hwang Chen-ku, interview with authors, January 1997). Other university presidents concur, especially Leu Hsi-muh of National Taiwan Normal University, Lin Yung-shi of Taipei Municipal Teacher's College, Ou Yung-sheng of National Taipei Teachers College, and Chen Jwo-min of National Changhua University of Education (Lin Yung-shi, Ou Yung-sheng, Leu Hsi-muh, and Chen Jwo-min, interviews with authors, January 1997). The real challenge may lie in shaping the reinvestment in higher education to support desired transformations into multipurpose universities by the more established national institutions and in linking all teachers colleges to universities. In one version, teachers colleges would become colleges of education within the framework of a university. These ideas are substantial in nature and have launched an important dialogue about how best to shape Taiwan's reinvestment in education generally.

Romania is restoring higher education. With the former rector of the University of Bucharest as president, long-overdue improvements are being instituted in student housing, in recognition of faculty, in restoration of their position and reputation, and in expanded educational opportunities for ethnic minorities. Funds are expected for needed infrastructure. Reform is expected to go forward as are management improvements and efficiencies. Graduate programs are getting needed attention. Underneath it all lie some tough issues. Scholars want access to Romania's communist archives. Romanian history was rewritten during the Iliescu, Ceausescu, and Gheorghiu-Dej regimes. Iliescu, the last of the tri-patriarchs, blocked research into the archival records. Trusted scholars were given carte blanche power and virtual monopolies over their specialties and privileged access to the archives. State archivists can block degrees by withholding access to needed records. Before buildings and laboratories are refurbished and constructed and even before respect for faculty is renewed, academic freedom must be restored. Here, the quarrel is not over annual budget increments or funding a pet project. The quarrel is over the resurgence of the freedom to know and to share knowledge basic to human and social survival.

From rightsizing to restoring, universities and colleges are rebuilding. They are rebuilding support externally for what they do, both in government and in the business world, and they are realizing the need to rebuild internally. The same old strategies no longer have the same old rewards attached to them. The realization that universities must master their own destinies or have solutions imposed from the outside is making higher education face the new realities globally.

BUILDING NEW ALTERNATIVES
IN AMERICAN HIGHER EDUCATION

Change requires new alternatives. These are found in new approaches to learning. As discussed earlier, research has identified the attributes of a quality undergraduate education (American Association for Higher Education, 1996). Quality is built on high expectations, diverse learning styles, and strong foundations in early years of study. A quality curriculum involves developing coherent learning abilities, synthesizing experiences, using learned skills, and linking education to experience. Quality instruction builds on active learning, assessment and prompt feedback, collaboration, time on task, and outside contact with faculty.

This view of quality has led to an alternative approach to learning. Current learning is heavily bureaucratic. Faculty and others engaged in providing the core of learning can be viewed in some ways as a professional bureaucracy based on expertise. Because their work cannot easily be measured, they are in the unique position of controlling both the content and processes of learning. In simpler times, this factory model worked just fine, educating the top 25 percent to provide the jobs for the remaining 75 percent. As we have argued elsewhere, the industrial age was compatible with and flourished under this model. But the information age makes this obsolete. This age needs everyone well educated and regularly engaged in advancing knowledge.

The inertia of higher education comes in part from the monopoly of expertise it has long enjoyed. But faculty are, if anything, entrepreneurial. They are fascinated by new problems. They are instinctively inquisitive. So why do some faculty resist change?

The resistance lies more in the organizations that faculty have built to house learning and the processes they have created to impart it (Seymour, 1996). Because there is little control over learning except by the professionals themselves, there is no easy way to make change happen. If the professionals oppose change, it will not come easily. A frustrated public and its representatives can easily turn to control, standardization, and simple algorithms to compare and contrast institutions. As Seymour observes, "Higher education is locked into a paradigm that focuses on resources, reputation, and a transcendent notion of quality" (1996, p. 11). In that paradigm, faculty maintain the right to define their responsibilities and the degree to which existing processes and paradigms constrain change. They also force change that is more radical than what would likely result from honest negotiation.

A clear alternative is the Malcolm Baldrige paradigm. In it, an award is constructed based on twenty-eight results-oriented requirements (Seymour, 1996). Eleven core values, ranging from learning-centers education to results orientation, are cross-matched to a weighted scale of seven criteria, ranging from leadership to student and stakeholder satisfaction. The core values are learning-centered education, leadership, continuous improvement and organizational learning, faculty and staff development, partnerships, design quality and prevention, management by fact, view of the future, public responsibility and citizenship, fast response, and results orientation. The seven criteria for 1995 were leadership, information and analysis, strategic planning, human resource development, educational and business management school performance results, student focus, and stakeholder satisfaction. With leadership as the driver and satisfaction along with school performance the outcomes, each of the other criteria are situated between these. An assessment is made, based on a proposal or report of a program from a school, by using the description of how core values and concepts manifest themselves against each of the relevant criteria. For example, using the criterion of student performance results, a program would demonstrate what its key measures for performance were, the actual results for their students on these measures, and how they compare to peers or other comparables. If the interest is stakeholder satisfaction, then key measures, such as success via job placement (if not actually working), evidence of advanced study one year after graduation, or percent of alumni giving to the institution could be specified. Actual changes from some baseline year could be provided, along with how these compare with peers. Core values and concepts would guide the development of key indicators.

Our concern is not the exact replication of this model. Instead, our focus is on initiating and developing other new and innovative diagnostic schemes, which relate to purposes and values and that allow an honest and straightforward display of failures and successes. The model can be as complicated or as simple as design and purpose permit. But a means of diagnostic assessment for organizations is central to genuine change in the information age. With information as the driver, organizations must become learning organizations, intelligent and able to use information and values to evaluate and adjust behavior as the organization evolves. The information explosion of the information age, appositive learning, and the need for global erudition and competency require new organizational forms. Richardson makes the case adroitly that change "is fostered by a decentralized, relatively flat organization, enabled by sophisticated management information, and responsive to a variety of market forces. I would note that this approach does not assume anything less than top quality in every undertaking" (1996b, p. 4).

Reaching New Learners at Home

In the information age, we must link with learners wherever they are. Providing education without access will not be good enough. Moreover, the linking of learning to the world of the learner's experience will clearly require that the burden of proof for access falls on the educational providers. This, of course, is a new point of view for most people except for those individuals traditionally involved in what we are calling distance learning. In addition, we will need to link not just with those of college age or above but also with those preparing for college. We must do this programmatically and in terms of what they learn and study, not just as targets of recruitment. This means working much closer with K–12 teachers and counselors. The current standards movement is forcing some of this, especially in the development of competence tests. But we are arguing here that it must be an extensive link, beginning from teacher education and ranging into partnerships in classrooms, learning from K–12 teachers as peers, and, the most difficult, moving away from the bureaucratic professionalism that has turned K–12 education into a lockstep routine that alienates both students and teachers. We are also arguing here that quick fixes such as charter schools, the Edison Project, and other innovations are fine. But they are not for everybody. They work in some areas and not in others.

Bureaucrats must also give up the penchant for standardization as the simple solution. Standardization was an appropriate model for the days when the select and homogeneous 25 percent went on to advanced study. But the information age will expect 100 percent to participate as lifelong learners. This is where the current national performance-standards effort runs afoul of real-life educational needs and systemic educational requirements. Teaching to a standard assumes a single learning style. Research shows styles vary. When a society tries to teach everyone, its approach must reflect the pluralism and heterogeneity that characterizes the world of actual learners. For this reason, several models, not one model, are needed. At the K–12 level, this means local approaches, most likely coordinated at the state level so long as funding and statutes require it. The lesson not to be lost is that schools must relate to the real-world students they serve, for knowledge will force this linkage in an age of appositive learning.

What about standards, competency, and the litany of traditional approaches to demonstrate mastery? Over time, they will fall as casualties of the marketplace. In spite of efforts at standardized competency, the competitive world of reality will reward accomplishments and recognize innovations. Pluralism, flexibility, fit with benchmark knowledge, these will be the drivers of the new age. To make a pointed comparison, flat-earth scholars became anachronisms in the Copernican world. We believe that the new age will be as Copernican to the exploration of knowledge and learning as Copernicus was to the exploration of the globe.

It is better to focus energies elsewhere, beginning where the students are and not where we want them to be. It is simply too easy for faculty to argue that they could teach better if students were better prepared. If they were better prepared, why would they need people to prepare them in the first place? If only the better prepared can learn, then who will provide the counter paradigms for this homogeneous cohort of well-prepared minds? Homogeneity breeds orthodoxy, and the new world needs heterodoxy and the clash of ideas, especially to advance appositive learning. This is not to argue that there is no place for this traditional view of learning. It is to argue that this view alone cannot shape the approach to learning for a global society.

Relinking to K–12 will require better ties between segments. Every K–12 school should have a community college or university partner. University faculty from all disciplines need to be in K–12 classrooms as colleagues, not as experts. K–12 students will require early exposure to advanced learning. Technology will be a useful but not a central tool in this relationship. It is faculty outside their classrooms and laboratories who inspire and impart new ideas at the same time that they learn from the refreshing enthusiasm of the eager learners. Secondary schools need reconfiguration. Much of what occurs there is the simple transfer of information. That is also true of lower-division university and college education, especially the freshman year. It is worth exploring what can be done to breathe life into the secondary curriculum, as its excitement seems to diminish by each passing day. High school was important and energizing when it led clearly to college or to jobs that satisfied the mind and interest of the student. High school was the vehicle to the factory of work or the factory of knowledge. But that is no more.

An example of the kind of partnering that works exists in Medina County, Ohio. The University of Akron has linked itself through fiber optics to the Medina County Schools, allowing simultaneous instruction to the twenty-six thousand public school students and other education professionals in the system. Eligible high school juniors and seniors can now take college courses for credit. The system is fully interactive; it connects students and faculty to two-way, real-time voice, video, and data transmission. An electronic board allows students and teachers to write simultaneously on the same board even though they are in different locations (American Association of State Colleges and Universities, 1997). This linkage is a simple example of the kinds of connections universities can make with K–12 systems.

The reform most sorely needed is the rearticulation of the curriculum and how it is learned for the needs of the new age. Technology will be an important partner, for it makes accessible what was locked in libraries or was otherwise foreboding or difficult to access. Now, students can learn about knowledge transfer early. If much of lower-division education could be taught by high schools and community colleges, then a bridge to advanced skills training (the community college) and advanced transdisciplinary learning (colleges and universities) can be designed, even as new knowledge is created.

Changes at the secondary level will trigger innovations at the elementary and middle school levels. Here, technology will play a critical role in establishing basics in the sense of language, qualitative thinking, and quantitative analysis. Much of this knowledge can be delivered electronically in a discovery and repetitious format that fits early learning. It can also be linked to homes and make better use of these ties than current public television channels do. More than one language will be needed in the global village, putting to a merciful end the controversies over bilingual education and the matter of official languages. The competition of the global marketplace will drive language learning back to the center of learning in elementary and middle school education. This is where the foundation for language and literature will be laid, along with the understanding of music, art, drama, and other forms of human communication. Along with this will most likely come the history of the whole world; as well as global geography and environments; world ideas and philosophies; the study of global societies and their cultures; and an introduction to the universe, its exploration, and the rapidly changing world of science. We will be educating citizens to be conversant with issues of the world, not just to be experts in a single culture and its particular nuances.

When curricula adjust to the new age, community colleges will play a critical transfer role. Though their basic function as the vehicle for transition to advanced careers or study will not change (Cohen, 1995), changing student populations and labor force demands will require increased flexibility to accommodate learning needs (Brawer, 1996). Driven by this focus on workforce training, community colleges are likely to redefine their customers as whole communities (Travis, 1995). With the increase of urban decay and the need to stabilize cities worldwide, community colleges will be at the front line of improving the infrastructure for the information age workforce. Small businesses are expected to grow from eighteen million to twenty-five million by 2000. Skills and management training will bring the community college even closer to the workplace than it has been. Some argue that it will become the fulcrum for the community network needed to foster community development and improvement (Travis, 1995). Cooperative ventures, pooled resources, and efforts to curry support for change within the community will characterize the adapting community college. As community college faculties age, focus must turn from preserving traditional jobs and retirement to turning the community college into a flexible horizontal organization able to adapt to the rapid changes likely in the new age. Some see the community college at the center of a K–14 system of community education and training centers, committed to lifelong learning, workforce training, and capstones of college preparatory studies at a quality and depth beyond the high school and at least as sophisticated as the lower-division education of today's better universities (Travis, 1995).

Academically, what cannot be taught well at the secondary level that is now lower-division education in colleges would easily fit the community college and its image for the future. Already well versed and successful in lower-division education, community colleges can put the finishing touches on introductory college learning. This would leave the university college and classroom free for transdisciplinary learning in less than a four-year format. Three-year colleges would be affordable, would probably require less housing and fewer traditional amenities, and would be geared for adult and lifelong learners. Classrooms would be linked to work and to residences electronically. E-mail, CD-ROMs, diskettes containing lectures and problems, and digitized video discs with demonstrations and laboratory experiments would accessorize a classroom focused on problem solving. Such a classroom would link naturally with the research and discovery required in appositive learning.

Undergraduate learning would be enhanced by problem-centered learning and participation in knowledge discovery. This approach would revitalize the undergraduate classroom and the undergraduate. Already, one of the authors offers a seminar open to any undergraduate on the future of the university. Students cover the literature, then break up into groups to design a university for the year 2020. The group designs are then presented and critiqued in class. After that, each student designs her or his own university. In all of this, e-mail keeps student and faculty connected, and the Internet links the student to digitized libraries, home pages, and the wealth of information about higher education available on the web. While students are in the design stage, the instructor is also available for individual tutorials. Because the instructor is doing research on the same topic, students are exposed to discovery regardless of whether they are seniors or freshmen.

Serving New Learners Globally
Through Innovative Links

Students over forty are the fastest-growing age group in postsecondary education. They represent new opportunities and challenges to colleges and universities (TERI, 1996). Between 1970 and 1993, this group grew by 235 percent to 1.6 million. "Overforties" increased from 5.5 percent to 11.3 percent of those enrolled in higher education over the same years. Most attend part-time, are white, female, and married. Their interest in further study is driven by increasing educational requirements for employment, changing life circumstances, and personal growth. Growth in skills-related courses among overforties was 45 percent between 1983 and 1991. Students over forty are a major constituency driving innovative approaches to learning, such as the Education Network of Maine, which provides access to courses and degrees via a statewide voice, video, data system. Overforties persist in spite of many obstacles from both work and family life. They generally have better grades than younger students. Forty-four percent of overforties received mostly A's in their course work compared to 9 percent of those aged eighteen to twenty-four.

Overforties could overwhelm the current infrastructure of traditional universities, especially when combined with the baby boom echo of those who will be college eligible in 2000. Both will be critical to the economic productivity of the nation and global competitiveness. They will have three doorways to education: formal programs of study; employer-provided study; and innovative access, largely through technology that links their places of work and residence to the classroom (TERI, 1996). Of these, employer education is the most competitive. It is the fastest-growing learning segment; it focuses on work-related needs; it is more innovative than traditional professional education; and its growth portends change in other education markets. It also includes Mode 2 learning in the apposition of work problems and related abstract learning.

Mode 2 learning occurs in the context of application and is transdisciplinary, heterogeneous in the skills participants bring to it, and sensitive to the broader social implications of research. Learners achieve quality by observing the degree to which the results of their learning endure, both intellectually and socially. Mode 2 learning fosters not only structured thinking but also creative insight, and it extends beyond the confines of disciplines and laboratories into the world of work and empirical experience.

Overforties will require changes in tradition (TERI, 1996). The social club orientation of traditional freshmen will give way to focused orientation that addresses setting goals, building on previous educational experiences, and scheduling around work and home, as learning becomes more connected with the off-campus situations of learners. Courses will need to be scheduled electronically for off-campus learning or at convenient times, ordinarily very early mornings, evenings, and weekends. On-line courses will significantly assist in scheduling and may well aid learning by allowing regular access when minds may not be exhausted. Overforties need less, not more, remedial work. Only 10 percent of overforties need this compensatory instruction compared with 13 percent of the regular-age students.

Their program interests parallel those of traditional students—business, health, humanities, and education. After these, overforties seek computer studies. Traditionals pursue the social sciences. At the graduate level, overforties differ in their interests. Education leads the list, with over 50 percent seeking credentials in this area. Business, humanities, social sciences, and health follow.

Once a curriculum is picked, overforties expect counseling, parking, assistance in aid and housing, and health services, and they expect better preparation of faculty and staff to meet their needs. Child care is also a pressing need. Juggling work and academics is not easy and is something colleges and universities need to address better. The typical overforty works an average thirty-eight hours per week. Trachtenberg (1997) puts it all in perspective: Baby boomers will be a disparate group. They will have varied and different expectations from traditionals. Active overforties will need exercise facilities meant for vigorous oversixties, not muscular twenty-somethings. They will want learning experiences available by way of museums, galleries, and theaters to be provided on campuses. They will have interest in residential facilities designed for them on or near campuses. If a medical facility is part of the campus, that will be a plus. Learning from home will also be attractive for those who want to stay in familiar surroundings. Most of all, they will provide an intellectual resource as the "already taught." Intellectual curiosity will drive them, and appositive learning will come naturally to them, given their years of workplace experience. They will challenge faculty, opt for no easy explanations, and likely have a passion for humanism and the other subjects for which their generation of doers had little time. It is unclear whether they will have a comparable impact on higher education to that of the GIs in the 1950s and 1960s. But their impact will be obvious and enduring.

Although we have come a long way in recognizing the older learner, overforties and other lifelong learners worldwide will require innovations in the delivery of instruction. One approach is via today's version of Thok's banana leaf, the satellite.

Some Additional Examples

In Europe, the first accredited university course by satellite involving face-to-face dialogue occurred in 1993. It was a course in safety and health at work and emanated from the University College Dublin (Keegan, 1994). It was used to reach out to those who work. Ireland has poor roads, and it is not possible for workers to drive to the capital from all over Ireland. The course covered law, chemistry, ergonomics, organizational behavior, and agriculture. It initiated in the audiovisual center at Dublin and linked to classrooms in Ireland's regional universities. It was designed for thirty students per site and was linked by cable to satellite, and it used projectors, audio-conferencing units, a telephone, and a fax. It was a basic audiovisual classroom. Because the course was on satellite, students could tie in from all over Europe via Dublin University. The satellite lectures and discussions were the course, and students paid for it via a university fee. Each student received two volumes of these lectures, given by leading experts in each area covered. The course involved a forty-minute illustrated lecture and twenty minutes of discussion. Tutors were at each remote site for follow-up and assistance. Only 0.4 percent dropped the course, and both students and tutors rated the course very good.

The open university presents another alternative. It really began in South Africa in 1946. But the better known program is the open university in England, started in 1969 and first offering courses in 1971. As of 1993, there were twenty-eight open universities in such places as Pakistan, India, Canada, the Netherlands, Indonesia, Costa Rica, and Portugal, among others. The open university in England leaves choice with the student regarding admission, study, place, time of learning, content, and mode of learning. In reality, it is contract learning (Holmberg, 1994). Most are large as universities go, ranging from 700,000 to 1,000,000 students in places like China and Thailand. Open university learning depends on carefully preproduced learning materials and mediated interaction between students and tutors. E-mail and fax are the more widely used supportive tools, as most of these universities developed their approaches before the days of computer networking. Computer conferencing has permitted the use of group approaches to learning in what was otherwise a largely individual exercise. Often, regular faculty develop the packages for these distance learning courses. This is especially the case at small universities, where distance learning is a clear adjunct to mainstream instruction. Some universities network with others to deliver distance learning. At Tübingen University in Germany, the university develops courses for use by other institutions, runs a department to research learning, and offers documentation services to those who deliver instruction. The National Extension College in Cambridge offers what it calls *flexistudy,* which allows individualized learning with appropriate teacher-contact time and the use of other university resources pertinent to the individual program of study. Evaluations and assessments are standard in open universities. Attrition occurs at the outset, by not showing up or by dropping very early. Otherwise, persistence to completion is the mode. The long-argued question of whether open universities are universities, or just substitutes for regular university learning, is increasingly moot. Open universities not only have sustained but also have flourished, providing an especially appropriate fit for those needing both to learn and to remain connected to the everyday world.

The fit between learning and work leads to innovation. In England, open universities offer traditional single-subject degrees, joint or combined two-subject degrees, modular programs in which you build your own program of study, and *sandwich degrees,* which are vocationally oriented and integrate periods of work and study—one year at work and one year at university. The latter are especially popular in business, science, and engineering, but there are also sandwich degrees in the humanities. These involve a year abroad and a year at home. Postgraduate study is also available. Academic work focuses on a dissertation at the master's level. Professional study varies but usually takes two years half-time or one year full-time. In education, certification can be obtained in one year. It involves periods of full-time study interspersed with periods of working in schools. Programs are available from the University of Durham, Keele University, the University of Leicester, the University of Sheffield, Heriot-Watt University, the University of Strathclyde, the University of Surrey, the University of Wales College of Medicine, and Northern College in Scotland, among many others. Joint programs are also available, including the partnership between Rose Bruford College, known for its theater programs, and the University of Manchester, as well as the partnership of Holborn College and the University of Wolverhampton in legal studies.

Most innovative from the early 1990s is the open university's conferencing system (CoSy) (Kaye, 1990). CoSy is a computer-conferencing system that includes e-mail, read-only conferences for posting information and written conversations, single-topic conversations, a scratch pad for editing text on-line, an address book of users, a conference topic directory, and a senior common room, where tutors and course team members interact to assess progress and improve instruction. CoSy grew out of a course in information technology and is now more broadly used.

Open university students stress the need to organize time for study within a busy work schedule, concentrate on materials, plan for timely completion of course assignments, and prepare for examination (Kaye, 1990). This is helped by face-to-face tutorials with television or other electronic information as backup. One key to successful learning is encouraging conversations within each tutor's group. As students fill the national chat space, tutors work at encouraging local interaction.

Nova Southeastern University in Fort Lauderdale, Florida, has a number of electronic classrooms, an electronic library, and instruction that revolves around Internet home pages. Computer-mediated instruction is part of both master's and doctoral programs in information technology. The electronic classroom emulates a blackboard session (Terrell, 1996). People sign in through a series of commands. The generated computer screen is divided into two: the professor gets the top two-thirds and others, the lower third. Names of all participants are displayed and students may, following a set of commands, electronically raise their hands to ask keyboarded questions or initiate keyboard discussions. This interaction appears valuable to learning.

The electronic library is a software system that interacts with the campus library and other library networks. Students may browse, do searches, order print copy, and have materials mailed to work or home for use. The easy access assists learning considerably.

Home pages are used to store tutorials, syllabi, examples of student's work, class notes, updates, and suggested sites on the web that are located worldwide. These resources encourage active learning and lead students to initiate searches for information at a more sophisticated and far-reaching level than in the typical classroom situation. Also available as aids are software analytical and informative packages, statistical packages, database systems, and grammatical support.

GLOBALLY ACCESSIBLE LEARNING

Current learners here and abroad are the test bed for developing new content, new techniques, improved support tools, and other innovations necessary to transform the learning infrastructure of higher education. As Dolence and Norris (1995) point out, mature organizations including higher education would rather miss an opportunity than make a mistake. To err is unacademic. But in a period of rapid change unprecedented in human memory, missed opportunities can be lethal. The obligation is to consider forward-looking innovations for clues to the future university. As noted earlier, distance learning is a time-weathered approach to bringing learning to the learner. We know it can work from entry to advanced level of study. Face-to-face interaction, whether direct or by some medium, is important to effective learning. Old seams between levels of learning set up barriers that inhibit learning, and a seamless solution seems necessary, including the revamping of curricula from kindergarten to graduate school and a redefining of roles at each level. Much of what passes for college study, which is the transfer of information, needs to occur elsewhere if college is to implant appositive learning. The gap between work, home, and school must be vastly minimized as must the compartmentalizing of learning that characterizes current practice. People will need to think all of the time in the new age and will need to have that integrated into how they learn. As Rossman argues, the university of the future must be a globally accessible institution, "more oriented to the particular individual and organized around basic problems of society" (Luhrs, 1997, p. 8). The current university is organized around subject areas. The problems that the world now addresses are interdisciplinary and must be resolved together on a global basis. To solve world problems requires bringing the great minds in the world together through education and research.

EDUCATING THE EXCLUDED

In the joint obligation to make America work better, one group of learners will require affirmative efforts to ensure lifelong learning, and that is the excluded learner. Often minority, but increasingly white, lower-economic class, living in family poverty, and female, these new urban poor are increasingly excluded from the fruits of learning. Regardless of whose fault it is, this growing permanent urban underclass and its rural counterpart cannot simply become flotsam on the sea of human change. Every mind wasted is a resource unused in the information age. The noncontributing represent more than welfare costs; they are drags on the productivity of the new age.

This is not just an American problem. Making the world better globally means facing the radical differences in education and lifestyle that differentiate the rural poor from the urban classes and the urban poor from their neighbors. The rural people of Africa, Latin American, and Asia, along with the urban poor of the world's metropolises, from Delhi to Capetown, are disconnected from the information revolution by their illiteracy and by the cost of technology.

In the United States, providing access to these groups does not lower standards, ensure unfair competition, or undercut the quality of American life. There are too many success stories to the contrary. Of the 5,500 students in the United States who have participated in the Minority Medical Education Program funded nationally by the Robert Wood Johnson Foundation, 2,500 have applied to medical school, and nearly 60 percent are in medical studies (Rivera, 1996, p. 6).

Globally, providing access will significantly improve the labor force and its competitiveness, something countries such as Singapore, Malaysia, and Indonesia clearly recognize in their economic rise. It is always worth remembering that the top half of the pyramid rests on the capacity of the bottom half for its stability, growth, and lifestyle.

Gates (1996) has talked about the problems associated with providing appropriate educational activities to society. He has called for affordable technology systems for the school and home. Providing the access and training that Gates and others recognize as essential for the millions of children worldwide will require private and public sector investment and support. Government bears a lead responsibility to educate the citizenry to the needs of the age, to provide an even playing field of opportunity, and to help overcome the disparities that exist when those who have control gain all of the advantages of education. Schools and colleges should forge partnerships, as many already have, to provide equipment and training that is current and state-of-the-art. Outdated contributions do not resolve the problem.

In our international interviews, we saw that educating for the information age weighed heavily on the minds of lead educators. These leaders sought strategies for educating their citizens so that their countries could become more competitive in the global marketplace. Smaller countries with resources, like Taiwan, have invested heavily in updating their educational systems and their teachers colleges, hoping to bring world-class education to the youth of their countries. The strategy of joint investment via resources from government and technology from business is the essential cornerstone for addressing this issue.

In the American experience, investment in the excluded pays off (Oviatt, 1997). There is the UCLA graduate whose father had only a second-grade education; the Salvadorean who graduated from Wellesley in 1992 with a double major; the former graffiti painter and delinquent who is at California State Polytechnic University, Pomona, under an educational opportunity program; the Ethiopian exile who largely supported himself in high school, was often in trouble, and is now completing a master's in business administration at the University of Southern California; and the Vietnamese young woman who had to learn English and had privileges taken away for every grade below an A, who is now a Brandeis graduate. These anecdotes tell the story about the gains society makes when it reaches out to and encourages the least among us to get a good education.

Strategic Responses to the Need for Learning

CHAPTER FIVE

Serving the Lifelong Learner

━⁓⁓━

In Part One, we made the point that learning in the information age will be a different phenomenon from learning in the industrial age. In Part Two, we look at several of the models that are currently being developed as well as several of the trends in higher education that will force change as they become stronger. This chapter looks at the changes in learning between the industrial and information ages. We present a way of looking at how the methods of education are changing, what we call *waves of transformation*. These waves develop scenarios of the changes that can occur as the academy adjusts to new age learning. These waves provide a framework for moving from a setting where learning in higher education typically occurs only once in a lifetime with the campus as the learning center to a setting where individual learners can both acquire a basic education and go back regularly or from time to time. This can be done either by reentering the campus environment or by accessing the campus from home or work through a variety of educational media.

TRANSITION FROM TIME OUT FOR LEARNING TO PERPETUAL LEARNING

The classic model of a college or university education is that a person who wishes to acquire a college education must go through a series of gateways. The first gate is the admissions process. The person applies to a desired institution, or perhaps to an array of different institutions. The objective of applying to more than one institution is to help ensure that out of several colleges or universities that the individual may wish to attend, one or more of them will accept the applicant. If the person is fortunate enough to have more than one college or university respond favorably, then the applicant can make a choice of which institution to attend based on personal choice and various inducements (for example, scholarships based on such factors as high school grades, participation in sports, test scores, or ethnicity). When all the offers are in, the applicant makes a choice.

The second gate is getting settled on a campus and into a program. Many high school graduates go away to college, which means a physical move out of their parents' home and into the campus environment. This is a major shock to some, and others adapt readily. Once on campus, new students need to plow their way through the campus bureaucracy to get involved in an appropriate study program and register for classes.

The third gate is surviving the grind. Fulfilling a degree requirement is a complex activity that involves taking courses from across the campus. Completing a campus's general education requirement, a college or school prerequisites, and then fulfilling the requirements of a major will take the normal student four or more years. All of this effort is rewarded by the conferring of a degree. Most students bid a fond farewell to the campus and leave, often to return only rarely for alumni events.

In this model, if there is a continuance of higher education, it usually takes the form of a graduate degree program, ordinarily at another campus. Many of the same gateways are repeated, and the normal result is the conferring of a second degree at a second graduation ceremony. Then they leave. And again, they probably leave this campus forever.

But in the information age, this separation between the place of learning and the learner is dysfunctional. The learner needs knowledge that is emergent as well as basic. Once the learner has begun to interface with the changes that occur in an information age organization, where new knowledge and the need for new knowledge is an ongoing reality, that learner will find the need to be updated on new knowledge. The natural place to go for such updating would seem to be the same institution that provided the original knowledge base and degree. Were that institution to provide such an updating service, both the learner and the institution would benefit from a long-term relationship.

If the institution is unable or unwilling to provide regular updating, its value is limited to the initial degree program. In the long term, this can alienate the learner and those within the learner's sphere of influence. The reputation of the institution can decline as a result, which may put it at a competitive disadvantage in the recruitment of new students (who will know that they will be better served in the long run by other, more progressive colleges or universities). This disadvantage could also affect the financial support from alumni and other donors. Yet, as Ringle and Smallen (1995) suggest, the technological age provides a magnificent opportunity, even for smaller, constrained colleges and universities. They suggest that the new age provides such institutions with a unique opportunity to develop and implement new programs and campus systems, which would allow them to distinguish themselves through focused applications. In this manner, they can attract new learners and help develop external relationships that will enable them to obtain resource security for the long term. A classic example of this strategy has been the University of Denver, which has grown its programs both on and off campus using every technological tool available.

This dynamic of change is one scenario. There are others, but the central point of all is that institutions of higher education must go through some level of transformation in order to ensure that they adapt well and effectively to the demands of the information age. This transformation process appears to be coming in a series of waves.

WAVES OF TRANSFORMATION

Transformation is not a single event. Change comes in a series of emerging events, or waves, each with its own particular impacts and implications. We identify several waves that colleges and universities are already experiencing as they adapt to new realities. Some of these events have already occurred. The presence or absence of a number of factors helps determine which wave is currently affecting a given campus—factors such as whether an institution is public or private, the presence or absence of a solid resource base, having a country of reference, and a variety of internal dynamics.

The wave scenarios we present may suggest a series of equally timed periodic events, occurring one after another. This is not our intention. The waves we describe do not come in equal intervals; they respond to the unpredictable push and pull of the changes that occur as the information age continues to define itself. They sometimes occur simultaneously. The point of using the wave metaphor is to suggest that these events have a dramatic impact on education. As a series of waves crashing onto a shoreline inevitably alters that shoreline, these waves reflect the relentless and powerful surges of a society that presses ever forward.

Squeeze Wave

The first wave of transformation has already hit many colleges and universities, particularly public institutions in the United States. As already noted, many colleges and universities are experiencing several external and internal pressures to change from their usual rules and procedures to a more responsive style. Pressures for different majors, on-line classes, workplace learning, and customized cross-disciplinary majors are putting a squeeze on the usual way of doing business in several segments of campus life. Administrations have been forced to cut administrative costs and seek new ways of performing administrative tasks with fewer people and reduced budgets. Academic units have had to reexamine their curricula, course loads, and credit hour production to find ways of increasing faculty loads and addressing shrinking resources. Campus support units have been among the hardest hit, with major reductions in force from student services to lawn care. No segment of the campus is spared, and it appears quite likely that the squeeze will persist for some time.

The bind that results from such forces has also led to an increase in campus turmoil. Various campus constituents have become increasingly alarmed at cutbacks to which there seems to be no end. Some campuses have seen the rise of faculty unionism and increased militancy among students who see reduced services and class offerings while their tuition and costs increase above the rate of inflation. Growing discontent among campus services personnel is also evident. And increased intrusion of the governing board into campus operations often accompanies the rising tide of concern. The turnover of top campus leadership is on the increase as college presidents and chancellors find themselves ill prepared or unsupported to deal with an increasingly hostile campus environment.

As we have suggested (Dolence, Rowley, and Lujan, 1997), those campuses that adopt strategic planning have a powerful weapon for helping deal directly with and responding effectively to these challenges. There is hope here of finding an important strategic fit with the environment and using that fit to help establish new resource connections and develop an appreciable level of campus stability. On the other hand, campuses that do not look at these challenges from a strategic perspective face a dimmer future.

FISCAL RESTRAINT, COMPETITION, AND THE GLOBAL ECONOMY. The political conservatism of the late 1980s and the 1990s has taken its toll in the budgets of colleges and universities in the United States as well as elsewhere. This substantive political swing to the right has forced federal and state governments to reassess their priorities for funding, as they also attempt to reduce the general tax burden. In a few states, the priority list has found higher education in a relatively favorable position, but in most states, higher education has done less well. In Colorado, for example, public higher education is behind entitlements, K–12 educational funding, and state prisons as a priority.

In these circumstances, public colleges and universities find themselves competing for fewer and fewer dollars, not only with other state agencies and programs but also among themselves. State legislatures often examine individual campus budgets. The ability of individual campuses to lobby effectively has become more and more crucial, as each argues why its budget requests should be considered more favorably than those of other state-supported institutions. These political realities and their related competitive activities may seem beneath the academy or undignified to some, but they are a fact of life for most public colleges and universities.

In the global economy, there is no particular tolerance for what many see as excesses of higher education. Although in some countries, such as Japan and Taiwan, healthy economies have meant more support for higher education, governmental control of resources remains a way of life, which can slow down or even prohibit change in their systems of higher education. The same is true for nearly every country in the world. The world may be changing in dramatic ways, but the academy is not directly benefiting during this paradigm shift as it did after the space exploration launched on the heels of Sputnik.

LEARNING PRIMACY, SCARCITY OF TIME, RETRENCHMENT, AND REORGA-NIZATION. The learners of the information age are different from the students of the industrial age. The primary concern of new learners is finding sources of education that help them understand one area of new knowledge well and completing that with general analytical skills. These learners need this information to help them better assimilate and deal with the demands of information age companies or information age situations. And they need it now. Because of the pace of change in technology-driven companies, many of these learners are not willing to go through the hoops of being admitted into a standard degree program and satisfying various prerequisites prior to gaining access to the knowledge and skills they may need. These learners are looking for alternatives, and there are many more alternatives for them to choose.

The impact on the academy of this new form of information demand has not fully been felt by colleges or universities, but the trends are growing, which suggests that an impact will occur sooner rather than later. As discussed in Chapter One, institutions such as the University of Phoenix not only offer nontraditional degree programs but also offer course-specific instruction. They offer it both live and on the Internet. These opportunities provide learners with a credible alternative to traditional higher education and can squeeze colleges and universities through the loss of enrollments and related revenue.

The natural tendency of institutions that face decline in their customer base is a series of retrenchment actions (Miles and Cameron, 1982). The problem with this response is that the institutions react from the viewpoint of decline, doing little to help overcome the weaknesses that contributed to the problem. Strategic planning would have them act in a more proactive manner, analyzing their strengths, weaknesses, opportunities, and threats and reorganizing so as to channel resources out of programs with minimal demand and shift those resources into existing new programs that better meet the needs of the new learner. Although some do this, most opt for the easier tactic, an across-the-board cut. In the long run, concentrating more on retrenchment than on proactive reorganization may prove to be a serious tactical error by colleges and universities everywhere.

Digital Learning Wave

A second wave of transformation is marked by an explosion of responses to the forces driving the first wave. Thousands of faculty around the world have seized the power of the World Wide Web as a primary tool for learning, research, and scholarship. On-line journals are emerging and expanding. This second wave is emerging from inside higher education and is potentially more profound than the first, because it is being driven by individual faculty initiatives. This is a salutary condition, for it indicates that any digital response derived for this group will necessarily be tied to quality and excellence, the inherent concern of scholars.

One of the more innovative ways of delivering information with an academic connection is the emergence of college level courses on the Internet. Since 1995, over ten thousand such courses have been indexed and listed on the web. These courses have been prepared by a variety of people, ranging from individuals who believe they have something of value to offer in a course setting to highly respected professors from around the world, who have made their on-campus course offerings available over the Internet. At present, there is little to no organization to these courses, but as we describe in the next section, the virtual university ideas that *are* being formulated for the Internet offer one promising format for organizing these courses for easy access and use.

PERPETUAL LEARNING TECHNOLOGY. The demands of the information age have turned the digital wave into a force for perpetual learning. As changes occur, those who deal with them in information age companies are constantly looking for new ideas and ways to help them better understand or better organize the phenomena they face. And since the information age is marked by increasing rates of change as well as by different forms of change, the information worker is forced to seek new information constantly. As there is no indication that this trend will do anything but accelerate in the future, the information age worker becomes a perpetual learner.

One reason so many of these new courses are available over the Internet is that several of the people who have developed them have done so because they believe there is a demonstrated need for such offerings. In many ways, these courses represent a way of getting immediate information without having to go through the hassles associated with traditional courses. These on-line courses are an ideal tool for the information age learner, as they are easy to find, easy to access, and can usually be accomplished on a flexible schedule. They may or may not carry certification or college credit with them.

ROLE OF FACULTY. As mentioned above, it is encouraging to note that many faculty in the United States and around the world are developing these courses independently. There may be a course here or there that has college or university sponsorship, but the majority of the courses currently found on the Internet are there because various faculty members from institutions all over the world have decided to use this medium as a forum for presenting particular courses or modules. This says that many members of college and university faculties around the world are far more interested and involved in developing tools for the information age than the institutions with which they are affiliated. Further, many of these faculty members are linked with information age companies and develop courses on the Internet in response to specific needs of information age workers.

This is very encouraging and exciting. It speaks well of the academy to partner with information age companies in a useful and educationally valid way. It demonstrates that the entrepreneurial ability of faculty to be in the forefront of developing and transferring knowledge persists and is the essential building block for strategic transformation in colleges and universities. Of course, these courses are still more random than organized or tested, and they may not be accredited. Without developing more formalized linkages between these creative faculty members, their institutions, the information age companies, and the accreditors, major opportunities are being missed at all levels, and the quality of the offerings that are available cannot be ensured.

Together, these first two waves of transformation are already reshaping higher education. They are realigning the academy with a rapidly and continually changing environment. This realignment is driving a fundamental redesign of institutions and systems. The Texas Agricultural and Mechanical (A&M) System is taking what it calls *strategic directioning* and linking it to budgets as an early response to the squeeze and the digital waves. Responses like this to the first two waves form the foundation of the third wave of transformation.

Virtual University Wave

The third wave of transformation involves new modalities for learning that use technology as the medium for delivery. Virtual universities are springing up across the globe. At present, we have identified fifty different models in three distinct categories. And the number fifty is up from just seven only eighteen months ago. They have sprung up on every continent across the globe. These virtual universities bring with them many challenges to twentieth-century traditions and the established practices of higher education. They are backed by private individuals or private sources (private colleges and universities, for example); or by national, provincial, state, and other governmental agencies; or by enabling initiatives aimed at making higher education more accountable, learner responsive, and outcomes based.

There is both excitement and reserve about the emergence of virtual universities. As Hayes (1996) suggests, the virtual university offers many advantages for participating colleges and universities. These include providing services to students who cannot travel to a campus, aiding employers by providing specific skills for their workers, and increasing outreach without increasing capital expenditures. As she also cautions, however, the virtual university may not be for everyone—the university campus experience continues to be a unique and valued experience for many.

The virtual university, in its current configuration, represents a variety of learning experiences. We believe they can be classified into ten different virtual learning environments:

Category One—Digitally Enhanced Module. This is a discrete learning segment usually smaller than a course that uses digital material, network research or scholarship, the World Wide Web, Internet, or other network resources to enhance the learning experience.

Category Two—Digitally Delivered Module. This is a module that is delivered entirely over the network or through other electronic means.

Category Three—Digitally Enhanced Course. This is a course that uses digital material, network research or scholarship, the World Wide Web, Internet, or other network resources to enhance the learning experience.

Category Four—Digitally Delivered Course. This is a course that is delivered entirely over the network or through other electronic means.

Category Five—Digitally Enhanced Program. This is a series of courses leading to a specific outcome (degree, certificate, competency) that uses digital material, network research or scholarship, the World Wide Web, Internet, or other network resources to enhance the learning experience.

Category Six—Digitally Delivered Program. This is a series of courses leading to a specific outcome (degree, certificate, competency) that are delivered entirely over the network or through other electronic means.

Category Seven—Virtual University Category I. This is an institution employing a core faculty, which offers more than one digitally delivered program. Examples of this type of institution include Athabasca University in Canada (http://www.athabascau.ca/html/info/au.htm); the University of Phoenix's virtual university, which augments its 19 learning centers (http://www.uophx.edu); the New School for Social Research (http://www.dialnsa.edu); and the Fayetteville Technical Community College (http://www.faytech.cc.nc.us/homeg.html). Each of these campuses offers standard, full-credit college courses to a global audience over the Internet.

Category Eight—Virtual University Category II. This type of institution employs a core faculty and concentrates solely on developing learning opportunities—including classes, personal learning, and simple topic development—all of which are delivered using digital methods. Examples include the Virtual Online University, a segment of Athena University, and the Athena Preparatory Academy, which lists 29 faculty members (http://athena.edu/vou.html).

Category Nine—Virtual University Category III. This is an institution with no core faculty, which is designed to provide and manage digitally delivered learning opportunities. Examples include the Western Governors University, created by the governors of 14 western states and scheduled to use resources from 21 different college and university campuses (http://www.concerto.com/smart/vu/vu.html). Another example is Jones Education Company, which has over 200 credit-based courses, 6 certificate programs, and 11 degree programs. It uses resources from 14 different universities and colleges (http://www.jec.edu/).

Category Ten—Virtual Learning Indexes. This is an index of databases, which describes different courses and different learning opportunities along with comparative requirements and price structuring. Virtual learning indexes allow knowledge seekers a choice of opportunities to develop or augment personal knowledge bases. An example is the Globewide Network Academy, which currently lists 251 providers, 771 programs, and 9,736 on-line courses (http://www.gnacademy.org:8001/uu-gna/index .html). Another example is the World Lecture Hall, which has listings for

over a hundred disciplines and thousands of course offerings (http://
www.utexas.edu/world/lecture/index.html). A third is the Internet University, which works with 30 providers and has over 700 computerized
courses (http://www.caso.com/).

The impact of the virtual university on the overall activities of
higher education is not yet known. However, as these many virtual
universities format their new way of providing higher education, they
set the stage for the other waves.

Global Wave

Another wave of transformation is being marked by the globalization
of higher education. Because of the many dramatic advances in technology, communication, and ease of travel, the educational experience
has rapidly become a global experience. Looking no further than the
Internet, the courses, training opportunities, and other learning experiences are potentially accessible to anyone throughout the world.

But globalization goes beyond that. Globalization means the combining of educational resources across international boundaries and
the pooling of resources to help create broader educational opportunities in a worldwide setting. This is an important step for the worldwide focus of information age companies.

To some degree, global activity is already in place on many campuses, setting the stage and creating opportunities for entrepreneurial learning and faculty involvement. For example, in many colleges
and universities, international exchanges of students and faculty are
already quite common. Some institutions, such as Tufts University in
Cambridge, Massachusetts, have established full campuses on other
continents. Joint programs in several discipline areas are already in
place that link campuses in one country to campuses in one or more
other countries. Though most of these programs require travel to take
part in both the cultural and educational experiences offered, other
types of programs exist that do not require travel, but they do broaden
perspectives, as they make the international educational experience
more accessible to larger numbers of people.

Finley (1997) states that internationalization is already dramatically changing the face of campuses in the United States and around
the world. He further states that the trend is getting stronger all the
time, forcing administrators and professors to rethink not only how
they can best accommodate the increasingly complex mix of students

on their campuses, but even how they present their subjects in the growing international environment.

CULTURAL AND LANGUAGE-BASED NETWORK LEARNING CENTERS. There is a movement in several countries to develop major cultural learning centers where the primary knowledge base of a particular culture would be accumulated and available for access by anyone interested in knowing about that particular culture. These centers are developing along primary language lines. They seek to compile all the information available that is written in a particular language for a particular culture. We believe that over the next five years, seventeen such centers (one for each of the major world language groups) will be up and running. A few are already in place. For example, the Virtual University of Oeresund in Sweden is developing a cultural learning center network for the Scandinavian countries in Northern Europe. Instituto Technologico Esquela Systema Mexico in San Jose, California, is developing a knowledge resource center for the Spanish-speaking world. Similarly, the University of Catalonia in Spain is developing a comparable center that focuses on Spanish culture. Also, the University of Montreal is beginning to develop a center that would encompass French culture and knowledge.

MULTIPLE-LANGUAGE LEARNING PRODUCTS. Globalization and the development of cultural and language-learning resource centers is forcing the publication of books, journals, and other academic materials in a variety of languages. Rather than printing materials in the central language of the author or the author's country of residency alone, publishers are having to use translators to rewrite the material in a variety of different languages and to some degree, with built-in cultural sensitivity. This has complicated the field of publishing, but it has also opened up larger opportunities for worldwide distribution and sales. As these opportunities become more viable, more commercial concerns will get involved. As virtual learning through international accessibility becomes more common, it is likely that commercial concerns will seek ways of expanding these activities through worldwide language-corrected media offerings.

Commercialization Wave

An additional wave of transformation will be marked by the commercialization of higher education. Providers will compete with each other and with traditional institutions for the best learning products.

Faculty developers will take their learning products to commercial providers, who will add value, enhance delivery, shape them into commercial learning products, and then share the revenues.

COMMERCIAL–QUALITY LEARNING PRODUCTS. There are several commercial companies that are already engaged in addressing the needs of individual learners. For example, Sylvan Learning Centers offer specialized learning opportunities based on the needs of the individual. Sylvan offers these services for all ages—children in kindergarten through adults in college. Their program is based on an initial assessment to determine what areas of knowledge need strengthening. From this assessment, they develop specific learning objectives with their client, provide individualized learning tools, and then do another assessment to ensure that the outcomes are the ones the client expected.

Another example is Virtual University Enterprises, a company that has an extensive web site on the World Wide Web. Virtual University Enterprises has identified knowledge bases throughout ninety different countries and has indexed them. Clients can use their indexes (for a fee) to discover and then take advantage of the learning bases that are available.

OUTCOMES-BASED LEARNING. One of the driving factors that is helping ensure success by the various commercial ventures, as well as other noncommercial enterprises engaged in similar services, is the issue of outcomes. As in the Sylvan example, these enterprises understand that the value of their services is in providing the client or learner with exactly what that person needs. Through initial assessment, those needs can become clarified, and through a postassessment, both the learner and the provider can determine whether or not the program met the client's needs. This quality assurance is one of the drivers of information age knowledge providers and is an interesting model for those within the academy.

ROLE OF FACULTY. College and university faculty are involved in many of the areas discussed in this section. Individual faculty members have been instrumental in developing basic products for which commercial providers then contract. The inducement for the faculty is either in flat up-front development fees or in profit sharing after a venture has proven profitable. These ventures tend to be beyond the activities in which they engage on their various campuses. In most cases, the college or university associated with a particular faculty member is mentioned only secondarily. In most cases, the institutions gain no benefit from the contribution of the faculty at all.

Although the activities of the faculty do keep information age methods and product development associated with the academy, many individual institutions lag in their support and development of these methods and products. This is both a threat and an opportunity. We believe that colleges and universities should recognize this and be responsive to it.

Personally Directed Learning Wave

Still another wave will be borne on the backs of the network personal computer and Web TV. In 1997, experts expected that 160,000 Internet TVs would be sold, with as many as 5.7 million in place by the year 2000. The overall cost to access the web and global learning resources will fall as much as 84 percent, making access to knowledge and educational opportunities on a personal level more of a reality. As we continue to emphasize, the demand of the information age learner for easy access to and use of major knowledge bases and effective, efficient, and convenient learning opportunities is a market demand that will be satisfied by connectivity that is already well into the planning and development stages. Personally customized learning that is on-line in a global setting is a clearly profitable venture, which for-profit providers like Phoenix University will recognize and exploit, especially if colleges and universities refuse the challenge.

Wireless Education Wave

An intriguing wave of transformation will be the emergence of wireless technology use in higher education. Today, there are at least 150 commercial satellites in service, generating $10 billion per year in revenues. By 2002, experts project that there will be close to 1,500 satellites generating revenues in excess of $100 billion annually. This method of communication, through standardized downlinking and uplinking, will potentially connect an additional billion people to the most sophisticated learning structure ever imagined. Because colleges and universities have some experience in satellite learning, either as providers or as users, this is an especially attractive medium for professional fields such as education and health services in traditional institutions.

Other Waves—More Developments, More Excitement, More Opportunities

Though the several stages, or waves, of transformation described here are substantive and revolutionary in comparison with the methods of knowledge transfer found in most colleges and universities today, one thing is certain: the technological advances that are moving forward today will lead to new applications throughout the information age society. There will be those in higher education who will seize upon these opportunities and will begin to integrate knowledge transfer using these new mechanisms. It will only be a matter of time before these advances take off or engender commercial sponsorship. Whether the several waves of transformation occur precisely as we have described here is really beside the point. The waves we have described are the ones that seem most likely to occur based on the current level of research and development with which we are familiar. We know changes are coming, and that transformation will not be limited to any given or certain number of transformational waves. The innovations that will create their own waves, providing opportunities and new methods for researching, gathering, distilling, and disseminating knowledge, will go far beyond what is described here.

This is the turbulent world in which higher education must determine its proper role. It is clear that individual faculty members are already leading the development of tools and mediums for new learning. Institutions are less adaptive, and the rest of this book will focus on this issue. If the strategic value of the new technologies is not recognized by institutions, they will not prosper in the new age.

CHAPTER SIX

Creating a Flexible Concept of Academic Organization

〰

Welcome to the second Renaissance. As we indicated in Part One, the world is in a period of such rapid economic evolution that business organizations change forms as quickly as market forces shift. Magsaysay (1997) tells us that a profound transformation in the foundations of society, work, and family is under way. The transformation clearly affects the academy as a major social organization. This chapter looks at several of the changes that are currently taking shape in colleges and universities throughout the United States and includes some interesting examples from foreign campuses. We examine these changes in the context of a rebirth of the academy, a renaissance in which particular campuses are redesigning themselves into new structural entities that are lighter on their feet and more responsive to the needs of the information age learner.

CONTRADICTION IN CURRENT STRUCTURES

The academy is changing, and the parallels to another time are striking. Knowledge, attitudes, and values are in a state of reformation. These were the conditions that prevailed at the beginning of the fourteenth century and that heralded the great historical age we now know as the Renaissance. The next two centuries saw the rebirth of civilization, a flourishing of the arts, and the rise of the individual. Original thinking flourished, leading to practical philosophies and pragmatic approaches to civil life. These same conditions predominate as we near the end of the twentieth century.

The realization that in creating computer chips, the main ingredients are the human ideas, knowledge, and skills reinforces Magsaysay's observations. In the highly competitive world of chips and software, the quality of the human factor is the decisive element. Jones (1996) tells us that in the new Renaissance, traditional lines between disciplines will blur, and new structures will emerge from the combining of several disciplines.

How are these new structures to evolve? How can campus leaders take a large complex campus and move it from one structural form to another? These are difficult questions that many campus leaders find not simply baffling, but at times, overpowering. At present, the structures that one observes in most colleges and universities are vertically integrated. They are also control based and hierarchical. Knowledge is compartmentalized by function, and information is often classified on a need-to-know basis. As Weinstein (1993) has observed and lamented, this kind of organization is slow to change.

In the world of higher education, all of this is complicated by the need for consensus, prompting one University of Wisconsin regent to observe that moving a university is like moving a battleship with one's bare hands. In such a setting, inertia, resistance, and the need for consensus all act to retard responses and dampen decisiveness. In other words, where process reigns, change must be sifted through rules and bureaucracy. These are conditions that exist on most campuses and are not necessarily confined to the administration, the bureaucracy, campus governance, or the faculty.

Duderstadt (1995) argues that changes in the academy are also retarded because of what colleges and universities have become. When the public pictures the educational process at colleges and universities, they see students sitting in lecture halls. Faculty properly see themselves as creators and guardians of knowledge and expect their students to apply themselves in achieving scholarship. As for the research university, the government sees it as a research contractor; the faculty see it as a resource; and the students see it as a source of prestige and skill, which will enhance their lives and ambitions. So the university is a conglomerate of diverse enterprises that some say is held together by a heating system and a computer network.

At times, these diverse forces come together in an incredibly complex amalgamation. For example, at the University of Michigan, the campus acts more like a conglomerate than a university, teaching fifty thousand students, operating significant federal laboratories, running a major hospital and health care company, overseeing several international sites and programs, being self-insured, and managing an entertainment company, the Michigan Wolverines. Although the University of Michigan is clearly one of the premier academic institutions in the world, through the years it has grown into a behemoth, with an amazingly complex structure, a labyrinth of bureaucracies, and a severe management challenge as it seeks to satisfy its multitude of strategic constituencies while furthering its academic accomplishments. Michigan is one of many examples, including the Ohio State University, the University of California at Berkeley, the University of Illinois, the University of Washington, the University of North Carolina at Chapel Hill, and others.

Countering this functional sprawl is an historical capacity to adapt. For example, Harvard University today is not the Harvard University of yesteryear. In today's world, Harvard University dwellers are entrepreneurial and transactional. Faculty are always pushing the limits to create new and more specialized programs. The issue is less the inability to change and more the necessity to transform change into opportunity for the entrepreneurial instincts of faculty.

Our everyday lives are intertwined with people from all nations and all walks of life. We see this in the labels on the clothes we wear, the vehicles we drive, the foods we eat, and the information and languages we use. These realities have increasingly placed globalization and multiculturalism at the center of educational change. Though everyone favors a curriculum rich in American thought and experience, we also realize that the educated must be conversant with the variety of human cultures in the global marketplace. This globalism also coincides with the information age. Few of us understand what kinds of changes these factors will bring about on campuses. These changes rise out of the shift of technology as an extension of human muscle to technology as an extension of the human mind. Because the mind is central in this new model, education is at the forefront of how such changes will unfold.

Even among the most flexible of organizations and people, old habits die slowly. In the case of the University of California at Berkeley (UC Berkeley), where economic and demographic changes are massive, the answer to the question, "What is to be done?" is in one of three alternatives (Kerr, 1994): take it year by year and hope for the best; take it year by year, delaying the harder decisions as long as possible; and, face the future all at once. Because the last option overloads decision processes and relies on the capacity to find overall solutions, it is an unlikely first choice. The remaining two options in reality are not strategies for quantum change. They are mechanisms to put off significant change. Herein lies the fundamental contradiction between the past and the future. The processes of the past handle gradual change. The processes of the future require quantum change.

STRUCTURES FOR QUANTUM CHANGE

Quantum change is not blocked by any lack of human talent. Rather, it is smothered by the inhuman organizations humans have contrived. Largely bureaucratic and mired in rules, present-day organizations do not necessarily bring out the best in people. When leadership expert Stephen Covey asks how many agree that there is more talent and creativity in their organizations than current jobs require, most managers agree (Magsaysay, 1997). Most present-day organizations are confining, are not necessarily rewarding of creativity, and are stifling of innovation. Organizations seeking to fit better with new market forces are moving from being guided by the bottom line to being open to ideas linked with new horizons. Liebig argues that innovative organizations seek inclusion of all classes and cultures, protect the natural environment, enable human creativity, seek actively to build a better world and more humane organizations, behave ethically, and transform knowledge by complementing reason and science with intuition (Magsaysay, 1997).

University as a Learning Organization

The image that emerges is a human learning organization. The metaphor for this organization is no longer the factory, but rather the space capsule—transforming as it wends its way through space, adapting to unexpected challenges, and returning to earth with mission accomplished or knowledge of what needs changing for success the next time around. When an organization has functioned in this way, the craft has jettisoned its fuel tanks, docked in space to conduct experiments, adjusted systems not functioning as expected, and improvised based on the best available information to complete its mission.

Magsaysay also contrasts the old and the new organizations. Twentieth-century organizations reflect and are characterized by stability and predictability, size and scale, top-down leadership, organizational rigidity, control by rules and hierarchy, closely guarded information, quantitative analysis, need for certainty, reactivity and risk aversion, corporate independence, vertical integration, focus on internal organization, sustainable advantage, and the capacity to compete for today's markets. Twenty-first century organizations reflect and are characterized by discontinuous change, speed and responsiveness, leadership from everybody, permanent flexibility, control by vision and values, shared information, creativity and intuition, tolerance of ambiguity, proactive and entrepreneurial initiatives, corporate interdependence, "virtual" integration, focus on the competitive environment, constant reinvention of advantage, and the creation of tomorrow's markets. The difference is about more than size. It is about learning to cast off control as the guidance system of organizations. It is also about ideas supplanting status and creativity replacing orthodoxy as the basis of a new mental revolution—a revolution in which the result is the humanizing of the organization. In a world where uncertainty is the only certainty, knowledge is the one source of relevant ideas essential for coping, and a learning organization is its seedbed.

Learning organizations address events as they unfold and shift direction as required. They acquire knowledge regularly, constantly upgrade and refine it, and improve the use to which knowledge is put. As learning organizations gain knowledge, they evolve their processes and assess results continually. Essentially, the basic learning organization is a shell in the same sense that a space capsule is a shell. Depending on its mission, this enabling shell takes on many forms, adapts to changing needs, and advances knowledge at the same time that it is using knowledge to navigate, conduct experiments, repair itself, and return with its payload. A learning organization houses and nourishes a knowledge infrastructure that acquires knowledge continually, enhances it, stores it, refines it, makes it available to anyone, and has the capacity for very fast evolution. The key to a jump start in such an organization is to use better the facilities and capacities that already exist.

Emergent New Organizations—
Looking for Scenarios That Fit

Becoming a learning organization involves more than a paradigm shift for higher education institutions. It requires a change in how we think about higher education, shifting the focus of that thinking from traditional to futuristic. Current thinking focuses on some historical definition of the educational enterprise that embeds it in processes and requirements that are largely disconnected from the rest of the world. The traditional higher education institution is, for reasons already discussed, encased in time and idealized practices that are extrapolated largely from the past. In contrast, a learning organization needs no boundaries. Instead, it needs a power source and a home base. Like the human brain's main function, the learning organization's core activity is processing information to extract new knowledge and usefulness. The organization must be geared to learning as it goes. This being the case, we see the university as a connective organization—an enabling shell or home base that can connect elements anywhere at any time. How it connects can vary.

UNIVERSITY AS A NETWORK. Dill and Sporn (1995) and Dolence and Norris (1995) describe such a college or university as a network organization. They see the academic institution as an intelligence power source with an unbounded set of linkages ranging from precollege programs to distance learning, electronic classrooms, learning modules, assessments of demonstrated learning, research laboratories and projects, economic development consortia, and global satellites.

UNIVERSITY AS A CONGLOMERATE. Dill and Sporn (1995) and Duderstadt (1995) portray the university as a conglomerate, which connects programs that range from education to entertainment. In this scenario, the university is the holding company, giving relevance to each of the connected nodes. This conglomerate has a central investment strategy that it uses to integrate otherwise very diverse or even contradictory activities. Like conglomerates of related and unrelated businesses, the education conglomerate buys units to blend its products into a profitable bottom line. If a unit fails to contribute, it is sold or spun off. In the world of knowledge, some products take huge investments to pay off. The top quark, one of the smallest particles of matter, is the classic example. It took more than four hundred scientists twenty years to discover. And we do not have much experience in educational spin-offs and buyouts.

UNIVERSITY AS A CONTRACTOR. Dolence and Norris (1995) also see the university as a general contractor or developer that customizes educational modules from teaching to research and service, which vary from constituent to constituent. This flexible university is con-sumer oriented and able to link resources from any entity willing to engage in custom-learning activities. Customized modules ensure the just-in-time learning essential for the lifelong, professional, or job-based learner. People, sites, and resources are bundled to fit a wide range of learner circumstances. The university acts as the developer of requisite learning resources and the provider of the necessary infrastructure for customized learning. Customizing can, of course, be costly.

UNIVERSITY AS A CULTURE. Dill and Sporn (1995) also propose the new university as culture. Drawing on evolving organizational theory, they surmise that the university of the information age will restruc-ture and redefine teaching, learning, research, and the faculty role. They foresee a new culture that addresses the clashes between disci-plines and professions, sciences and humanities, graduates and under-graduates, and distance as contrasted with campus-based instruction. The new culture recasts these formerly competing forces into a new architecture for learning—an architecture that addresses a world of rapidly changing information and expertise. Indeed, as a reviewer of this book put it: "The university must be very flexible and needs to be consumer oriented and needs to be able to link resources. The exist-ing culture therefore must change. . . . There will be a great swirling of students among institutions, public and private, many offering live instruction through electronic technologies."

UNIVERSITY AS A MARKET. Clark (1995) speaks of the university as a market. Although he uses terms such as conglomerate and federal, he alludes to the university primarily as a place where market-type activ-ity flourishes. Like the *souk* or the *mercado* of the Mediterranean and Latin America, the university is a marketplace where people bring goods or services to sell or trade, where there is a loose price structure, where consumers bargain over what they need, and where the result is a consumer-driven market. Decentralization and loose restrictions give the university as market the flexibility to strike bargains with its customers. Markets, like universities, develop a sense of character over time. Given discretionary space, an institution can develop its own strengths, lend character to its activities, and expand or contract its specialties as market demand varies.

STRATEGIC UNIVERSITY. The notion of a strategic university emerges from van Vught's (1995) discussion of managerial changes in higher education. Focusing on quality, he presents the view that a worldwide management revolution is under way in higher education, as universities adjust to the imperatives of economic decline and the need to respond to public opinion and social expectations. These stimuli are moving universities to assume responsibility for their own strategic fates. This proactive behavior includes quality and accountability as integral to change and the constant search for strategic opportunity. Although the bureaucratic rules that can result from management can take a university too far in becoming a business, responsiveness to public needs and problems can take a university to better recognition of the opportunities and strengths that it can match to meet the hyperactive educational requirements of the information age.

We have described the future university as network, conglomerate, general contractor and developer, culture, market, and strategic shaper of excellence. In each of these scenarios for university change, there is one common element. Above all, the university of the future is *connective.* The future universities will be porous—open to the movement in and out of people, problems, and ideas. These universities will also have no monopoly on knowledge and expertise; instead, they will be one set of actors in a world driven by information vendors. Future universities will be discontinuous, creating and disbanding activities and structures as they deal with the broad marketplace of ideas. They will link through strategic partnerships and collaborations to bring the best available talent to bear on a given issue. They will contract learning modules worldwide. And they will broker solutions as strategic players in the world of ideas. Ideas, intellectual property, innovations, talent, solutions, and learning systems will replace the current institutional units as the essential infrastructure of the new university.

Innovative Changes Under Way

Alternatives to old ways are already evident as many colleges and universities respond to the demands of the new millennium. For example, the University of California at Santa Cruz was innovative at birth, relying on a cluster college concept for its physical and programmatic layout. Boards of study were designed to group faculty by interest rather than by discipline in the need to coordinate programs. The Evergreen State College in Washington for years has been a theme-oriented college with multidisciplinary faculty and programs. Prescott College at its inception in 1966 organized around five interdisciplinary teaching and research centers. New themes annually guide what the centers emphasize for those enrolled. The University of Wisconsin at Green Bay began by focusing the curriculum on the environment and weaving this focus through its initial four colleges and concentrations within them. From the beginning, team-taught courses were encouraged. These innovations occurred in the 1960s, when student unrest gave rise to more open and less traditional means of teaching undergraduates. The Experimental College at Tufts typifies these more participative and customized-learning programs to broaden the curriculum. Here, students and faculty joined in cross-disciplinary seminars, courses, or workshops that could be taken for credit (Levine and Weingart, 1973). Today, most universities have options for individualized and multidisciplinary degrees at both the undergraduate and graduate levels.

Potential Lessons from America's World Neighbors

Innovations are not solely American either. There are several interesting international examples of colleges and universities developing innovative new ways of adapting. For example, in Peru, where universities have been traditional and controlled by elected assemblies of professors, staff, and students, new legislation will change that (Stinson, 1996). New institutions will be private enterprises, with corporate rather than elected leadership and staff. This will enable fundraising and give flexibility to the curriculum, so that nontraditional subjects may be studied. The Universities of San Ignacio de Loyola and the Peruvian University of Applied Sciences are among those moving in this direction.

Incorporating New Modes of Learning

Today's learners are going to spend their lives in the next century. They will need different skills. According to Ehrmann, Renwick, and Hebenstreit (1994), they must know how to frame problems when facing unfamiliar situations, to communicate well and with people from other cultures, to work effectively in teams, and to learn through deep learning. By deep learning, Ehrmann, Renwick, and Hebenstreit mean that students actively relate what is being learned to previous knowledge and experience, search for patterns and underlying principles, check for evidence, and tie it to emerging conclusions. This is appositive learning, and it needs different supporting pedagogies (Ehrmann, Renwick, and Hebenstreit, 1994). Communications used to be taught in rote form, using a classroom, blackboard, and audio laboratory. Now, audio and audiographic conferencing, two-way live video, and an electronic classroom with chat spaces can put students in touch with a heterogeneous group of other learners to practice communication with while learning the subject (Young, 1988). Although real learning requires time to evolve or jell, the technologies of fax, e-mail, keyboard conversations on split-screen monitors, video tapes, and diskettes with topic-related scenarios or data sets can all enrich the interim environment between exposure to new information and the development of a reflected response or solution (Cerf, 1991).

Up to now, using "new" techniques meant relying on typewriters, library books, studios, or internships. In the future, computers for simulation, design, composing, and analyzing; CD-ROMs; videos and on-line access to digital libraries; data banks; search engines; and the Internet will link the workplace to the classroom. This will add significantly to learning by doing. Directed instruction (now delivered mostly through traditional methods, such as the lecture, the slide projector, the overhead, and the textbook) will be augmented significantly by lectures on diskettes or CD-ROMs and by on-line electronic classrooms that provide communication by keyboard, supplemented by e-mail, chat spaces, and computer tutorials. In these new modes, access will be available around the clock and from workplace or residence, if desired. Already at the University of Illinois, select courses are offered in this way through the Sloan Center, with student tutors working the e-mail and chat spaces in the off-hours for the instructor.

What happens to the quality of learning in this new mode? Treisman (1985) at UC Berkeley demonstrated that collaborative learning among African American students works. Those who had failed basic math and science courses that were traditionally taught produced levels of achievement on par with those of any other student group when exposed to group learning. In addition to the efficacy of group learning, there is evidence that technology assists oral learning. Smith (1990) studied a control group in a conventional audio-based language laboratory, while the experimental group used e-mail and computer conferencing. The oral performance of the experimental group was superior. An external evaluation of the Annenberg/Corporation for Public Broadcasting project, designed to develop new instructional ways to a degree, found that a majority of faculty and students thought that e-mail provided communication as good or better in frequency and usefulness than other forms of on-campus communication (Ehrmann, Renwick, and Hebenstreit, 1994). These findings validate the utility and the capacity to assist learning that are contained in new technology. For universities with old physical plants, with demand beyond campus capacity, with off-campus instruction programs, and with the need to link work to the classroom, technology is a valuable knowledge- and skills-increasing partner for the future.

At the level of individual universities or systems, we have previously looked at changes within the California State University system, which involve a major effort to cope with expected large enrollments, the desire of business and the external community for applied knowledge and skills, and increasing demand for access. A three-year compact was reached with the governor to provide a 4 percent budget increase beginning in 1995–96 plus $30 million in lieu of a fee increase. A Cornerstones Principles Project was undertaken to address excellence in teaching, access, effectiveness and accountability, as well as linking learning to society's needs.

These Cornerstones Principles underlie five study themes—being student centered, achieving demonstrable results, effectuating lifelong learning, achieving institutional effectiveness, and financing quality. Whether these particular criteria and principles survive unchanged to guide the system or not is less significant than the realization that one of America's largest comprehensive university systems will not replicate the past as the basis for educating students for the new century. More likely, active learning among students will be encouraged, and outreach and distance education will grow, using new technology to respond to off-campus demand. Efforts to keep quality teachers, to ensure that students pay a predictable tuition, to make sure graduate students pay more of their own costs (which are now subsidized by undergraduate tuition and fees), and to institutionalize performance accountability will put the California State University system among the first in rank for evolving into a university of the future. As principles rather than goals, these elements should allow flexibility at the campus level to adapt change to internal strengths that better match their service area environments.

The land grant colleges and universities report another approach to change. In the National Association of State Universities and Land Grant Colleges' (1997a) Kellogg Commission Report, "transformational change" is a central theme (p. 4). Transformation involves seven action commitments, which are to revitalize partnerships with elementary and secondary schools, reinforce the commitment to undergraduate instruction and general education, comprehensively address the personal development of students, link education to career, provide high-quality education at affordable prices, define educational objectives better, and expose undergraduates to discovery in learning.

If you dig beneath the standard language of academics in most of these innovations, you see that the underlying theme is connectivity— connecting better with governors, government, communities, students, within the curriculum, between work and the classroom, and with the core of quality faculty.

BALANCING COSTS AND RESOURCES

None of these ideas just posed are free. Change has a price tag, especially in a public university system for which users have paid only a fraction of the actual cost of learning. Tuition, like the subsidized price of gasoline, has gotten us into bad consumptive habits. We want full-tank education for one-third tank prices. As just noted, the California State University system has sought to stabilize fees and then shift to a fee system with predictable but reasonable prices. That translates into offloading state funding to students and making the system essentially a state-seeded one.

The land grant colleges and universities have also worried over cost. For years, these institutions have sought ways to cut their own costs and find new revenue sources to keep tuition manageable. But from 1980–81 to 1994–95, the average tuition for public colleges and universities has risen 234 percent (National Association of State Universities and Land Grant Colleges, 1997b). At the same time, household median income rose 82 percent. Several options for dealing with costs are currently practiced. Two-thirds of colleges and universities offer at least one monthly payment plan. Nearly 70 percent accept credit cards. Eighteen percent offer special pricing or payment plans. Fewer than 10 percent offer discounts for cash payments. A similar proportion allows students to pay in full and up front for a degree at the entry-level price. Kent State in Ohio has an optional payment plan that ensures fees will not go up while a student is an undergraduate.

The California State University compact with the governor of the State of California poses an interesting alternative. Universities promise to keep fees stable and the state compensates for the difference. Compacts can become a vehicle for customizing cost and revenue issues by institution or system, so long as colleges and universities demonstrate a genuine concern for containing costs and keeping quality.

Cross-subsidies are also in for review. It is typical for undergraduate revenues to subsidize graduate study. Because of the smaller faculty-student ratios; the research required; the laboratory, library, and other learning-accessory costs, graduate students have never paid full cost. It would be very significant and quite likely prohibitive to do so. Consequently, undergraduate revenues subsidize graduate education at varying rates. Cross-subsidy also occurs at the undergraduate level. Professional school fees are often higher and sometimes subsidize low-enrollment areas in the arts or humanities. Liberal arts colleges serve as the warehouse for many undergraduates until they major and pursue a degree in another school. Consequently, there are times when arts and sciences subsidize professional schools with tenured faculty and dropping enrollments, as for example, in education. Though cross-subsidy is practiced and its effects are complex, continuing the old practice without a current assessment seems open to challenge.

Decentralization is another related factor. Cross-subsidies, differential tuition, and other similar practices often make sense when a university is centralized. Balance is achieved by central reallocation of resources through the annual budget. But if higher education is to move to a flatter structure and become a performance-based learning organization, decentralization may make sense. This would devolve cost issues to producing units, a practice not uncommon in businesses that are restructuring or rightsizing or reengineering. Devolution and decentralization are practices worth considering as costs and revenues are addressed. If "each tub were on its own bottom" in terms of enrollments, time to degree, requirements of other units for home unit degrees, faculty head count, and the like, efficiencies would have to accrue as units balanced revenues against cost. Units would have to be more price sensitive and consider how high they could raise prices for the education they provide. Though seen as risky by some higher education administrators, this is a common calculation for most businesses. This perspective is not to make colleges and universities run like businesses but rather to make higher education aware of the limits that cost presents to students, families, employers, and other consumers of higher education.

EVOLVING FORMS IN AMERICAN HIGHER EDUCATION

In a 1996 review of undergraduate education (Division of Undergraduate Education, 1996), the National Science Foundation reports that research on effective methods of instruction indicate that active, participative, and collaborative techniques, which engage students in real problems and issues, enhance learning. Student-centered active learning and demonstrated performance are the variables that correlate with learning and competency. This suggests that curriculum alone or support services by themselves do not push learning. In combination, they do.

Active learning on real and difficult issues is not easy or low cost. At Harvard, science students learned poorly in standard lectures. Basic concepts suffered. So the instructor used tests to expose student conceptual deficiencies, then used peer instructors to identify student deficiencies and log them on a computer. Students then talked with other students about their misconceptions and tested one another's knowledge. The result was enhanced learning for all and less reliance on the lecture format (Division of Undergraduate Education, 1996). Here, we see that active learning and guided pedagogy weaves in with subject matter requirements to enhance understanding.

In Virginia, state government attracted Motorola, IBM, and Toshiba to locate in the state. Part of the collaboration was to include education and training funds as pieces of the package. This included funding for a microelectronics laboratory in the Virginia Commonwealth University engineering school. It also led to linking town and gown via an industrial advisory group to work with faculty and to design new curriculum to prepare students for jobs in this emerging sector.

Sometimes such activities lead to commercial spin-offs from high technology or biotechnology research and learning (Trani, 1997).

At Florida Gulf Coast University, a new university has been built with the intention to provide one-fourth of instruction by distance learning. Three of every five courses required of all juniors and seniors in arts and sciences will be interdisciplinary. These interdisciplinary courses, such as a course on the environment, might include political scientists for public policy, economists for understanding the economic effects of the environment, historians, and ethicists. All graduates of arts and sciences will have a bachelor of arts in liberal studies, with concentrations in typical subject fields. The business dean intends to tie in top business executives, drawing from over a hundred Fortune 500 retired executives within twenty miles of the university. By connecting across the curriculum and with the external world, Gulf Coast will offer an innovative learning environment (Trombley, 1996b).

At Rensselaer Polytechnic Institute, studio classrooms are used in calculus, chemistry, and physics. Equipped with individual computer workstations, students may complete in-class assignments and lab work. Brief lectures expose students to key concepts and studio work is used to apply these concepts. Learning is improved as is student satisfaction.

At the Sloan Center for Asynchronous Learning Environments at the University of Illinois, technology drives significant innovation. Based on the view that students need immediate feedback when they are studying, access to teaching assistants and faculty is provided by technology around the clock. Because students perform better in settings that encourage active learning and offer teamwork skills, networked computers and required software are used to enhance learning. A total of fifty-two undergraduate courses like this were supported in spring 1996. Software included web browsers, asynchronous conferencing, and proprietary courseware and software. Lecture material and notes, on-line programs, simulations, multimedia, CD-ROMs, interactive homework, and quizzes are used to teach courses in biology, economics, and genetics. Students use on-line individual discussions, nested discussions, virtual documents containing both information and graphics related to the course, and pose questions to on-line round-the-clock teaching assistants for quick response. The result is virtual assistance in the course. Group projects, group interactions, real-time simulations, computer conferencing, and continual monitoring of student progress all lead to effective learning.

The Central Oregon Center is a partnership among the Oregon State System of Higher Education (OSSHE), the Oregon Office of Community College Services, and Central Oregon Community College to bring bachelor's, master's, and professional degrees to central Oregon. The area is growing and needs regional services. Because of its geography, travel is difficult, heightening the need for educational services. Central Oregon Community College provides facilities and the Oregon Education Network provides technology to bring in the resources of other Oregon colleges and universities. Although the regional ambition is for a four-year institution, the practical aspects of Oregon's public finances have replaced that idea with making the center serve the purpose. Under the center, Eastern Oregon State College delivers upper-division courses. Two private colleges, three OSSHE campuses, and the Oregon Health Sciences University all offer courses at the center. These partnerships offer alternatives for those without direct access to higher learning in Oregon.

In California, eleven strategies emerged in 1996 from the California Higher Education Policy Center (1996): preserve the state's investment and target better-prepared undergraduates; use existing campuses well; use private institutions by providing student financial aid; increase student fees moderately; reallocate funds to priority programs; accelerate student learning; fund cost-effective technology for instruction; have admissions based on achievement; assess student learning for demonstrated performance; seek teachers with teaching skills; and deregulate colleges and universities. These ideas prompted the Cornerstones Project described earlier. One can argue whether these changes are profound or superficial. But the challenge that gave rise to Cornerstones is to revamp the system in a major way that is more than cosmetic.

In Colorado, the University of Northern Colorado put together a Rocky Mountain Teacher Education Collaborative between faculty in science, mathematics, engineering and technology, and education and K–12 master teachers to improve instruction in these fields. The focus is on improved precollege preparation as a means of enhancing science understanding in the college-bound.

Liberal arts colleges also face their challenges, especially as science and technology have grown, often muscling out the humanities and the arts. While this has happened, the liberal arts remain rooted in integrated scholarship. The liberal arts deal with the values, visions, and vices of knowledge in ways that integrate them with the reservoir of human knowledge and that critique both their value and utility. If anything, new science has spotlighted the liberal arts. Cloning has led to questions of ethics. Medical advances have raised issues over who should receive the limited supply of available organs for transplant. Interdisciplinary work has created new fields. Solid state physics merges with materials science, chemical engineering, and computer science to produce new techniques. The study of how smooth liquids become turbulent involves mathematics, physiology, atmospheric science, and galactic structure (Ruscio, 1987). These examples of crossing disciplines are enhanced by the integrative culture of the liberal arts college. Logical completion and consideration of the meaning and value of new fields can thrive in the liberal setting and pose interesting issues for the extension of present knowledge and epistemology.

Interdisciplinary work is often done in environments where there are no disciplinary departments. The Biological Imaging Center at the California Institute of Technology is an example of this. The center develops new technology for seeing inside organisms and applies this knowledge to important biological issues (Wheeler, 1997). Mathematicians watch cells become chick brains and ponder how this relates to ideas in developmental biology. Magnetic resonance imaging makes it possible to see inside living organisms, making it no longer necessary to kill organisms to observe them internally. It lets scientists watch animal brains as they develop in the womb. A physicist who specializes in how metals conduct electricity at low temperatures works with a physician studying animal multiple sclerosis. These examples show how important appositive learning is to advancing human knowledge and addressing real problems simultaneously. They reflect transdisciplinary knowledge in the making.

Duke, Purdue, and Ohio University have Internet master of business administration (MBA) programs in place. Nearly three hundred institutions offer some form of virtual degree. Market-sensitive institutions such as the University of Phoenix offer on-line services especially for those who work or cannot conveniently take set-time colleges courses. The Internet provides easy access and the capacity to make use of rich course materials. The process enhances communication and conversational learning and assists student in active learning (Rudenstine, 1997). Driven by for-profit institutions like the University of Phoenix and by market pressures for work-related and mid-career learning, traditional universities have begun to heave to on technology-driven learning.

New educational organizations need to be global. In economics, information, politics, and social relations, we are intertwined with world cultures whether we like it or not. The best response for higher education is to broaden the perspectives of students to the cultures of the world. Whatever their majors, students need to learn about the relative aspects of other cultures. This will have clear effects on foreign language instruction and its importance for effective communication. Although everyone expects a curriculum that is centered on the American experience and the knowledge of the western societies that spawned it, comprehending the variety of human cultures is a necessary adjunct, both for understanding those cultures and for a broader understanding of America. This new understanding will drive American competitiveness and contribution to the global marketplace of ideas and things.

In Virginia, all of these ideas have sketched expected new practices in colleges and universities. Student-faculty contact will increase with technology. Televised instruction, complemented by digital materials from the library and computers in students' rooms, will facilitate greater frequency of contact and interaction. If students do not understand a lecture, it can be replayed and the instructor queried face-to-face in discussion or by e-mail. Faculty will interact with students from their offices and in other small discussion locales, freeing the use of traditional classrooms for a range of purposes that will enable responding to more students. Because the student center is linked to the library at George Mason University, students integrate better into a learning community. The library will become more of an information switching station than a warehouse. Libraries digitally linked will be more heavily used because of the convenience of on-line access. This will improve the quality of ordinary learning. As new Ph.D.'s with better teaching preparation are hired, the faculty will enhance active learning and turn study and analysis into a partnership that extends beyond the simple transfer of information and into discovery. In all of this, the access to global technology and databases will contribute significantly to the quality of learning.

The disciplinary system is already evolving and becoming transdisciplinary, as research requires cross-thinking and the application of concepts from other fields to understand complex issues. To encourage the flexibility required by this rapidly changing knowledge, some colleges and universities are decentralizing, especially in Canada and Europe.

Innovation is benefiting from the flexibility and capacity to save and move resources around as priorities shift. Leadership in these institutions is increasingly proactive in support of innovation. As the Virginia Commission put it: "To be blunt, the present arrangement does not encourage or reward cooperation, risk-taking or innovation. It tends to equate effective leadership of colleges and universities with acquisition of resources: staff, buildings and money. The institutions seldom act together because they jockey for competitive advantage among themselves. They tend not to take chances or innovate" (Virginia Commission on the University of the Twenty-First Century, 1989, p. 17).

CONCLUSION

Higher education is undergoing important changes in its structures and processes. If there is a theme underlying the scenarios of change we presented, it is that the new form centers around innovation and connectivity. By whatever names one campus may apply to them, these forces will become the core of the future university. For lack of a better term, the future university will become the New University of Organized Responsibility Units in a loose decentralized relationship, connected by information sources, knowledge and curricular sources, research and knowledge-creation sources, and assisting and support services. It will use seed money to support academic units, which will first blossom and then move on to be replaced by new problems and new issues of educational and social concern. It will pioneer global literacy through its research, active learning, and technological links to institutions around the world. It will be guided in all of this by the linkage of internal strengths and areas of distinction to external opportunities, along with a careful analysis of the cross-impact that will result. This theme is discussed further in Chapter Thirteen, where we present our practical steps for using strategic planning as a tool to guide this change.

CHAPTER SEVEN

Achieving Strategic Fit Between Strengths and Opportunities

⁓⁓⁓

As previous chapters have shown, the challenge to change can be threatening to faculty, administrators, and support staff. Campus leaders from every quarter of the college or university sense this but are often at a loss about how to proceed in strategically restructuring their campus to meet better the needs of the information society. This chapter looks at several of the issues that campus leaders should consider as they make strategic choices among the various paths their institution may choose for the future. These choices often touch on traditional excellence and other practices of the past that served the college or university well during the industrial era but may not serve well in the new millennium, especially as new knowledge requirements become better known.

RECOGNIZING ESSENTIALS

We have argued before that colleges and universities should be responsive to their environments because external forces set some of the parameters of long-term survival (Rowley, Lujan, and Dolence, 1997). Part of that argument was that institutions must be more market driven in deciding what course offerings make sense, as they try to match the challenges and needs of the environment with the capacity and purpose of the academy.

No matter how great the pressure on the academy to be more responsive to the changing needs and demands of society, the academy cannot afford to abdicate the important role that colleges and universities play in research, in the encapsulation of knowledge, and in its dissemination. Although we make the point here that some basic research is already taking place beyond the walls of the ivory tower, it would be a major mistake to conclude that the role of basic research has passed from the academy. This is not true now, nor is it likely to be in the future. The real issue is determining the appropriate mix of research—research that is directly within the control of the institution, research that is directed from outside the academy, and research that can involve both of these conditions.

Research is not the only essential in developing a more cohesive and mutually beneficial fit between institutions of higher education and the external environment. Information transfer and direct service to the external environment are also areas in which colleges and universities must find new matches and new relationships.

UNDERSTANDING THE REAL OBSTACLES CAMPUSES FACE

It is one thing to identify the need for change and another to be able to effect change. There are many forces both inside and outside the academy that support change as a means of improving operations, education, research, and service. There is also a large body of those who sit on the fence, not getting involved in one side or the other for political, judgmental, or special-interest reasons. There is another body of people who just do not care.

These different forces present significant opportunities as well as some very serious threats to those who seek change. Sometimes, no matter how grave the issue, internal inertia and interests will resist changes in the status quo. Administrators and faculty who face these obstacles are often frustrated and disillusioned by deep-seated opposition, whether it is vocal or not. When one group can see so clearly that change is essential, yet at the same time they fail to rally support for thoughtful and constructive innovation, it is easy to become disillusioned.

Resistance to change does not prevent change. Change occurs regardless of the support or opposition to it. The issue of concern is how that change will occur. Campuses that are able to come together in a meaningful way to examine the pressures for change can then develop a common process for change to occur. Change brought about in this way can be significant and beneficial. On the other hand, campuses controlled by those who want to maintain the status quo will often experience major disruptions, including cutbacks in programs and staff. It is fascinating that sometimes some resisters who are forced into change continue to oppose anything that could lessen the negative effects of that change, even when it is clear that the changes will take place. After the change has occurred, there often will still be attempts to roll it back.

These are sad but not uncommon events on campuses around the world. The academy is a prized and comfortable place for many to reside, build careers, develop roles in their chosen disciplines, establish friendships and family roots, forge bases of power, and contribute to society. So when external forces press for change, one response is resistance or indignation. But if history teaches us anything, it is that when two forces decide that combat is preferable to cooperation and mutual problem solving, the stronger of the two will prevail, leaving the fate of the vanquished to the whim of the winner.

It soon becomes a question of who is stronger—the forces that resist change in the academy or the other forces, found both inside and outside the academy, that push and lever change. It is also important to note that the academy is becoming more fragmented. In the face of this, some campuses are able to respond with innovations, as others dig in. Still another group sits on the sidelines, waiting to see which way the winds will blow, positioning themselves to move to the winning side when a winning strategy becomes apparent.

Yet, overshadowing all of this diffraction is the reality that the information age *needs* major academic partners to discover, distill, and disseminate new research, new knowledge, new learning opportunities, and new service involvements. There are enough of these opportunities that no one needs to be a loser in the information age, unless one chooses it. For this reason, we emphasize ways to assist institutions in transforming themselves.

Understanding the forces that push campuses one way or another is central to developing a scenario for a more compatible relationship with the need for new ideas and information. Comprehending these forces begins with the most crucial of a college's or university's internal and external environments—the central groups or individuals that control external funding and the forces that drive the internal campus and its programs. As we argued at length in our previous book (Rowley, Lujan, and Dolence, 1997), strategic change occurs best when an institution is able to adequately match its internal resources with the needs and demands of its most important external partners. When a campus moves from being provider driven to consumer oriented, it can achieve greater harmony with its most relevant environmental forces, both internal and external. This will help ensure long-term survival.

Dealing with Declining Public Support

The Western Governors Association issued a report in 1996 that spells out the problems facing higher education, particularly in the area of public funding (Western Governors Association, 1996). In this report, they express the importance of developing a higher educational system that is supportive of a changing society and its allied economic community. At the same time, the report highlights the inability of state governments in the United States to support higher education at the level it purports to require.

The decline in support of higher education at the state level is partially a response to a growing concern in state legislatures about getting adequate return on their investments in higher education. This concern wends its way through the political process, from election issue to public policy expectation. As long ago as 1983, when *A Nation at Risk* was published, higher education had been told that the general public is increasingly dissatisfied with the products and methods of higher education in preparing its students for the needs of society (National Commission on Excellence in Education, 1983). There have been other calls more recently for the academy to be more timely and responsive in the curriculum to the massive changes occurring globally (Leslie and Fretwell, 1996; Kaufman, 1993). Marshall and Palca (1992) have written that when governmental bodies detect major levels of criticism of the programs, services, or agencies they support, they reduce their support.

Clearly, another contributor to the erosion of funding support comes from the shifting of social-program funding from the federal government to state governments. Beginning with the Reagan years, the federal government has worked hard to shift the load of social entitlements from federal to state. As these shifts have occurred, states have had to spread their thin resources over larger demands and have had to reprioritize. Add to that the growing conservatism throughout the country, with its accompanying push for lower taxes and less governmental intrusion, and the states find themselves stretched for resources as never before. Hence, they call for those dependent on them to make sacrifices and economize. Higher education has not been exempted this time around.

REPRIORITIZATION. As states reprioritize, education is not first on the list. Even in the area of education, K–12 and higher education are not classified together, and K–12 usually ranks above higher education in most states. Ahead of education are entitlements, the mandated responsibilities placed on states by the federal government, the courts, or previous obligation.

For example, in Colorado the priority order in recent years has been entitlements first, followed by K–12, prisons, higher education, transportation, and then everything else. Davies (1997) suggests that this type of prioritization exists nationwide. This puts a severe additional strain on publicly funded colleges and universities through repressive taxing and spending laws. An example is Colorado's Amendment 1, passed in 1992, that set California-style limits on tax increases as well as on spending increases in a formula that is keyed to the sum of the rate of population growth and the increase in the Consumer Price Index of the Denver-Boulder metropolitan area. Such measures do not help support the level of services required by a rapidly growing population. This is particularly true when the population growth is faster in the underclasses than in the middle and upper classes, putting greater strain on entitlement programs and leaving even less for those programs further down the priority list. The money does not stretch far enough to meet the needs of publicly funded higher education in most of the American states.

DECLINE OF PRIVATE COLLEGES AND UNIVERSITIES. Decline in funding is not only a problem for public institutions. Private institutions also are finding that it is a mistake to take their funding sources for granted. There are limits to the amount of tuition any college or university can charge (with very few exceptions), and the need for private colleges and universities to ensure that their students are satisfied with their educational experience has become more and more of an issue over the last several years (Rowley, Lujan, and Dolence, 1997). As competition continues to increase among private colleges and universities for top students, the accompanying imperatives to improve student services and provide state-of-the-art educational opportunities continue to mount. The demands of the information age only heighten these pressures.

Also, private colleges and universities need to be more and more responsive to donor groups and endowment grantors. As any members of these groups become dissatisfied with the operations or results of institutions they have traditionally supported, they seem to be more and more willing to pull back funding and support, leaving major voids in the institutions' funding and damaging their reputations as well. The latter can be fatal in the long run.

LOSS OF STATUS. All of these conditions contribute to a general loss of status for colleges and universities, particularly in the United States. Although higher education may still be viewed as a valuable asset, it is not viewed by everyone as the preeminent asset it once was. When examining the benefits of various programs throughout a campus, one becomes clear that many of these do not lead the participants directly into the job market as one might otherwise have thought.

For example, though MBA programs around the world continue to provide an increasing number of graduates for the marketplace, many students have begun to question the degree's usefulness. Not so many years ago, an MBA was seen as a guarantee of a good job. Today, many MBAs are looking for work right along with non-MBA's. This is particularly true for those students who upon graduation from a baccalaureate program go straight into an MBA program. For these students, the lack of meaningful business experience following the acquiring of a bachelor of arts or sciences degree is a major hindrance in securing a well-paying, high-prestige job in business even with an MBA.

Business is not the only program in which students question the value of their degrees. Many arts and sciences majors, as well as a growing number of education majors have real difficulties finding suitable jobs following graduation. For them, it is easy to look back on their collegiate experience and question the value of the time, effort, and money spent on an education that does not appear to be relevant to the emerging job opportunities of the information age.

Those graduates who have professional training in areas that support the information age appear to have the edge when it comes to applying their educations to life after college. Nevertheless, most engineering majors, computer science majors, medical and health industry majors, along with most undergraduate business majors, find jobs in their chosen fields of preparation.

Earlier, we identified the loss of status in the world of research and development as an area in which the academy must be concerned with its image. Particularly in the field of information technology, much of the basic research that is done today is done within the confines of company laboratories and to the general exclusion of the campus academic. Because of the centrality of this field in the emerging paradigms of the information age, for the academy to be left out of this or to be just a convenient and narrowly confined project partner erodes the traditional position of higher education as the primary source for new knowledge.

PUBLIC CRITICISM. Horne (1995) tells us that as criticism of higher education continues to mount, politicians, government officials, and others who believe they have a stake in higher education have begun to question what goes on inside the classrooms and laboratories of higher education. Botstein has even made the charge that the general education students receive at most colleges and universities is "artificial, arbitrary, tendentious—even imposed and essentially dispensable" (1991, p. 10). These are harsh criticisms indeed, but they underscore the decline in support that most colleges and universities have overlooked.

Public institutions have come to this juncture after years of open and generous support from governments and publics. Private institutions have always needed to be more sensitive to outside criticism, because they depend on donors to take up the slack in budgets that tuition has not been able to cover. Public institutions have always enjoyed a modicum of sheltering by state legislatures and other regulatory bodies, ever since the explosive demand for higher education following the successful launch of Sputnik in the late 1950s. So not only do most colleges and universities view the present criticism as harsh, they also view it as new.

Certainly, many within the academy hope that this is a blip on the radar screen and that it will subside as the public comes back to its senses and understands the values, philosophies, and mores that have always come from the academy. Yet, such a hope may be very much misplaced in the dramatic shifts of values, techniques, and expectations emerging from the information age.

Lifestyle Challenges

The college campus has become a haven over the centuries for the creation, distillation, and dissemination of knowledge. There is something quasi-religious about a campus. Often, references are made to "hallowed halls." Chapels stand as part of many campus settings, and the activities that thrive on a campus often inform the notions of right and wrong that one carries through life. Parklike campuses are more the norm than the exception, and beauty and solace are part of the ambience.

The professorate has preeminent status, as it should. Those admitted to its ranks have passed tests, endured preparation, and obtained impressive certification. These are the stalwarts and beacons of knowledge. They have come as bearers of knowledge. Administrators are largely tolerated, and staff are necessary to support and expedite scholarly pursuits. Students come to learn and to leave enriched, both intellectually and practically. This is a comfortable world by design. In practice, it tolerates very little external intrusion.

Yet, this very world is challenged by an increasingly hostile external environment. Questions about what happens in the classroom, why students are sometimes ill prepared to enter a competitive job market, and why costs keep going up but quality appears to be going down are often seen as invasive and are not well received by the keepers of the flame within the academy.

Interestingly enough, on most campuses, administrators attempt to shield their professors from the immediate effects of external criticism. Now, as institutional governing boards begin to take more involvement in the activities and inner workings of the campus (Gardner, 1995), there is less shielding of the faculty from the growing disenchantment of externals. Some choose to ignore this criticism. Others feel that if the criticism gets too rough, cooler heads will intercede and not penalize higher education.

Governing boards that wish to preserve a tradition, campus administrators who understand the penalties that may result from being innovative and who choose not to challenge the status quo, and campus bureaucracies that seek to preserve the powers and controls that they have achieved over the years are all capable of being recalcitrant and hostile to change. In earlier work (Rowley, Lujan, and Dolence, 1997), we discussed campus politics, and particularly negative politics, as a very real part of campus life that can be inimical to strategic change. Others have made a similar point (Dooris and Lozier, 1990). Pfeffer (1992) tells us that groups use politics as a method of seizing control of resources to ensure that decisions will be made in a preferred direction. Although there is nothing inherently wrong with politics (Birnbaum, 1991), in its negative form, it is always a source of conflict (Hardy, 1991). As a governing body, an administrator corps, a bureaucracy, or a faculty decide that it is going to resist change, especially challenges imposed on it from outside power bases (such as state legislatures, or grant-giving entities), it will usually resort to political activity. Depending on the issue and the campus involved, that activity could be a force that can hinder meaningful change or a force that can thwart change through negative politics and exercise of veto power. At the heart of the issue is the preservation of a style of life that is not only comfortable but also conferring of status and respected by many.

Traditions That Hinder

Finally, there are traditions that can hinder substantive change. The degree system can become exclusive and rigid in the face of changing fields and student expectations. The mark of a well-educated person is often associated with the degree that person possesses. A baccalaureate degree is fairly commonplace among most major business and professional employees. In business management, an MBA is still both a common and a preferred degree. Master's degrees are still important qualifications in many professions (health care, education, psychology, and social work), a medical degree is still the required minimum to attain certification in medicine, and a J.D. is required to practice law. A doctoral degree is certainly necessary for membership in the academy itself. Granting degrees is the coveted right of accredited qualified colleges and universities. Degrees granted by unaccredited or upstart institutions are never given the same degree of respect as those that come from well-known and well-regarded colleges and universities.

The problem here, as pointed out earlier, is that the demand for knowledge by information age workers in an information age economy and a global society does not necessarily fit the narrow confines of existing degrees. Not only is the changing knowledge base not well covered in classical degree programs, but the need of the information worker to get specific knowledge on an on-demand basis is at direct odds with how most colleges and universities structure their certification and knowledge dissemination processes.

Narrowing disciplines is another phenomenon challenging the attempts of most colleges and universities to become more useful to information age workers. When one looks at the way we currently run doctoral programs, both in the United States and around the world, the pattern for training the professors of the future has varied little over the past century. Doctoral candidates are given huge reading lists of all the basic literature in their chosen fields, are asked to participate in seminars in which that knowledge can be discussed among other doctoral candidates or with senior faculty mentors, and then are tested to prove that the basic knowledge of the field has affected the thinking and skills of the future professor.

The capstone of any doctoral program is the dissertation. For centuries, the research and writing of a doctoral dissertation has been the final rite of passage for granting of the terminal degree. But what types of dissertations are usually required? What is the subject matter they cover? Who is it that reviews them and passes judgment on them? What sort of use is the dissertation put to once it has been accepted? The answers to these questions are disturbing in that they all involve a process that narrows already specialized academic fields. In an age in which broad analytical and cross-disciplinary skills are particularly valued, a dissertation that narrows seems counterproductive. And the knowledge that has been generated, though new knowledge, tends to narrow disciplines further.

In terms of the impact of this century-honored tradition on the information age, the outcome is not quite as straightforward. In a new age in which change is clearly the name of the game, new knowledge based in new theory is sorely needed. We have come to believe that the more leisurely paced academic output in emerging fields is a reason why research into information age methods and knowledge bases has started to come from sources other than the academy. Unless colleges and universities that engage in doctoral preparation can restructure their programs to encourage their students to study emerging issues in the information age, there is little hope that the academy will produce a new generation of professors who will be prepared for the problems and conundrums of the future.

Tenure continues to be the lightning rod of change, discussed further in a coming chapter. It is a controversial reality in American colleges and universities and can be—but need not be—a tradition that hinders. There is growing concern among state legislatures and other state educational regulatory bodies that tenure is more an obstacle to accountability and effective campus management than it is a positive aspect of academia. The defense of academic freedom has not played well, particularly when legislators remark that academic freedom is also guaranteed by the First Amendment. For those who believe this way, tenure is a special privilege that is disproportionate in a general economy and an excuse for undeserved pampering and minimal workload requirements. From this, it is easy to see why there would be legislative or governing-board movement either to eliminate tenure or to reduce personnel costs.

Needless to say, faculty's broad and often hostile fear of losing tenure is one of the reasons many professors are looking at unionism as a method of forestalling or eliminating the threat altogether. It is worth noting that tenure may not be the underlying issue, because union contracts make it difficult to fire anyone, tenured or not. Regardless, the time and energy spent on this issue polarizes the campus and puts it at odds with its environment.

STRATEGICALLY DEFINING THE CAMPUS ROLE

Despite all of these obstacles to change, many colleges and universities are making the transition to the information age. Those who are farsighted enough to do this are providing leadership, and their initiatives are welcomed in the business and policy worlds and among the academics who participate in these innovations. Those who struggle to find appropriate niches, but who have significant resource bases behind them, will eventually make the transition and develop appropriate relationships external to the campus. We believe there will be several colleges and universities that will resist changing right up to the bitter end. For this group, we cannot be hopeful about their future. It is likely that many of these institutions will end up being consolidated into larger, more aggressive systems (particularly those institutions in the public sector) or may simply be forced to close their doors (most likely in the private sector).

We do not see the dynamics and forces of the information age as supporting mediocrity or reactivity. Koch (1996) has stated that enterprises in the new age will succeed when they seek to add long-term value rather than to go for the easier short-term profit. Those institutions that fail to address and respond adequately to the needs of the information age society will have difficulty surviving over the long term. Who will survive and who will not ultimately comes down to individual campuses, their faculties, administrators, and governing boards. It will also depend on campus propensities for change, the resource base of each, and the levels of connectivity that already exist between the college or university and information age entities. Our prescription for change is that each campus must build its own strategy by assessing its own external opportunities and threats. Each must compare these to its internal strengths and weaknesses. Each must look for cross-impacts, and through fairly broad and participative brainstorming, each must let campus constituents build a working consensus by focusing on specific issues. Enrollment management is always a good place to begin, for it is a common problem and involves both the external environment and internal elements. The California State University task force approach is another. In their case, four major issues were turned over to task forces. How a campus initiates change or what kind of nomenclature or organizing structure it follows is less important than following the major steps for strategic planning (see Dolence, Rowley, and Lujan, 1997).

Change Will Vary

Higher education in the information age is not about discarding everything that has preceded it in the industrial age; it is about shifting over time from one basic paradigm to another. Though the information age is upon us, it is upon us in degrees. Not everything will change as the basic economic and political systems change, and many institutions will be able to prosper in their present condition well into the next decade without dramatic change. Although it is certain that the demand for older-style institutions will decline over time, and eventually perhaps all institutions will become significantly different, some colleges and universities will survive in the new millennium without radical changes. We do not say this as an antithesis to what we have talked about throughout the book. This statement simply recognizes the individual variations from one campus to another and also within a given campus. Some are in more fortunate circumstances than others, and the differences in circumstances will temper how they interact with the needs of an information age society.

CASE OF THE LARGE RESEARCH INSTITUTIONS. As we began to look at in Chapter One, we believe that there are a core of colleges and universities that will survive relatively unchanged because they are already outstanding institutions or have sufficient resources to survive for a long period of time without feeling the needs for major change. Moreover, some within society will continue to seek a traditional college education, either because their parents believe it to be essential or because it offers living and learning conditions that are valued. The mix of these factors suggests that major research institutions such as the University of Michigan, the University of California at Berkeley, the University of North Carolina at Chapel Hill, and others of this magnitude will most likely not feel significant demands to change substantially in the near future, though some may change on their own.

VARIANT OF THE SMALLER RESEARCH INSTITUTIONS. Institutions such as the Universities of North and South Dakota, Montana, Idaho, or Vermont present a different matter. Their research roles are far more focused, and they come from states with finite resources. In the past, federal largesse helped them grow research programs that are now threatened by federal belt-tightening. Agriculture often provided additional resources for these institutions, permitting them to acquire national respect, if not reputations. The squeeze of federal resources will afflict these campuses significantly, and the requirements and costs of big science will threaten their science base. Many of these institutions will be reduced to regional universities, providing focused excellence in subjects and problem areas existing in their home regional environments. Even in these cases, if an institution's strengths are in rural life, forestry, mining, family farms, and dairies, the future will require restructuring and redefining a role for which there is sufficient demand and enrollments.

CASE OF THE EXCELLENT PRIVATE SCHOOLS. Likewise, most of the Ivy League schools, Northwestern and Stanford Universities, and other private schools with deep pockets and world-class reputations will not be placed under scrutiny they cannot easily defend against. Even among these schools, movement from an orientation in industrial age academics to information age academics is already occurring in select programs. Many of these institutions are characterized by dynamic and entrepreneurial faculties and administrations. The degree of change, however, is unpredictable and depends on the openness to new ideas and the willingness to fund innovative faculty and projects. There are also a number of highly regarded and well-endowed smaller private liberal arts colleges that will most likely survive relatively unchanged due to the presence of dedicated alumni and parents of students across the world who value the benefits of the traditional liberal arts education they provide. We believe, however, that the demand for such an education will decline as more and more information age learners seek different ways of achieving their educations and find fields of interest that these schools do not offer. Most of these campuses will change because they will want to, not because they will be forced to.

ALL THE REST. Davies (1997) tells us that many students will select Ivy League or the most prestigious liberal arts colleges because of their excellence. He states that all other institutions are at risk. It is the large group of state-supported research, comprehensive, and teaching colleges and universities where the impact of external pressure will more likely force change. Small, less well-endowed private institutions will face some of the same issues. Here is where public, governmental, and regulatory criticism will be most keenly felt. It is these institutions that will choose early whether or not they wish to make substantive changes to accommodate their crucial external stakeholders or whether they will dig in and try to ride out the tempest. We believe it is this very last group that will fare the least well but have the opportunity, if they act now, to recast themselves for the long run. As campus militancy clashes with external demands, it is probable that external funding sources will begin to take harder and harder stands and reduce resource allocations. Ultimately, institutions with diminishing budgets, dropping enrollments, high percentages of tenured faculty, marginal degree programs particularly at the graduate level, technologically minimal capacity, too many programs, and a divided campus will be forced to act. They will have to change, consolidate, or close up shop. The irony is that those campuses that close will have had many opportunities to prevent their fates but will have chosen to dig in and defend what was in the end indefensible.

Academic Changes Under Way

Some information age changes already are occurring, particularly in the central utilities of a campus and in outreach. The most notable changes so far are occurring in the campus library, in student access to learning, and in campus laboratories.

LIBRARY REFORM—THE VIRTUAL LIBRARY. There are many factors driving changes in the methods of acquisition, dissemination, storage, and use of library collections, not least of which is the reduction of resources campuses make available to their libraries as a result of general resource tightening. It is the rare campus that tends to value its library very highly when prioritization occurs. Even if increases come, they are modest compared with those of the rest of the academic structure of most campuses. Yet the cost of serial subscriptions (journals, newspapers, and magazines) continues to go up; new book costs continue to escalate; and the general expenses of keeping up the facilities, staff, and utilities all go up. The crunch comes quickly, and many libraries have begun to look for alternatives.

One of the significant advances has been in electronics. More libraries are able to share resources through larger networks, such as the Colorado Association of Research Libraries system in Colorado. Such a system allows libraries to identify more easily holdings throughout the statewide area, which includes most of the major public as well as private colleges and universities. Interlibrary loan has grown tremendously as a result of such database systems, and the result has been a lessening on demand for each individual library to hold major collections.

Another major advance is the digitizing of major library collections. Of particular significance is the digitizing of the Library of Congress, the largest library in the world. Although work thus far has been confined to new additions and serials, eventually the entire collection could be digitized and made available through a worldwide mechanism such as the Internet. Digitizing is also occurring at the libraries at the University of Michigan and the University of California at Berkeley, the University of Minnesota, and the Ohio State University, among others. Eventually, this virtual library system could significantly alter the makeup and use of campus libraries throughout the world. The beginnings of this significant change are already in place in most academic libraries. It will likely culminate in fingertip access to most of the essential references and databases required for research and learning.

LABORATORY INNOVATIONS. Laboratories are undergoing slow but significant change. Computer simulations replace noticeable amounts of lab table work in fields such as chemistry and biology. Computerized learning labs are used to teach mathematics, both at the precollege and college levels. The Mathematics and Science Teaching Lab at the University of Northern Colorado links eighteen hundred classrooms in 126 school districts with software that teaches basic arithmetic and algebraic thinking through repetitious problem solving. Music technology labs are being used increasingly to teach music theory and some aspects of playing particular instruments and also to provide interactive sessions in which student performance is compared digitally to the work of the masters. These innovations use keyboards as simulated instruments and can assist in learning a range of theory and techniques from understanding staccato to playing the cello like Pablo Casals.

ACCESS AND THE OPEN UNIVERSITIES. Open universities, as discussed in Chapter Four, are those that offer open admissions, open programming, and open pace of studies (Kirschner and Valcke, 1994). Several such institutions now exist around the world. One of the more interesting ones is the Open University of the Netherlands. According to Kirschner and Valcke, this particular institution has developed a program that centers around individual courses, which are available to learners in a distance learning environment (the only requirement being that the learner be eighteen years or older). The individual learner chooses a program of study, then selects specific courses, which the university delivers through distance delivery media and didactic techniques such as interactive telecommunication or courses on the Internet. The student can choose a personal pace of learning and can also choose from a variety of learning paths. The hallmarks of this distance program (there are no resident students) are flexibility and providing the learner with a "learning adventure." Although the institution decides the content and materials used in each course unit, the learner is given as much latitude as possible to help ensure that each learner achieves the goals he or she is seeking. Technology is a central part of open learning.

CONCLUSION

What we have argued in this chapter is that threats and opportunities characterize the challenges of the information age. Those who act proactively to find and leverage opportunities in their external environments to areas of their internal strengths and distinctions will evolve and survive in the long run. Forces against change exist in many forms. Forces for change also emerge in a variety of shapes and sizes. The force field of the new age pushes one way, then the other. Without a strategic decision-making process, such as we have outlined, in place, an institution will be weak to respond and will become increasingly subjected to the expectations of environmental stakeholders, who will exert their external power. This can be extremely dysfunctional for the campus. But if campus leaders unite, and if governing boards, administrative corps, campus staff, and faculties together develop a strategic solution that exploits available opportunities, then the campus will shape its own future. Then, positive change will follow to preserve the integrity of the institution. The choice is up to each campus, but the outcomes will impact society generally.

CHAPTER EIGHT

Expanding Channels for Instructional Delivery

T echniques for information transfer change dramatically, almost on a daily basis, and this trend will continue into the
future. In higher education, we are beginning to see that what has
occurred in nontraditional centers of learning is beginning to show
up in the classrooms, libraries, and laboratories of the more traditional
colleges and universities around the world. Changes regarding the
learner are clearly on the way.

We believe that for all of its pros and cons, the lecture method of
teaching will endure, though its use may be guided by a better understanding of how well it conveys particular subject matter and for
which settings it is beneficial. Other forms of transfer will become
more commonplace, because different methods will be needed to meet
the widely ranging demands of new learners. This chapter examines
several of these methods and discusses their uses by information age
learners. We also consider some of the alternatives today's learners use
as the competitive world of information evolves.

FUSING THE EDUCATIONAL COMMUNITY WITH THE LEARNER ENVIRONMENT

In the previous chapter, we stressed the importance of colleges and universities working to align their areas of distinction with the emerging demands of information age companies and other information stakeholders. It is obvious that the requirements of the information age worker will only partially be satisfied by current practices in higher education. For those areas in which the learner can find the necessary knowledge in higher education, so much the better. When learning needs cannot be satisfied by traditional systems, however, one can either not get the knowledge at all or get it from some other source. We stress again that this Hobson's choice diminishes support for higher education and undermines its role as society's font of knowledge.

The only reasonable choice is for higher education to change its pedagogy to be more useful to the knowledge worker. According to Dillman, Christenson, Salant, and Warner (1995), approximately 81 percent of the adult workforce (in the United States) sees the importance of getting additional training or education for their work. Of this number, 75 percent are interested in getting this additional training or education from a college. Over half are looking for credit courses, whereas 75 percent are interested in noncredit courses. This is a huge demand that will affect every college and university, not only in the United States but also throughout the world. In this regard, several ideas are already surfacing about what might need to take place in higher education for it to be more compatible with the needs of the knowledge worker.

VARIETY OF STUDENTS AND LEARNERS

The new millennium is demonstrating that there is more than one kind of student seeking knowledge. These new learners are turning to universities, community colleges, proprietary schools, company universities, on-line institutions, and other sources of knowledge, teaching, or training. These learners can be divided into three distinct categories— the traditional college student, the graduate learner, and the nontraditional learner. Each has its own particular needs and expectations from the academy.

Traditional College Students

There is and will continue to be a large number of eighteen-to-twenty-two year-olds who seek higher education on college and university campuses in the United States and around the world. As we noted previously, there is also a stable cadre of young people, parents, and fervent alumni and friends of traditional colleges and universities all over the world who value the experience of "going away to college," of being educated in a traditional setting, and of making this their bridge to adulthood. This traditional student will seek full, daytime schedules of course work and look to achieve a degree at the end of a four-year experience.

On the surface, it might appear that there is no earthly reason for colleges and universities to change if their student body of the future is essentially their student body of the past. But although there is and will be a cadre of high school graduates who will seek a campus experience, it is a mistake to assume that these students are no more sophisticated than their predecessors. These seekers of a traditional-style education are nearly all computer literate, worldly wise users of the Internet, fully aware of the competitiveness of the job market, and in some ways, more job and technology "street-smart" than their predecessors. They expect their college or university experience to prepare them adequately for a successful career after college. Most are aware of the criticisms of the academy and know firsthand of the competition between colleges and universities for the brightest and the best of high school graduates. This all goes into making the new age high school senior different from the graduate of twenty or fifty years ago. Some of them are passive seat time learners. But many new age freshmen view their higher educational experience as more of a right than a privilege, are assertive about what they must get to do well after college, and hold their institutions to a higher standard than in the past. The growing sophistication of this group and their openness to active learning will transform traditional learning. If nothing else, technology will see to that.

Graduate Learners

In contrasting learners and students, the graduate student is more of a learner. Learners are active in designing their programs of study and in their studies. Unlike undergraduates, this group is focused, mature, and not as tolerant of academic requirements that seem to make no sense. They know what they want by and large and will find a graduate experience to meet *their* needs. As graduate programs have come to realize, the potential graduate student is more demanding and selective than in the past. As a result, many graduate programs are not growing or are in decline. Doctoral education is especially under challenge, because a national decline in the demand for new professors has reduced the appeal of expensive and labor-intensive graduate programs.

This new learner is currently challenging the traditional graduate school. Because graduate competition is becoming more acute, the challenge is to determine the unique abilities of any given graduate program to meet the needs of the society it serves. To adapt, graduate programs must scan their external environments for opportunities, assess their internal programs for excellence and distinction, revise their missions accordingly, consider their resources, then match their efforts with the needs of information age learners.

Nontraditional and Adult Learners

The fastest-growing group of learners are nontraditional and seek education outside the setting designed for the full-load, daytime, primarily resident undergraduate student. This adult learner goes back to college to attain needed knowledge and a degree during the career years. As suggested in Chapter One, the information age has spurred on this group because of the demand for a better-educated and flexible workforce. Many nontraditionals look to their local college or university to supply the knowledge they seek. Some are disappointed when they discover that the local academic institution is not really geared to accommodate them.

These individuals differ from others in several significant ways. These learners want an education on their terms, not the institution's terms. They often want their education during off-hours, at alternative sites, and convenient to their own time schedule. Because seeking an education for most of these people occurs in the face of other life responsibilities, such as a job or family obligation, they want an educational experience that will accommodate them and not an experience to which they must accommodate. Bronner (1997) tells us that institutions such as the University of Phoenix, which caters to adults only, are carving out an impressive niche serving this type of nontraditional student.

Many of these individuals are not necessarily seeking a degree. Some may wish to take advantage of a single academic discipline, program, or course and may, for example, see no value in a general education. Others find quickly that in order to be allowed to take the course work they want, they must wend their way through a range of prerequisites.

Because these learners are adults, including those thrust into adult roles at an early age, few feel at home on the traditional campus. Teachers on traditional campuses often come across this growing group of learners, whose needs are distinct but whose abilities once burnished are evident.

If not satisfied, this group of learners is the most mobile and the least loyal to an academic institution. This group will leave one college and seek another until they get what they need. This is the group that has given the greatest amount of support to the proprietary colleges and for-profit universities. They have also taken advantage of company opportunities to achieve what they need from company colleges or any one of the growing number of alternative educational providers.

Colleges and universities should know that this group is the early prototype of the information age learner and represents the most current and immediate interaction between educational institutions and the information age. If this group is dissatisfied, their support for the academy will decline. This dissatisfaction will spread to potential students of all types, to funding sources, and to policymakers. Moreover, as these learners rise to levels of decision making, they will be influential in how the business and professional world views higher education.

KNOWLEDGE DELIVERY MODES AND METHODS

The primary transition that many colleges and universities need to make is to move away from a provider-driven perspective and toward a more consumer-driven orientation. This means that most higher educational programs should examine what subject matter they offer, why they offer it, who it is designed to benefit, how it is taught, and what the expected outcomes should be. Traditionally, these questions have been the purview of the faculty, supported by their disciplines and institutional accreditation agencies. In this model, there is little that attempts to match offerings to demonstrated needs of knowledge seekers. This has to change if colleges and universities are to develop more comprehensive means of meeting the needs of knowledge workers.

This is not to suggest that the need for reform comes only from the emergence of the information age. The most common method of teaching today is the lecture. Yet, there is a growing body of literature that suggests that lecturing is not always the most effective method of knowledge transfer (Guskin, 1994; Chickering and Gamson, 1991). For one thing, lectures provide little opportunity for interaction. This reduces the opportunity for the learner to question what is being said either from the viewpoint of argument or to gain better understanding. Lectures are normally the product of a lecturer's design for a course or a subject. As a provider-driven methodology, the lecture may not correspond well with the needs of the learner nor best convey understanding of the subject.

As Kember and Gow (1994) tell us, today's students (including the traditional college student as well as the other information age learners) are no longer passive receptacles of the information their teachers wish to share with them. Many are becoming vocal about the usefulness of the information their teachers give them, and some are beginning to take a more active role in demanding that the knowledge conveyed be useful and meaningful. Kember and Gow further tell us that the lecture method of knowledge transfer will insufficiently satisfy learner needs. In enrollment-sensitive private colleges and universities in particular, there is a movement toward listening more seriously to these concerns and responding in ways that ensure integrity of the discipline while meeting the needs of the learner.

Another concern is the ability of the current classroom to meet simultaneously the needs of the traditional learner and the new learner. As the information age develops more knowledge and requires its workers to update themselves continually in that knowledge base, a challenge to the traditional degree program will arise, as students begin to question the value of a degree from an institution that is not willing to keep that degree current. We believe that marketing demands will eventually force many colleges and universities into a position where they will have to provide their graduates with opportunities for educational updating in order to provide legitimacy to the initial degree. According to Dolence and Norris (1995), many colleges and universities will need to reorient themselves from being a "time-out" learning center, in the form of a multiyear program in which the student is expected to devote full-time to study, to becoming a perpetual learning center, where learners return continually to refresh their knowledge. These forces will bring change to the classroom and the curriculum.

Traditional Classroom—the Same, but Different

During an interview with Appleberry, he expressed the idea that many colleges and universities should begin to consider a major transition from the way the classroom is used today to other uses. He even indicated that in some settings and for some courses, the classroom is unnecessary. We agree with this view. The growth of technology; the demand for more relevance of the material for the learner; the increase in student assertiveness for an active role and partnership in learning; and the growing core of progressive faculty with new ideas, who are developing new pedagogical methods, are all forces for transforming the classroom.

We doubt if the classroom, a basic and time-tested tool of learning, will go away completely. There are many situations in which it is important for learners to get together with a professor to develop certain knowledge. It may even be practical for some large introductory courses to continue to rely on lecturing as a quick means for conveying a standard body of knowledge to a large group. We believe that both of these primary tools of teaching, the classroom and the lecture, will diminish as other methods aided by technology emerge and the efficiency of those methods is demonstrated. Examples of these include the electronic classroom, on-line learning modules, and self-paced or mastery-oriented learning.

POOLING THE PROFESSORATE. There are a variety of factors driving the need to reexamine how we use the resources found in the professorate. A major concern is economic. Depending on the discipline involved and the rank a professor has attained, salaries for professors range widely. For a beginning, tenure-track assistant professor in English, a beginning salary might be $28,000, whereas a full professor holding a distinguished chair in medicine might command a yearly salary of $280,000. Most salaries range in between and to the lower side of this scale. Based on discipline and rank, one college or university might have a younger liberal arts–dominated faculty and enjoy a relatively small payroll, whereas another college or university might have an older, highly distinguished faculty including more of the professional disciplines and be saddled with a very high payroll.

Tenure is another element of the academy that makes it difficult for colleges or universities to maneuver their salary obligations easily, and as general salaries increase in disciplines, most colleges and universities have no choice but to match these increases in peer institutions year to year or risk losing their best professors. In an age in which resources are becoming more and more constrained, many colleges and universities are looking for viable alternatives to help ensure that they can continue to provide high-quality faculties, while maintaining or reducing overall costs. Pooling is one idea that may have some useful implications for this increasing administrative dilemma.

In pooling, a core of the best professors are placed in a central talent pool and then shared among a variety of institutions. The potential for sharing contracts among several institutions exists because most college and university faculty members in the United States contract on a year-to-year basis (as opposed to long-term contracts or lifetime contracts, which do occur in several countries around the world). Without having to contend so much with tenure or alter basic salary models, a variety of institutions could use the best professors in an expeditious and mutually advantageous manner. This may be accomplished by the professor physically being on a variety of campuses over a term, by electronic transmission, or by some combination. In this manner, each institution would share the high cost of a top professor and would reduce the burden of one campus having to pay entirely a top professor's large salary. Each of the participating institutions could use their junior or specialized faculty to meet remaining teaching needs in the discipline. The cost of covering these other classes would go down, freeing resources for the institution.

This pooling technique holds promise for sharing the expertise of the best minds within disciplines. This would enhance quality. A top educator might conduct classes by interactive teleconferencing among several colleges and universities at the same time, sharing expertise with a large number of learners on a given subject. Other faculty, whose mix would vary by campus, could complement the curriculum locally. This approach provides quality, enriches the faculty, and adds substance to the knowledge being conveyed, while reducing cost.

USING THE BEST INTERNATIONAL PROFESSORS. The idea of pooling could also extend to the use of international experts in various fields of education. With the advance of technology, language barriers can be reduced if not overcome altogether, allowing colleges and universities access to professors from every corner of the globe, who could become visiting or even adjunct faculty. In a world where internationalization of commerce, transportation, and communication is occurring at a highly rapid rate, the advantages of having an international faculty, a faculty whose expertise is world renowned, could add significantly to the resource base the institution can use to improve its competitive advantages.

Institutions around the world could use these global "best" professors in a variety of ways. Interinstitutional contracts, resource-sharing agreements, exchange programs, individual contracts between a certain professor and a college or university somewhere else in the world, and networks could all be used to establish connections. As with pooling, the demand on the home campus for high-level professors in a variety of fields would be lessened, allowing for resource distribution to help support areas and programs of excellence.

INCREASING THE USE OF TECHNOLOGY. Today, more and more classrooms have the capability of delivery through some level of technology. New campus construction, as well as remodeling activities, almost always include new wiring schemes to allow classroom access to computer networks, communication systems, and interactive television. Older classrooms are exchanging asbestos for retrofitted technology. More and more colleges and universities understand that newer methods of delivery need to be incorporated into their existing physical plant and teaching modalities.

As Appleberry noted, the use of technology is growing substantially outside the classroom. Computers at home and in faculty offices connected to networks that open up communications to the department, the college, the institution, and the world beyond make it possible for faculty members to maintain close contact with students and colleagues any place and at any time. This use of networked computers offers a wide variety of ways to expand the learning opportunities for learners and faculty alike. For example, one professor in a rural nursing program at University of Northern Colorado, who uses interactive television to deliver a course throughout northern and eastern Colorado, also uses an Internet chat room where students chat with one another on regularly scheduled occasions. The professor acts as a passive observer, responding to specific questions or adding specific thoughts from time to time, as learners discuss the material and its application among themselves. This is only one of many examples that show how enterprising faculty can successfully integrate new technological techniques into their courses and programs to enhance the learning experience. As faculty move away from their dependence on the classroom as a primary site for teaching, they will use their time more efficiently to guide learning of individual students, groups of students, or outside learners, as well as increase their research time.

Students too are interacting with technology. It is not uncommon for students to show up on campus with a computer setup ready to install in a dormitory room or apartment. From there, many connect directly to the Internet and have the capacity of connecting to anything the university or college might have available as well. If the campus has already been wired, students are able to sit at their computers at home or in the dormitory and connect directly into the library, faculty e-mail, or even interactive classes and chat rooms. In more progressive settings, these activities can be augmented by access to the Internet and the World Wide Web, allowing the student access to an entire world of database resources and knowledge-gathering opportunities.

More publishers are producing high-quality interactive course materials. These tools increase the learner's desire to study and the quality of that study. For example, one publisher now produces an interactive CD-ROM introduction-to-management textbook that allows the learner to read the book, view short videos, query the use of words and terms, and quiz themselves on the material. With this type of material available to the student to review and learn at a personal pace, it seems silly to waste classroom time on lectures that are not nearly as interactive, engaging, or interesting. This frees the classroom for other uses—for a seminar; for small-group tutorials; for problem solving; or as a laboratory for simulation, role playing, or experimenting with ideas on management techniques. Time set aside for this class could also be used for providing management experience in the field. Students would test the situations depicted on the CD-ROM in actual settings, with or without other students, and then come together periodically in the classroom or in smaller groups in the instructor's office to cement what they had learned.

INCREASING THE USE OF LABORATORY TIME. Looking again at the management CD-ROM example, the learner gains primary information through electronic media that can be accessed whenever it is convenient and as many times as is necessary to obtain mastery of the information. Because this type of learning allows each learner to digest the material in a convenient, comfortable, and self-directed manner, the learning should be nearly optimal.

Because the learner masters the basic material prior to class time, other activities that cement the material should dominate class time. These activities might include small-group discussions, small-group seminars, experiential exercises, question-and-answer sessions, multimedia presentations of supporting materials, guest speakers, or field experiences. Regardless, class time presents an opportunity for the faculty to make the learning experience come alive for the learner and to foster active learning. It seems like a wise move to turn the classroom into a place where the learner can play with the material, test it against a variety of referents, and gain the insight of peers as well as faculty so that the material can become more meaningful and relevant.

The problem here is obvious. Too many knowledge providers are comfortable with only one form of knowledge transfer, the lecture. For the new methods to be effective in the classroom, institutional initiative is important. When a college or university makes a decision to be more user-friendly and more concerned with the positive outcomes of the educational experience for their learners, its best strategy is to provide incentives for faculty and to fund the early pioneers in innovation. Others will follow, once they see that change has its rewards. Faculty development programs have been successful in encouraging transition; they are even more successful if they extend to other members of the faculty community. Staff and graduate learners often are willing and able to improve learning. They should also be encouraged and recognized. Faculty, administrators, and support personnel all need to reorient their thinking from creating an environment in which they can all "do their jobs" to creating an environment in which the learner is an active partner in mastery of subject matter.

Additional expenses may be incurred initially when the campus goes through a training-and-reorientation process and then modifies classrooms for a larger number of uses. Even in the face of budget cutbacks and program eliminations, such an expense would be easily justified if governing boards, administrators, and faculty leaders understood that the remodeling could well result in increased enrollments and in new learning opportunities that the campus could then offer the community. We realize that recommendations like these are difficult to implement and that many faculty leaders, administrators, and governing boards do not realize that the need for change is so strong. They often fail to recognize that a reorientation of the dimensions we describe here is really necessary. As we have suggested throughout, the changes coming with the information age are not going to subside or diminish. Changes are already under way, whether individual members of the academy are ready or not. Individual campuses that adapt to those changes will, along with a growing number of commercial providers, give the learners of the information age the learning they desire. If successful, these institutions will grow. Possibly, the number of students left to be educated could be so small that the recalcitrant campuses will suffer significantly.

Challenging the Notion of Seat Time

"Seat time" or in-classroom contact hours involve the amount of time an administrative or academic body requires of a course at a given level of credit for it to comply with accredited or other standards. It is formula driven. For example, a three-hour semester course might be associated with forty-eight hours of seat time. This amount of time is reserved in the schedule of classes and describes the amount of time a student should expect to be in a classroom receiving instruction during a semester. The start and stop times for each class, the number of days a week set aside for the class, and the number of weeks in a semester, taking into consideration holidays and other disruptions, all should add up to forty-eight hours.

The regulatory reason for seat time is to ensure that a student receives enough contact with a professor in a classroom setting so that the material advertised in the course description is adequately covered. Also, by standardizing seat time, there is the hope that there would be little difference in the content, requirements, and practice for one course as opposed to another, when both are listed as having the same credit hours. The scheduling reason for seat time is that regimenting classes to conform to a particular arrangement allows the institution to plan for the use of its classroom and laboratory resources in the most efficient manner. A faculty reason for seat time is that specific expectations for student contact are easily established, and research and service times can be scheduled around classroom expectations. This is the central determinant in setting a faculty member's workload and schedule for any given term.

The problem with seat time is that it is a preset schedule that fits the needs of the regulators, the institution, and the faculty, but not necessarily the learner. Seat time does not take into account the varying lengths of time that different learners need to absorb the material effectively. Seat time may prove to be inadequate or overly generous, given the individual learner and that person's understanding of the subject matter. Seat time also does not take into account the amount of learning that takes place outside the classroom, be that in the form of homework, group meetings, library time, or individual time with the course instructor one-on-one. In other words, seat time is an artificial and largely bureaucratic measure of learning.

From a teaching perspective, seat time represents a set of constraints that results in the instructor filling dead time with trivia or in the instructor not having enough time to present the requisite substantive knowledge adequately. Besides, seat time is not a guarantee of effectiveness in transferring knowledge from relevant sources to the learner. The bottom line for the knowledge manager is making a connection between the learner and the proper knowledge base and then facilitating the transfer of that knowledge so that the learner develops a competency within it. The time involved is really irrelevant to the process.

Now, the issue becomes one of which point of view should prevail. Realistically, it is unlikely that those who advocate seat time will give up much ground in addressing this issue. However, as technology advances, and such things as log-on times are easily recorded, these may displace seat time as the measure of approximation. As more and more campuses become involved with meeting the needs of their learners, there will be an equally strong pressure to revisit the seat time requirement. The best hope for eliminating the requirement altogether is in the development of more accurate assessment tools that measure demonstrated learning and indicate the proficiency of the learner. Time can then be eliminated as a controlling force, and the learner will simply indicate a readiness to undergo the assessment. When assessment tools are reliable, then seat time requirements should go away.

Degree Alternatives

The degree program serves as the capstone of the college experience. In addressing the context of the information age, it has several flaws. First, it should not be necessary for a learner to enter a degree program to access knowledge—especially when the knowledge needed is unidimensional and not part of a major knowledge base. Further, it should not be necessary for a learner to meet the prerequisites for a whole program or course just to get access to the one course or part of a course that contains the specific knowledge sought. In an environment where the learner seeks competency in a particular knowledge base, and where no degree is sought, the learner should be able to access the material until competency is reached. If the learner cannot do this, that learner will seek alternatives. One of the many rules in marketing is that a customer will go into a store twice. If on the second visit the customer cannot find the goods or services sought, that customer will not return. Given the competitive environment that colleges and universities will face in the information age, turning away interested learners will begin to do irreparable harm and could diminish the customer base on which the institution depends.

Second, time-bound and residency-based degree programs do not serve the perpetual learner. Because the knowledge changes rapidly in the information age, competency gained from a current degree program will be out-of-date in a relatively short period of time. Finality and ongoing competency are illusions. The learner in nearly every new age field will find the need to resample the knowledge base from time to time, to update in order to maintain currency. Though a degree can signify competency at one point in time, that same conferring institution needs to provide a pathway for keeping the lifelong learner up-to-date. This will mean restructuring degree programs and the departments that support them. The institution can benefit through this by maintaining an ongoing relationship with its alumni in a meaningful and mutually beneficial way. This will also ensure that faculty maintain ongoing currency in their fields through research and participation in information age issues and concerns.

Virtual Classroom

If we could dispense with the traditional idea of the classroom and its requisite seat time, "the classroom" would become any place at any time in which learning interfaces with the knowledge base. This can occur on the job, at home at night, on vacation, during a break in weekend activities, during travel, and certainly, in formalized learning facilities during formally scheduled times. Learning can be opened up to anyone at any time through the uses of current and future technologies. This more widely defined classroom promises to be an extremely competitive learning environment, one that would meet the needs of the information age worker to a degree we only dream of now.

A virtual classroom philosophy would require major philosophical and resource base shifts for a college or university. This shift would involve modularizing knowledge into segments that could be accessed through something like the Internet or via telephone. Interaction with faculty would also be electronic and could involve scheduled chat rooms, unscheduled e-mail exchanges, subject matter software, simulations and other supportive materials, and on-line tutorials. By tracking participation and progress electronically through a log-on system, any learner or any faculty member could easily access a record of progress and establish appropriate assessment opportunities, especially self-paced mastery modules in which assessment precedes moving to the next module. The setup could be costly at first, but the competitive advantage such a shift could provide the campus would repay development and operational costs many times over.

Knowledge Cafeteria

The term *cafeteria* is used in today's colleges and universities when the learning process is not very popular. It implies an almost randomized course selection process that is hard to plan for, hard to build degrees around, and hard to regulate. The lack of structure associated with cafeteria-style education suggests a chaotic state that most educators properly find offensive. Also, from a learner point of view, cafeteria-style education does not offer many clear pathways toward degree attainment, and it is easy to waste time on useless offerings that do not add one way or the other to the goals a learner may seek.

For the programs associated with degrees, cafeteria-style learning is most likely a waste of time and resources. It is preferable for institutions and learners to come together in an understanding of precisely what is needed to achieve a degree or to master a set of modules and then get on with it. If anything, reducing unnecessary requirements and providing opportunities to take modules that do not add substantively to the degree attainment should be a paramount concern. Pressure is building in several states, especially the Western Governors states, to reduce the time and requirements needed to attain a degree.

The *knowledge cafeteria* we propose is quite different. Institutions need to rethink themselves in information age terms to be versatile. As we have indicated, the growing demands of the information age worker, the increase in competition especially from commercial providers, and advances in technology are all both threats and opportunities. In considering the opportunities associated with the new age, colleges and universities are gold mines of knowledge. This knowledge, both historical and current, can be shared outside the confines of degree programs through a knowledge cafeteria, which could take the form of an electronic inventory of all the knowledge bases represented not only in the college library but also throughout the faculty, institutes, special programs, and centers for excellence of a campus. These knowledge bases could then become accessible by anyone, internally and externally. This is an opportunity to share scarce resources on an individual campus or on a network basis. It provides revenue-generating outlets for all areas of a campus's knowledge core and also provides external consumers with a greatly expanded knowledge resource.

Such a drastic change in philosophy and process would certainly add to the currency and value of the degree program, as the interaction between the knowledge providers and the external constituencies would help ensure ongoing currency in all fields. This additional dimension of college and university activities would also help develop an ongoing relationship with degree recipients, because it would be natural and easy to continue the relationship beyond the time a degree is conferred.

REDISTRIBUTING RESOURCES
TO SUPPORT AREAS OF EXCELLENCE

All of the techniques we have discussed in this chapter are designed to do a variety of things. They propel institutions into a more meaningful role in the information age; they help define programs that are more learner friendly; they redistribute and redefine the use of academic talent; and they help campuses determine the most optimal use of their resources.

This matter of optimal use of resources is of particular concern for most colleges and universities today as a result of governmental belt-tightening. The options described in this chapter allow for each campus to do two things—reengineer themselves to meet most effectively the demands of their learners and information age partners, by reducing their dependence on duplicative or arcane methods and practices; and redistribute saved resources to support those areas of excellence that best match the ability of the institution to survive and prosper. By developing and promoting these areas of distinction, the institution can attract additional resources, which will help build and sustain it during uncertain times. In these ways, today's colleges and universities can become more relevant and more viable in ways that shape the information age.

ALTERNATIVES TO THE ACADEMY

Although it is our basic hope that colleges and universities will develop strategies and tactics that will help them transform their roles in the information age, we recognize that other forms of education are also emerging. These alternatives represent a very real threat to the long-standing ownership rights to knowledge creation and distribution that the academy has claimed for centuries. These new forms will not just persevere, they will grow in strength, status, and market share. As a result, the more traditional colleges and universities need to be aware of and consider not just ways to compete, but even ways to cooperate, perhaps through strategic alliances. Absent initiative from colleges and universities, these competitors will focus on keeping their competitive advantage.

Corporate Universities

Many corporations have established educational centers in their ongoing training and educational activities. The initial purpose of these centers was to provide training for their employees regarding new manufacturing or service techniques or to update them on changing practices and formats. Another purpose has been to help develop an educated employee base that provides a company with a competitive advantage. Over the past several years, these centers have expanded and changed dramatically. In some instances, companies have established their educational centers as separate educational campuses, resembling small colleges. Today, there are several corporate universities throughout the United States and around the world, which help the companies that own them develop an employee base that has access to exactly the type and quality of information the company knows they will need to keep the company competitive.

This growth has not only broadened the scope of corporate education, but it has also helped to shape it. As more and more of these companies have expressed concerns about the quality of the education their new employees bring with them from colleges and universities (Horne, 1995), several of these companies have begun to structure their own educational programs to rival those acquired on college and university campuses. Several are saying that they would prefer to educate their employees from the beginning of a college career themselves rather than have to reeducate new employees who do not come to them with the language, mathematical, social, managerial, or computer preparation the companies believe they should have received in their college preparation. Some are even beginning to talk about becoming accredited.

Defining the Corporate University

A corporate university provides specific training and educational opportunities for its employees. These institutions are designed to help assure the strategic direction of the company as well as provide a significant educational benefit for its employees. Contrary to what many in higher education and political circles believe, the prime motivation behind the explosion of corporate universities does not appear to be dissatisfaction with colleges and universities. In fact, significant partnerships with colleges and universities are common in the corporate university sector.

Jeanne C. Meister is president of Quality Dynamics, a New York City–based organizational development and corporate education firm, and founder of the Corporate Quality University Xchange newsletter. Her book, *Corporate Quality Universities: Lessons in Building a World-Class Work Force* (Meister, 1994), was the result of a three-year research project involving thirty American companies that are known for their outstanding training facilities. In 1997, Meister surveyed one hundred corporate university "deans" (the persons responsible for the strategic management of the corporate university) to determine among other things the major contributions the corporate university made to the organization. The top five are as follows: enhance job performance (37 percent), communicate mission-vision and values (31 percent), develop a world-class leadership program (24 percent), establish systematized education processes (18 percent), become an agent of change for the organization (13 percent).

Motorola University

Motorola University (MU) presents an interesting model of the corporate university. MU was officially inaugurated in 1981. MU is more important than ever, as 120,000 new employees are expected to join

Motorola in the years between 1996 and 2001. Today, MU represents a massive corporate effort that has developed itself into a wide variety of parts and applications. The following examples demonstrate how a corporate university, such as MU, can become a major and extremely substantive undertaking.

GALVIN CENTER FOR CONTINUING EDUCATION. Motorola dedicated the Galvin Center for Continuing Education in Schaumburg, Illinois, in 1986. The facility utilizes 133,000 square feet of space and houses eighteen classrooms, thirty-six breakout rooms, a two hundred plus–seat auditorium, seven training laboratories, a distance learning classroom, a video conference room, and a full-service cafeteria. The Galvin Center was named for both Bob Galvin and his father, Motorola's founder, Paul Galvin.

MOTOROLA UNIVERSITY WEST. MU has established two major campuses in the United States, MU East and MU West. Motorola University located its new MU West Education Center in the Arizona State University (ASU) Research Park. ASU will offer its College of Business Technology MBA at the center. The Joint Arizona Center for Manufacturing Education and Training, a consortium of the engineering colleges and major companies in Arizona, will also make use of the center. The facility encompasses 100,000 square feet and includes fourteen classrooms, six mini-classrooms, sixteen breakout rooms, computer and manufacturing laboratories, a two hundred–seat auditorium, IBM, UNIX, and two Power Macintosh laboratories, a fully equipped teleconferencing center, message center, dining and lounge areas, and administrative offices.

OTHER CAMPUSES AND OPERATIONS. MU has also established an impressive international presence. It currently has campuses in Europe, the Middle East, Africa, China, Taiwan, and Korea. The expanded MU has proven its worth to Motorola and is now able to develop and deliver actively more customized programs both nationally and internationally. Motorola even has its own publishing house, Motorola University Press.

Some of the course offerings at MU include basic management, writing for results, effective writing, Chinese tutoring, project management, and successful office management. Although a number of these courses are purely business training courses, others look surprisingly like courses that might be taught at many traditional colleges and universities. Instead of relying on the traditional colleges and universities to provide this education for their employees, Motorola is providing it on its own.

Arthur D. Little School of Management

Another interesting example of a corporate university is the one created by Arthur D. Little Consulting, who also recognized that a superior workforce means maintaining a strategic advantage. Its School of Management (SOM) was begun in 1964 and received regional accreditation in 1971 from the New England Association of Schools and Colleges. SOM is currently a precandidate for accreditation from the American Assembly of Collegiate Schools of Business. SOM students span the world, with an average class of 65 from up to 28 countries. Since inception, SOM has had over 3,200 professionals from over 115 countries.

SOM operates an intensive eleven-month program in three terms, which they call phases. Phase one, seventeen weeks in length, focuses on managerial skills. Phase two, fifteen weeks in length, focuses on management functions. Phase three, thirteen weeks in length, focuses on integration and application of management skills and functions. Additional educational activities in this area are also conducted by the Arthur D. Little Consulting School of Management and the Master of Science Management (MSM) Program. Courses in the program include managerial skills (seventeen weeks), management functions (fifteen weeks), business process reengineering, orientation and team building, financial management, ethical issues in management, entrepreneurship and new ventures, strategy formulation, management of technology, management information systems, human resources management, transnational negotiation skills, international marketing, creating a learning organization, organizational behavior, operations management, and strategic market research. As is true at Motorola University, many of these courses parallel the business offerings in most major United States colleges and universities. They even have their own master's program.

Faculty in the MSM Program include practicing Arthur D. Little consultants, who bring their practical problem-solving approach into the classroom, and visiting professors from leading Boston-area business schools. MSM students work at solving actual ongoing business problems currently being worked on by Arthur D. Little consultants in client sites around the world. Tuition is $27,000; books and fees are $1,800. An optional summer preparatory program costs $2,000 for Program I—math, accounting, and computers, and $2,500 for Program II—intensive English, math, accounting, and computers. Admission to the program requires a completed application form, official university transcript, two recommendations, fluency in English (a recommended Teaching of English as a Foreign Language test score of 550 for non–English speaking students). GMAT score reports are encouraged but not required. Again, the similarities between this program and many college and university MBA graduate programs is striking.

Bank of Montreal's Institute for Learning

The Institute for Learning, located in Toronto, is another interesting corporate example. It was established in 1994 to help the Bank of Montreal cultivate an organization of excellent learners by instilling a spirit of lifelong learning and organizational renewal. Its value to the Bank of Montreal and its impact have been immediate. Not only has the institute already achieved its 1997 goal of providing five training days per bank employee, but it has also increased the depth and range of learning support significantly. The institute's Diane Blair reports that over 70 percent of the learning support provided by the institute now occurs beyond its walls, at or near the workplace or embedded directly in day-to-day work. This type of corporate college is not as much a mirror of the traditional higher education system as Motorola University, but it does represent another company's choice to spend its money on developing its own educational (and, admittedly in this case, training) program rather than rely on or ally with local colleges and universities.

Warning Signal

Not only does the growth of the corporate university mark the advent of a well-heeled, potentially major new competitor for college and university students, but it also denotes the further deterioration of the relationship between the academy and its external environment. Rather than seeking cooperative agreements or determining how the vast resources of the academy can be used to help provide a proper education for information age companies, most colleges and universities have kept their distance from this emerging, powerful new educational force. Unlike the academy, however, business has traditionally been used to forging alliances. One possibility that could occur, should colleges or universities fail to reach out, would be that companies with complementary interests may form significant additional alliances among themselves, building mega–educational centers, which could potentially create an even bigger threat to the academy. That threat would be most evident when these mega-centers use their ample resources to hire away the academy's best minds.

VIRTUAL LABORATORIES

The college and university laboratory has traditionally been where the core of basic research has occurred. This has also been the site where many students have been able to develop a deeper understanding of subject matter by engaging in experiments that test certain hypotheses against actual responses. But the world of the laboratory is also changing with the advent of new technologies and simulations. Some of these new technologies can make the use of the traditional laboratory obsolete, whereas other technologies make them more useful and productive. These changes represent what colleges and universities face, as they make choices among competing elements for resources to carry the educational process forward.

Increased Uses of Simulations

As noted earlier, simulations are used in a variety of settings. Though not all of these simulations are computer based, most are. Some of them offer major advances in the knowledge transfer process and deserve a major look by college and university academics and administrators.

For example, one chemistry simulation allows students to perform a variety of experiments using different chemicals and compounds and assessing the results. The activities are the same as in traditional labs, but there is no exposure to dangerous chemicals or the expense of replacing them after the experiment is done. Another clear advantage is that the experiment can be conducted over and over again, until it is done right, without concern for exposure or cost.

In business, simulations are available that put learners in management positions and have them make management decisions. The simulations can inform the students of the implications of those decisions and set up the context for a meaningful group or class discussion.

These are just a couple of examples from different areas of the campus that demonstrate the potential for the use of experiential exercises that have relatively low costs but high impacts on learning. These simulations are not necessarily bound to a classroom or campus setting, making them even more attractive to learners in the information age.

Internet Networking

One of the greatest contributions of the Internet has been in the development of improved communication devices. E-mail, video communication, and video conferencing are examples of the ways in which information technology is improving our ability to communicate with each other on a worldwide basis. These methods have clearly provided new media for information providers and information seekers, and their use is expanding exponentially as the twentieth century comes to a close.

Still Other Alternatives

Other forms of educational alternatives include the virtual universities (discussed earlier), the opportunities available on the Internet, and the potential for the developing interactive learning techniques that come from an increased use of computers in classrooms from grammar school through college. According to Microsoft's Gates (1996), these will only expand in the future. As these alternatives become available, the academy should be proactive and develop ways of using them effectively in the learning-transfer process.

FOCUSING ON DISTINCTION

The opportunities for engaging in meaningful knowledge transfer will only become more broad and diverse in the years ahead. There will be literally thousands of choices for colleges and universities to pick from in designing their own campuses of the future. This should be seen as an exciting time, when individual campuses can make their own long-term connections to different elements of the information age society and economy.

One note of caution is in order here, however. We believe that it would be a grave mistake for each individual campus to try to do everything that is being done, to cover all the areas that are being covered, and to offer all the programs that are being offered. The result would be a sameness from one campus to the next, mediocrity as thin resources are spread widely, a lack of innovation, and the cloning of campuses. This is what happened during the major explosion of higher education in the late 1950s and 1960s when the United States, in particular, responded to the Soviet launch of Sputnik with a major push toward improving education from grammar school through college. The cloning of successful campuses that occurred then did open up greater levels of opportunities to more students, but it also curbed individuality and uniqueness, which had marked much of higher education.

We believe that responding to the information age will be effective if it is strategically done. There is just too much going on in the new era—new ideas, new methods, new needs, and new learners—for any one campus to be able to respond adequately to all of these. In addition, the tendency of funding agencies to restrict or reduce support will force individual campuses to find those areas of excellence that they can hold out to their communities as highly valuable and contributory to society's needs. This will let these campuses concentrate their limited resources on distinction. Finally, the demand for ongoing changes and improvements will keep those institutions that attempt to do too many things guessing at what will happen next, and on what front. This would be an academic and administrative nightmare, and no institution would prosper under these conditions.

We have the view that niching emerges as the best solution for colleges and universities that want to adapt appropriately to the information age. By recognizing the needs and wants of the information age economy and society and by providing a focused set of knowledge bases, methods, and interactive opportunities that are grounded in excellence, campuses can distinguish themselves and respond to the new age effectively. This should also help institutions develop stronger relationships with their resource providers, reducing criticism and concern. This will have the salutary and strategic effect of enticing support from those served in ways that increase resources and strengthen areas of distinction.

Re-Creating Higher Education Through Strategic Choices

CHAPTER NINE

The New Learning Infrastructure

With the need for change identified in Part One and with the emerging models and trends discussed in Part Two, Part Three looks at some of the options today's colleges and universities may wish to consider as they look at how they will prepare themselves for the new millennium. This chapter looks at the academic infrastructure of colleges and universities and begins to suggest what they may need to look like in the future as they seek to serve the information age learner and the information age society.

Subject matter changes as society changes. The information age will bring major changes in society and will bring new categories of knowledge and new fields of interest that will reshape the curriculum. Along with this comes the reality that some fields of knowledge will no longer be as relevant to the society of the information age as they were to the society of the industrial age. This will mean that the resources allocated to old disciplines and professions will be pared back and some will be eliminated. The pattern will vary from campus to campus. These changes provide both opportunities and threats to the academic core of colleges and universities. This chapter explores the various options available to these institutions for making decisions about the curriculum in the information age.

REPLACING THE COURSE

A *course* is a unit of academic measure. It pares down knowledge in a discipline or profession and organizes it to meet academic criteria. Among the criteria that a course must have are: enough time allotted for the information to be presented; a certain number of "hours" that will represent a measure of completion; a logical step in relation to other related courses leading to certification or degree accomplishment; and an economic variable used for pricing by students, faculty, departments, schools and colleges, and institutions.

As we have already noted, the course is the central unit around which schedules are built, majors are designed, work assignments are decided, and degrees are ultimately conferred. There is an assumption that a course (as a building block in any of these categories) comprises an essential amount of knowledge. The completion of the course implies that the student, or learner, has achieved a certain level of competency in that subject. This competency is denoted by a letter grade or a "pass" or "fail" notation on an official record. This system of measurement has been in place for some time and has served the industrial age fairly well.

Regardless of its widespread and common usage, this system has some problems. These problems will weaken the process of transferring academic knowledge in the information age. Other for-profit providers are already transferring knowledge within certain curriculum areas and will gain a competitive edge, should the academy not ensure that knowledge is transferred in the most effective way possible.

The first problem is that, as an artifact of the industrial age, the course is defined by "experts." Those who control the academic offerings of a college or university also reserve the right to design the course. As a curriculum base encompasses an entire subject matter, a course is an orderly segment of the base of knowledge that academics determine is appropriate for students to learn. In the information age, the learner may wish to have exposure to the entire subject matter or particular segments of it, and the course may not always meet the learner's needs.

Second, the course reflects the time preferences and constraints of the faculty and the institution rather than the learner. Even though some institutions now offer courses that are more time sensitive (through a vehicle such as continuing education), most courses are time bound and specifically scheduled with little chance for the learner to alter the time needed to complete a course (either up or down) or to determine when it would be more convenient to take the course. This will pose an impediment to the information age learner, who is driven by the need for rapid updates, midcareer expertise, and lifelong learning. For those who are also place or work bound, this represents a major obstacle.

Third, the course is primarily an economic unit of measure rather than a competency measure. Courses are designed to fit particular requirements of seat time, also an artificial measure of student exposure to and comprehension of the learning process. A one-, two-, three-, four-, or five-hour course relates directly to a formula that determines the tuition an institution can charge people who take courses at that institution. There are also minimum and maximum requirements for a critical mass of students taking a course. These are also economic and relate to the resource base of the college or university. We see serious problems with a system in which an information age learner is prevented from obtaining needed information that a particular college or university has, but cannot provide, because a course did not "make." To make means that a course must enroll a minimum number of students required by the institution for financial or workload reasons.

Fourth, the course is often constrained by prerequisites and may even be limited to people in certain disciplines. For example, one of the authors regularly teaches a course in strategic management. This is a capstone course in the business curriculum and is very difficult to access. To get into the course, a student must be a senior and a business major. In addition, the student must have previously taken two courses in accounting, one in finance, one in marketing, one in organizational management, one in statistics, one in business law, one in computer information sciences, and one in production management. No one who has not completed all of these other courses, no one other than the business majors, and no one outside the university may take this course *for any reason.* Such exclusivity is dysfunctional in the information age. In this environment, if a bank president wanted to take this particular course because of a belief that it might lead to doing a better job running the bank, that person would not be allowed to do so. This example is one of many that demonstrates how the academy has built a wall around the educational process. Yet, in the age where knowledge is king, learners will find a way to get it. If the university is not willing to provide the local bank president with the information sought, that executive *will* get it elsewhere, reducing the service capacity of the university, as well as its revenue.

Fifth, the course is saddled with a common evaluation system. Nearly every course we are familiar with contains both a common grading and evaluation system. What this does is develop criteria on which the institution can certify successful completion of a course. It has nothing to do with learning. With a common evaluation system, each person taking a course takes exactly the same exams, writes the same model of paper, or gives the same type of presentation to allow the course evaluator a common ground on which to make a statement regarding how a person has performed. This sameness allows a comparison of learners and not of what the learners learned or mastered. Performance on any of these evaluation mechanisms may or may not have anything directly to do with the amount of material the student actually learned. Just as individuals learn differently, they test differently. Further, for the information age learner, it may only be important that a segment of the information be learned. Finally, learners do not all begin at the same level of prior knowledge or understanding.

In all of this, courses remain the basic implements with which colleges and universities conduct their activities and reflect their prerogatives, needs, traditions, and resource allocations. When courses are more important than the content of curriculum and the learner's needs to access that content, courses are dysfunctional. For the new age, colleges and universities should refocus curriculum and base it on the module. These modules would be the building blocks of a curriculum for demonstrated learning. They should be flexible and open to combinations that meet the faculty-advised learning plan for the new learner. In this way, learners may shape their learning in terms of what they need to know. If this is done with the assistance of knowledgeable faculty, there is no breach of excellence in such flexibility. Assessment of learning also needs to be learner centered. It should reflect the needs of the learner and enable the learner to demonstrate competency, using such techniques as those being developed in the California State University system, in the Baldrige program, and in the assessment practices emanating from the American Association for Higher Education.

This is a nontraditional way of looking at knowledge transfer in colleges and universities. Its implications for grading and determining mastery are important and rooted in existing efforts to improve assessment and measures of demonstrated competency.

FOCUS DEFINED—CAMPUS BY CAMPUS, DISCIPLINE BY DISCIPLINE

Every campus needs to develop its own particular set of curriculum bases that reflect those areas of excellence each particular campus has been able to build. As we have stressed throughout, it is a mistake for any given campus to attempt to be all things to all students. The resources simply are not in place for that to happen, and the needs of the new age are so broad that excellence requires focus.

As each campus is able to build a curriculum based on excellence, it will create a reputation of distinction, separating the institution from is competitors. When marketing based on distinction kicks into place, campuses that are truly excellent in chosen areas will set the benchmarks in those fields and will have a clear competitive advantage over those that do not. By introducing the reality of the market to the institution, each campus will be continually challenged to keep its programs of excellence up-to-date and contributing to the growing body of knowledge. Everyone can benefit from this type of competition. Those campuses that are unable or unwilling to maintain a leading edge within a particular discipline or profession will be the ones that suffer.

Strategically Integrating Information Age Needs into Campus Decisions

The notion that the market should control what occurs in the academy is repulsive to some academics. But this is not the real issue. For centuries, colleges and universities have developed methods of discovering knowledge and effective ways of sharing that knowledge with the world. No one wants that to change. There are also areas of research that only colleges and universities can successfully continue. As the world's greatest think tank, the academy is expected to encourage intellectual discovery and promote human understanding. None of this should change. If anything, these areas of distinction will blend better research and teaching in a strategically developed curriculum of distinction.

We argue that the academy can no longer conduct its affairs in isolation. The growing levels of knowledge, their interconnectedness, new knowledge bases, and the facilitation of knowledge transfer are changing as in no previous time. This is what colleges and universities must respond to, if knowledge is to advance. That response will be effective when institutions are more sensitive to the needs of the institutions, companies, workers, and learners of the new age.

The marketplace is now a world marketplace, connected by instant communications and easy travel. Barriers imposed by national boundaries are coming down all over the world, and the impact of these realities on the economies of the world and the societies these economies affect is dramatic and substantive. Individual cultures reel from the impacts of the information explosion. A world economy with a worldwide system of communication challenges old ideas and old methods of interaction and transaction. There is no way that colleges and universities in any sector of the world can escape these changes. Moreover, colleges and universities are part of the economic system. They depend on resources generated by the greater economy and are expected more and more to add their own value to those resources.

We have argued throughout this book that colleges and universities must be connected and responsive to their external environments and must contribute conspicuously to the knowledge sector of global society. They do this by developing partnerships that tie external resources with internal strengths in a way in which both entities can benefit. This means moving away from making all the decisions about what the knowledge base should look like and how it should be shared to *including* those outside the ivory tower and its academic processes in determining what the mix of curricula should be and how it should be shared.

Cooperative agreements should in no way be viewed as abandoning academic autonomy and secularism in any way. These connections are built on intellectual and knowledge-based excellence, not on the political beliefs or religious orthodoxy that led to secularism and the separation of church and state. The resulting ties open up the thinking and creative processes rather than smothering them. This gives each campus a new identity and new lines of communication, which should help inspire the creative minds of academic researchers and broaden the scope of the work they do. Being environmentally responsive helps sustain the strategic viability of the institution by broadening its base for resource acquisition. It also creates important interdependencies that strengthen colleges and universities through ever expanding stakeholders.

Linking Traditional Disciplines with Information Age Needs

The traditional academic disciplines change constantly. Institutions, units, deans, and academic review bodies are continually asking questions about the viability of certain subject areas and making hard decisions about closing particular programs down, while also supporting growth areas. This has been particularly true recently, when in state-supported institutions, external funding has not matched internal needs. The most common response has been to pare back those areas that are not growing or that are costing more in institutional resources than the value of the benefit they provide.

This externally imposed reshaping of the institution has been hard for many, but it has gone forward nonetheless. As we have proposed (Rowley, Lujan, and Dolence, 1997), the effectiveness of this restructuring rests basically on both the ability of the institution to do substantive and thorough strategic planning and the ability of the institution to make those changes based on their own particular fit with their most crucial environments. For those colleges and universities that are successful in adapting such a plan and in achieving such a fit, their longer-term future is much brighter than is the future for those who do not achieve this strategic end. Regardless, the imperative is that colleges and universities stop focusing exclusively on their inward desire to research, distill knowledge, and share that knowledge in areas they choose to pursue. Instead, they should support only those areas in which they can achieve excellence and in which they can meet the needs of their most important environmental partners. Strategic choices in the information age continue to challenge the pursuit of excellence because of the increase of international economic interdependence and the increasing speed with which the changes are coming. Quick, timely, competent responses are not easy to come by.

The challenge to support traditional areas in which colleges and universities can achieve excellence *and* meet the knowledge needs of the new society requires a delicate balancing act for the campus. The answer lies in integration. By combining the best of what colleges and universities do with what the information age needs and wants, areas of traditional excellence can improve rather than just continue, and support for them and the new fields of study they generate will emerge. This allows an institution to maintain its relevance to its traditional base and to carve out a reputation in the brave new world of the information age.

Benefits of Campus Niching

One way to achieve integration is to downsize and focus. Rather than trying to clone the major research institutions around the world, institutions could lend quality to utility by doing fewer things well—things that match strengths and distinction with specific needs in their service areas. Knowledge will be both useful and better understood when it is exposed to the crucible of appositive learning. It is worth noting that areas of excellence define themselves in a competitive environment by challenging the paradigms of the knowledge providers with other models and other methods of knowledge development and delivery. These other models and methods provide the user of knowledge with the ability to choose. When learners consistently choose one program over another, the chosen program will gain a competitive advantage. In a logical world, the provider of the chosen program will continue to upgrade it and support its advancement. The provider of the second-place program will have to make hard decisions about whether or not it will be economically feasible to enhance and restructure its program to exceed the capabilities of the competition. The strategically available option is to divert the resources used to support this program to other programs for which excellence can set the benchmark and provide the competitive advantage.

This natural selection process, described by organizational population ecologists Hannan and Freeman (1989), implies strategic program review as a way to assist niching, even if the pressure for this comes from external forces. Clearly, the better way to accomplish this would be through strategic choice—determining what areas of the knowledge market give a particular institution the greatest potential for serving and setting the benchmark. Strategic pre-event thinking is absolutely required for preserving resource bases, avoiding campus strife, and responsively shaping the institution's reputation for excellence and distinction in both knowledge development and transfer.

Because niching is not now the norm among colleges and universities in the United States and around the world, movement from general education to specific education requires fundamental reorientation on the part of trustees, administrators, faculty, staff, and students. It involves the focused span and depth of issues and participation that characterized the California State University Cornerstones Principles project or the Texas A&M strategic directioning effort, which was designed to guide in budget allocations. It is worth noting here that the easiest transitions are those that the institution can initiate and make over time. The hardest ones are those that are externally imposed and that force the college or university into a position of making hard choices among the curriculum, colleges, departments, and faculty.

Niching that is built on a reputation for excellence in select and important areas of a campus's academic offerings provides real direction for the whole campus community. This process gives hope to those institutions around the world that are not among the elite of the academy. By establishing themselves as the choice of excellence in a regional or local service area and by cementing the supportive relationships with the external environment that results, these institutions will find relevance and stability in very unstable times.

TREATING TENURE AS A RESOURCE

We turn once more to tenure, which has become a bone of contention that often clouds the issue of effective campus change. Most of the controversy comes from the reaction of those who work outside the academy and make a modest wage but have no job security. With business restructuring, many are laid off and many more are concerned that they will be. They see that their tax dollars are paying for tenured faculty and protecting the faculty from the very hardship that they and their families are experiencing. In addition, faculty are reasonably well paid, at least in the eyes of a middle class undergoing real income decline. And a faculty workload, no matter how well described, remains light in the eyes of a public that sees teaching three classes three days a weak as minimal in comparison to their workweek.

It is also unfortunate that tenure has recently become an economic issue. The constitutional right to speak freely is essential to both good scholarship and good teaching. Tenure emerged as an umbrella for academic freedom in education and a defense against censorship or from capricious firing. After World War II, McCarthyism and the "red scare" led to virtual witch-hunting by some elements in Congress. This severely endangered higher education. Course content was being perused, and many immigrants from Russia and Eastern Europe, often targets of the witch-hunt, were on college faculties. Serving that purpose well, tenure's mantle of protection has gradually expanded over the years. Today, many outside the academy see tenure less as a shield for scholarship and more as an unrealistic protection from the realities of a restructuring economic world.

Preserving Tenure—Productivity Is the Key

Tenure is a resource. It ensures an experienced and skilled faculty and gives stability and expertise to knowledge and education. As mentioned earlier, in 1996 a review of tenure was undertaken by the University of Minnesota regents. Faced with the need to downsize, the regents sought a revision of the tenure code in order to be able to dismiss faculty in marginal programs set for elimination.

In other examples, Florida Gulf Coast University and the University of Arizona International are both building new faculties without tenure. The Georgia regents have approved a posttenure review process to take place every five years. Although not directly tied to program reduction, these reviews will grade professors and rank them, a practice that could have job-related consequences down the road. In the Minnesota case, as faculty rebelled, the regents reduced their tenure revision to apply only to the law school and its thirty-five faculty. The troublesome provision that would have allowed the regents to fire someone in an eliminated program was deleted. It does allow for lowering base salaries during times of financial exigency, but this may only be done collectively and with approval of the faculty senate.

This retreat demonstrates the political volatility of tenure. Nevertheless, economic forces and changing market demand require a tool for restructuring and reduction when revenues cannot pay for the cost of doing business. As knowledge evolves, some fields of study become less useful, less relevant, or outdated. Being forced to keep faculty whose expertise is in these declining areas is inefficient. Magrath of the National Association of State Universities and Land Grant Colleges makes the point that stubbornness on internal matters and procedures invites external regulatory intrusion. Magrath argues, "Tenure must be carefully scrutinized now by the academy, so that narrow political interests do not impose on us destructive changes" (1997b, p. A60). Elsewhere, he makes the important case:

I believe passionately that self-regulation within our universities is infinitely more preferable than external regulation from state legislatures and government agencies. While this is not the only topic before us, the tenure principle—particularly as guaranteed lifetime employment— needs to be addressed and, at the very least, modified. A number of universities are doing this, and, like it or not, this is a public issue both in fact and perception and will not go away. There is much misunderstanding about tenure and how it works, but it is clear, I believe, that careful modifications are in order—if they are undertaken *internally* in a collaborative partnership of dialogue and trust among faculty and academic administrators, hopefully supported by governing boards that avoid the dangerous and destructive temptation to take charge on their own. [1997a, p. 5]

Opposition to this view is widespread. Much of this opposition is rooted in the view that "this too shall pass" or expresses itself in the strategy to pressure administrators, regents, and public officials in a political effort to forestall change. Sadly, this can be destructive to collegiality, shared governance, and the wisdom of internal initiative. Posttenure review is gaining respect as a reasonable way to ensure continued scholarly growth and excellence, making tenure a resource for sustaining excellence. So long as faculty help develop the criteria, this review is a wise step forward. If budget cuts are the issue, many campuses already have rules governing financial exigency, which permit termination in severe financial circumstances. In such cases, the faculty senates play important participative and oversight roles.

Both Byrne and Chait (1997) offer an alternative based on protecting academic freedom and providing flexibility for such things as financial shortfalls. They argue that tenured or not, faculty deserve the protection of academic freedom. This protection can be provided by a peer-dominated review panel: the faculty makes a clear case that a violation of academic freedom has occurred; the burden of proof then shifts to the institution to show that it has not done so; an oral hearing occurs before the review panel; a decision is rendered; and still-disputed claims can be turned over to arbitration. This would separate protection of academic freedom from the financial and salary aspects of faculty service. This approach would reasonably provide for the appropriate protection of scholarship and the flexibility needed for effectively managing the institution. It is worth remembering that contract law and other protections related to job security, job rights, and job performance are already in existence in both the public and private sectors and can serve in similarly clarifying the rules of separation for financial reasons. Finally, the right to sue ordinarily remains an option. As we mentioned in the previous chapter, unionized faculty have the job protection of a contract, and most contracts greatly restrict the grounds for dismissal.

A few institutions have no tenure. The Evergreen State College in Olympia, Washington, is one such example. Originally criticized for this and often maligned with charges that it would not be able to keep faculty and allow for their scholarly and professional growth, the Evergreen thrives and its faculty are satisfied. No major problem involving either financing or academic freedom has yet arisen there. Hampshire College has had a similar experience in its evolution.

In our view, tenure has value and should be preserved. The controversies that challenge it around the United States are leading to interesting outcomes that range from no changes at all to complete elimination of the system. These controversies present the opportunity to reenvision the role of faculty tenure in the context of a campus linked as much by technology as by the classroom, with the technological capacity for faculty to teach at more than one site simultaneously, and with the increasing need for teams to research the most interesting and pressing issues of our time. Moreover, the few abuses of tenure must be addressed: no one can afford to pay good money to someone who is no longer productive, up-to-date, and a contributing member of the academy. We believe that tenure must refocus on academic freedom as an essential guarantee and its continuance dependent on productivity and performance using measures that the faculty have helped design. By incorporating methods that guarantee that a person will continue to be productive before and after being granted tenure, tenure can continue as an important guarantee of academic freedom. Jointly defining these guarantees will be difficult, but we believe it is a labor worth pursuing, both as a protection of an excellent faculty and as an important message to society as a whole, which has intruded more than ever into the life of the campus.

Bridging Faculty from Declining Disciplines

Tenure, doctoral preparation, and departmental segmentation all make the transition difficult for individual faculty members when issues of program elimination, departmental consolidation, and management flexibility arise. The narrower the field of specialty or practice, the more difficult it becomes for faculty to be flexible and adaptive to the consequences of institutional reorganization.

We believe that one answer lies in the basic discipline and with those who are associated with it. We have already called for revisiting the elements of doctoral preparation. Similarly, we believe that the basic disciplines need to rethink their independence from, and relationships with, other disciplines and professions. The key here is to open disciplines up to the transdisciplinary learning required by the new age. Permanent departmental structures need to give way to learning teams of scholars, brought together by common interests and working with students as partners and aides.

It is interesting to note that there is an identifiable body of common knowledge already shared among a variety of disciplines. In the strategic management class we described earlier, success depended on the learner's knowledge and skills in a wide variety of disciplines, including psychology, sociology, anthropology, economics, history, political science, and mathematics. These are all areas outside the general business curriculum. Within the business curriculum, the successful learner must have active knowledge of accounting, marketing, management, statistics, computer science, finance, international business, and business law, among others. Even with all of these interdependencies, it is worth underscoring that in most colleges and universities, the teaching of this particular course is often the exclusive right of management faculty. And in that faculty, teaching is the exclusive right only of those who have been trained in the strategic planning and strategic management curriculum. This is particularly true in those business schools that have achieved American Assembly of Collegiate Schools of Business accreditation, in which case the accreditation looks at the qualification of instructors and professors who teach courses in business programs as one of the conditions for granting or renewing accreditation.

A broadening of such criteria to allow greater flexibility among disciplines is essential. It should make little difference whether a course in strategic management is taught by a management person, a marketing person, a finance person, and so on, *as long as that person has an adequate preparation in the topic areas.* Adequate preparation will depend heavily on the ability of those who control the basic curricula to broaden the scope of the discipline rather than continually narrowing it. If this were to occur, faculty in declining disciplines would have the ability to move into related disciplines. This would bring fresh insights into the field. The increased flexibility would also allow the institution to downsize or eliminate programs and disciplines that will neither achieve excellence nor add to the overall balance of excellence. This would allow program changes without continual layoffs of narrowly trained and unadaptive faculty. This is a simple idea, which is difficult to achieve given practices of tenure, the exclusivity of discipline certifications, and the reluctance to support or accept change easily.

EFFECTIVE PROGRAM REVIEWS
BASED ON INFORMATION AGE NEEDS

As tenure evolves, administrators bear a special burden to protect scholarship, teaching excellence, and research quality first. The loosening of traditions should not be a license for capricious management. The curmudgeonly professor with high standards and a lesser personality must be judged on the former. Poor scholars who are popular personalities must also be judged on the former. From this, it is easy to see that fairness is a function of the process used to review, because reviews are needed not so much to punish as to reward.

Effective reviews begin at the unit closest to the scholar; they are participative as to goals and expected results; they provide ample time for accomplishment; and they are conducted by each level of the institution from the scholar's home unit to the trustees. This is a common practice. It is almost always in the faculty code, and its results have been generally salutary.

A good process, however requires good information—information about class content, the role of courses offered, evidence of effective teaching, quality research, and useful service. These criteria will not change. What they reflect and measure will change. Among the things that faculty will do and that must be reviewed are effective use of technology, currency and significance of what is taught, active scholarship, research that drives teaching and active learning, inclusion of undergraduates and graduates in research projects, evidence of appositive scholarship, and contribution of scholarship to improving the quality of a society or a community. Peer review will need to be augmented by stakeholder review. If appositive scholarship involves using knowledge to resolve real problems, then those involved in and affected by that scholarship should participate in the review.

Should traditional tenure be replaced by overt guarantees of academic freedom, faculty may well become much more mobile. As we have suggested elsewhere, a Nobel laureate may be sought by several institutions. With technology, the laureate can teach on the web and be available at any number of sites. That same laureate can be involved in several research projects simultaneously. What meaning would tenure have for such a scholar? If students have the choice between a web course from the laureate versus one from Professor *X*, why should an institution impair that? Better yet, why offer something of lesser value to students? This fluid, free agent environment—once academic freedom protections are in place—will turn teaching into a market phenomenon. People will seek the best knowledge rather than the average knowledge. Demand will be a major influence on who faculty are and what jobs they have and for how long.

This market aspect of scholarship will make scholarship and knowledge creation the most competitive part of the information world. New knowledge will drive the university. New technology will shape how it assists in the discovery and transfer of knowledge. The lines between teaching and research will blur. Professorial ranks will become less meaningful, as students become partners rather than objects of learning and teaching. Contracts may replace tenure as a framework for employment, and their length could vary by subject, by individual scholar, and by which universities are interested in that scholar's work. Busy scholars will hire agents to seek and iron out contracts, perhaps providing a role for displaced faculty and administrators. Laureate faculty may have a team of designated mentors, who work directly with learners via e-mail, telephone, two-way video, and in face-to-face sessions, while the laureate scholar travels from site to site and engages through technology to individual concerns. Mobile digital libraries will assist in much of this. A mobile unit with proper computer access to a worldwide library will assist those in out-of-the-way places so that they may also benefit from new forms of instruction.

BALANCING ACADEMIC RESEARCH WITH INFORMATION AGE NEEDS

As campuses adjust to traveling faculty, on-line modules and courses, team research projects, classes linked to the workplace, electronic classrooms available twenty-four hours per day via e-mail and chat spaces, peer mentors for assistance when faculty are occupied, and on-line chats with faculty while doing homework or solving a problem, their posture toward research will also change.

Information Age as an Opportunity for Research

Technology will be a stimulating partner in research. Bringing data to one's fingertips, permitting ongoing discussions with interested scholars and colleagues on a research team, and blending research and real-world problems through appositive learning will make research more productive, more sophisticated, and more immediately useful. Moreover, the great puzzles of our time will now be more open to solution. Over four hundred faculty took twenty years with largely early generation technology to discover the top quark. Better technology, appositive scholarship, the use of teams, the testing of ideas as they emerge in classrooms and chat rooms will mean that problems as unwieldy as the Human Genome Project will be more doable.

More important, an information age society will grasp the meaning of sophisticated things more readily and mine their implications more thoroughly. Instead of worrying about who owns what piece of intellectual property upon discovery, universities will become partners in unfolding the implications and facilitating the discovery, growth, and distribution of new knowledge and discovery. Just as the new community college will become a community development center, the university will become a research and technical assistance commons, serving its own institution's students, students anywhere in related fields, businesses, other research entities and universities, and venture investors growing information for the information age.

Living Libraries and Computer Centers

We alluded earlier to how libraries will be revolutionized by all of this change. Historically, libraries have been a kind of passive post office that moved information around. Libraries increasingly will have to become as mobile as the information they need to provide. The future library will be an information switchboard linked worldwide. As computer and technology centers will provide the basic hardwired and satellite backbones and platforms for digital communication, libraries will be the platforms for processed information. They will be digitized with local printer capability, which will displace many books. Printed books will remain available, but their use will diminish and turn them from mediums of information into artifacts for use in specific circumstances. Like the writings of Chinese scribes, books will become art forms, still meaningful but for different reasons.

A good example of what is taking place is the National Library of Information, an evolving project to integrate the Educational Resources Information Center and the Institutional Communications Network into a coordinated source and central clearinghouse of printed and digital information. A one-stop shopping center, it will advance the instant access to needed information that has been processed and is ready for general access.

As access expands, librarians will become research assistants and guides via complex information networks. For a fee, libraries will do sophisticated searches, edit data files, and provide other services designed to present information to a user in a readily useable format. Subscriptions will link specialized users to the library and provide them with periodic information of additions, changes, new discoveries, and other useful bits of information essential to the currency of scholars and their scholarship.

Market-Oriented Research Faculty

Ivory-towerism, or the tendency to concentrate almost exclusively on what is happening within one's own research and teaching, is a hard tendency to break. The traditions of academic freedom and the hallowedness of campus life are strong magnets that can confine and isolate academics. There is little in this tradition that supports interaction with the outside world on an ongoing basis.

Many faculty are *project* oriented. They teach classes for twelve weeks or so, complete their association with the elements of those classes, and then move on. They work on specific research projects and seldom spend an entire lifetime seeking paradigm truths. Among other things, the common reward system—especially that part of it concerning publishing—encourages short-term thinking and short-term project completion as opposed to long-term research or teaching outcomes, which are difficult to measure or reward.

In the information age, external partnerships will suffer from project orientation. Particularly on an institutional level, partnerships are built over a longer period of time. The notion that a faculty member might interface with the same learners over a span of several years, as those learners continually update both knowledge and skills in a discipline area, is currently viewed as unrealistic. Yet, this type of ongoing relationship may well be what the lifelong learner will require. For the institution to be relevant in the information age economy, such a relationship may well have to occur.

For reasons like these, institutions must redefine their relationships with their learners and consider a broader scope of relationships, ranging from degree-oriented to lifelong learning partnerships. As institutions reorient their philosophies to permit such relationships, they will also have to find ways of coping with changing faculty relationships. As the utility of tenure changes and faculty become accessible via technology, ways to let faculty move from one institution to another or be simultaneously available to several institutions will be needed. Colleges and universities will need to develop new rewards, research incentives, and knowledge base updating capabilities. They will need to redesign physical facilities in order to facilitate changing and flexible faculty roles in a new market-oriented world of knowledge transfer. Preparing students to achieve degrees as well as working with them over the longer term add to the scope of what a college professor does.

Treating Students as Partners in Academic Research

Throughout this discussion, we have talked about the importance of reorienting the curriculum, the faculty, and the institution to match the knowledge needs of the information age. An important part of this discussion needs to be the role of the knowledge-consuming learner in this process. Information age learners will be more active in learning so that the knowledge they gain becomes effective in their information age jobs.

Because they will be more active, they will also take more responsibility for the knowledge they wish to acquire. This means that they will have a much more substantive interest in the discipline or profession than their predecessors. This will have ramifications for admission, advising, study plans, majors, learning settings, classrooms, technology, and curriculum and will require that colleges and universities rethink the match between their perceptions of students and actual student expectations.

The term "learner" fits better than the term "student" because it implies active learning. The information age learner has an active interest in the subject matter. Likely grounded in work or a career, this learner will wish to blend real problems with academic knowledge. This desire for appositive learning turns the student into a partner in learning and makes the student take responsibility for learning. This creates an entirely different relationship between the knowledge consumer and the knowledge provider and offers the opportunity for active and cooperative enhancement of knowledge. When this relationship is developed to extend over a longer period of time, the ongoing interest of the learner is not only in understanding "the basics" but also in being updated through added knowledge over the long term. Because the motivation of many of these learners is related to the work they are doing in information age companies, the opportunity to do ongoing research will provide major opportunities for both the learner and the faculty member to learn appositively.

Learning appositively and changing the academic infrastructure to encourage it is an example of the paradigm shift the information age brings. It highlights how colleges and universities must shape internal adjustments to meet the needs of the new age more effectively. Rethinking the curriculum, the new process of knowledge transfer, the shift in faculty role, and the active involvement of the new learner show how substantial and wide-ranging the changes in infrastructure will be. Deciding early to make the necessary changes to build the new relationships discussed here will advance the reconfiguration of higher education significantly.

CHAPTER TEN

The Faculty, Facilities, and Administration of the Future

～∿～

As we have noted throughout, we strongly believe that the colleges and universities of the future will be very different from what they are today. Yet, the differences that will emerge will not be the same across the academy. Some campuses may strongly resemble their current forms on the surface, whereas others will have gone through substantive modification much more obviously. Regardless of the degree of innovation, the institutions that survive and prosper in the information age will all be different. That difference will reflect the environments and learners they serve.

The people and facilities of the information age colleges and universities will also reflect information age needs and demands. Professors will teach and research differently, and among other things, their training will need to reflect these changes. Faculty may no longer be based at a single institution. They may be contract entrepreneurs, who "free agent" their talents on the open marketplace. The campus is unlikely to grow in physical size, but programmatically, it will be infinitely larger, as partnerships within the virtual university become more prevalent. Administrators will have completely new challenges in the future, the chief of which may be replacing the current administrative structure with one that is more responsive to the needs of the academy of the future. This chapter looks at the ramifications of these issues, as today's campuses become tomorrow's centers of knowledge.

FACULTY OF THE NEW MILLENNIUM

The faculty of the new millennium will reflect the needs of the information age as well as some of the traditional needs of academics and their chosen disciplines. Just as some campuses that refuse to change will go away, the same is true of the professorate. There is little evidence to suggest that the current mind-set of a large number of today's faculty will survive long into the future. Today, there is a lot of concern and a lot of rhetoric about the importance of preserving academic freedom and the traditional structure of disciplines. With the declining support of resource providers, it is highly unlikely that this mind-set will prevail into the future. As we indicated in the previous chapter, the current attack on tenure in the United States will most likely bring about some changes in the tenure system, removing some of the concerns that have generated public criticism.

This is not bad news. By this, we do not suggest that the rich tradition of original and basic research is about to go away. On the contrary—in the information age, innovation will be one of the stalwarts of successful campuses. Original and basic research will continue to prosper and flourish. Given the stance of the United States Supreme Court over the past several decades, adjustments in tenure will not harbinger the end of academic freedom. Free speech and freedom of the press will continue to support all the tenets of academic freedom and the demands of the new age, including new philosophical ideas, new technological methods, new explanations for human behavior and health, the ability to replicate forms of life, and the exploration of the universe.

Protection of Academic Freedom

We do not believe that in the information age, the freedom of expression in print or in the classroom will be abridged. Such intrusion would be dysfunctional to the interests of a knowledge society, for it would narrow inquiry and discovery. In an era where change comes quickly and substantively, the need to debate and explore on an intellectual basis will be even more crucial than it is today. The classroom, regardless of the form that it will take, is the ideal place to conduct such activities. We believe that the modifications to tenure that we have suggested will highlight the particular freedoms needed for free inquiry and will affirm them more substantively than is the case today. If the academy is to be the font of knowledge in the information age, it must be freer than it has been to cope with the speed, range, depth, and sophistication of information in this new age. Such issues as cloning, life in the universe, altering the human immune system, freedom of information on the web, and human experimentation already test the current capacity and the current practice regarding freedom of speech and ideas. The age of ideas can hardly be the age of thought control.

What Information Age Faculty Will Enhance

The redefined tenured faculty will be responsive to resource providers and the social forces that affect higher education. They will be more concerned with the quality and the relevance of the fields of knowledge in which they work and whose tenets they share with their constituents. They will look for ways of integrating the knowledge bases with which they interact. They will be more concerned about how the integrated knowledge base addresses important emerging questions than are those specialists who splinter and segment their fields of study. This faculty will be highly productive, and that productivity will be more apparent to those who monitor the academy.

This faculty will be conversant and proficient in a number of methods of knowledge transfer. As the use of the traditional classroom declines, the interaction among faculty and learners will be more individualized and based on the particular needs for individualized knowledge transfer and assessment. Technology will help reduce the drudgery of the administrative sides of the job and will help organize and coordinate the educational activities that will occur between professor and learner. This will allow the professor to spend much more academic time with individual learners or with smaller groups of learners.

The increasing use of laboratory and field settings to examine and solidify learning experiences, along with the continual development of optimal group techniques and interactions, will help make the learning experience meaningful, realistic, and relevant. Having students interact with the people, places, companies, and other external entities that they will encounter in the real world will add substantively to the learning experience.

The faculty of the future will also find ways of involving learners in all types of academic research. Previously reserved for the professors alone, or shared with select graduate students, this area will be opened up to include learners at any level of academic preparation. The advantages in becoming more involved in research at any level is that the learner will develop a much more thorough understanding of the materials involved and will become more of an active partner in the knowledge transfer process. Because research will be part of the ongoing effort to understand and explain the emerging phenomena of the information age, new learners will benefit greatly from participating in knowledge as it evolves (Tratjenberg, Henderson, and Jaffe, 1992).

Involving the learner in all levels of research will also have a major impact on the faculty member. Active learners will make it possible for faculty to accelerate their research agendas. These learners can help faculty disseminate findings through journals, scholarly meetings, and other media for information exchange. The learner will have the chance to build skills and a reputation via trade journals, the popular press, the Internet, and other avenues of information transfer with which the learner will be associated. Though rules will need to evolve that protect the rights of faculty and learner to the information they create, this activity will clearly improve both the productivity of faculty members and the knowledge transfer process between faculty and learners.

Graduate Learning

The pressure to change graduate and professional learning is driven by more than simply the Internet. It is much more substantively driven by the lack of jobs for many of those with disciplinary terminal degrees. The taxi-driving Ph.D. in English is the typical parody of this situation, but the issue is real. Academic leaders at the California Institute of Technology have urged cutting down the number of Ph.D.'s. The Kellogg Foundation has supported designing an interdisciplinary doctoral program for educational leaders seeking to move beyond the narrow professional boundaries of education's Ed.D. degrees. Washington University is scaling back its doctoral admissions across all the major fields of study. This has improved student quality and helped keep the time to graduation between seven and eight years. However, Washington is a private university with resources to help fund this approach. Many larger public universities may have trouble doing this, given their sunk costs in tenured faculty, laboratories, and their need for affordable entry-level teaching assistants.

Some institutions are eliminating doctoral programs. The University of Rochester phased out chemical engineering, mathematics, linguistics, and comparative literature doctorates. The University of Chicago intends to cut its education doctorate. The University of Northern Colorado eliminated programs in teaching biology and chemistry. The available choices for potential students will continue to decline as low-priority programs are eliminated, largely for financial reasons. The real question here is where funding will go at the graduate level, as excellence drives the market.

There is also growing concern over graduate pedagogy. Some urge turning the dissertation into less of a tome. Others urge its deletion. Most agree that fewer students better trained and more actively involved in research and problem solving would improve things. Then, there are the voices calling for better teacher training as part of the doctorate. Most Ph.D.'s work in places other than research universities. In these other institutions, teaching is important and is currently being criticized. So, better training in teaching and improving the quality of the doctoral experience as an apprenticeship seem to be the underlying themes. Students observing good teachers, joining with their faculty in research, copublishing, and demonstrating mastery beyond the dissertation are among the most desired elements of reform.

With the growing number of multidisciplinary fields, education that broadens knowledge beyond narrowly specialized disciplines and subdisciplines seems necessary. For mathematicians to watch chicks' brains grow and then to be able to relate their findings to developmental biology, it is important that they have knowledge of biology and various life-forms in general. For physicists to be able to help mathematicians understand multiple sclerosis, it is even more important that they both have broad knowledge that crosses disciplines. If the use of fractal geometry extends outside mathematics to medicine, psychology, and other fields and opens new areas of conceptual sophistication, then transdisciplinary learning becomes a critical aspect of knowledge generation.

The cost of all this also matters. Typically, graduate education has been subsidized by undergraduate revenue. This cannot go on because of the rising costs of undergraduate education. The California State University system is calling for graduate and professional programs to pay more of their own way as an essential reform. Clearly in professional areas, it is in the interest of employers to assist in this regard. At some institutions, professional degree students are subsidized by their employers. As the classroom-to-workplace linkage grows, it will grow first at the professional and midcareer level, where employer self-interest is obviously tied to the education of employees. In addition, businesses and some professions have long practiced providing equipment and other forms of capital support for graduate and professional training. This avenue will also improve in potential as the workplace linkage is reinforced by colleges and universities.

In order to manage effectively the types of activities we have outlined, we must change the preparation of professors. There is currently a tendency for doctoral preparation to narrow the academic discipline, which creates further splintering of the field. Also, only a limited number of institutions engage in training their doctoral candidates to be effective teachers. Both of these problems are serious enough that those colleges and universities that prepare doctoral candidates for positions in the academy need to address them and develop revised doctoral programs to prepare graduates to teach and communicate effectively with information age learners and environments.

We believe that research conducted in a doctoral program has to be seriously augmented to include a broader transdisciplinary perspective and that research should prepare the new doctoral candidate for the important tasks of integrating knowledge bases within current and related fields of study. Successful doctoral research should include topics that cement knowledge bases together and find new interconnections and areas in which emerging information is creating new knowledge bases altogether. Not only does this help make the doctoral study more relevant to the world the new doctoral candidate is about to enter, but it also prepares the candidate in areas in which learners are more likely to have questions and research concerns.

Outside schools and colleges of education, it is rare to find doctoral preparation programs that educate their candidates to be effective teachers. The common method of learning to teach is by being a student and observing the teacher. Some institutions include a mentoring component to this method of teaching the teacher, but such methods do little to instill new methods and modalities of knowledge transfer. It does little good to mimic an old-style professor if what new professors need are new styles of working with the information age learner. What does work is to expose doctoral students to the campus's best teachers, to videotape the students as they teach, to critique their performance in light of good teacher praxis, and to develop a personal effective teaching plan with hints, cues, and good practices for each Ph.D.

It is unclear where the training should come from, but many campuses have a faculty development or research center. A good example is the Center for Instructional Development and Research at the University of Washington (CIDR) at Seattle. Housed in the provost's office, it provides teaching training to new teaching assistants, new faculty, and other faculty. Their techniques are based on research of current practices. Assistance is personal and confidential. Those with poor teaching evaluations are referred to CIDR for help. Those referred benefit themselves, and they also contribute to the research on effective teaching. We posit that doctoral preparation programs already have access to programs like CIDR and to world-class knowledge transfer experts through networking, the Internet, and on their own campuses. In addition, as colleges of education struggle with the demand to prepare K–12 teachers better, the methods and techniques developed for this purpose may have applicability to doctoral preparation. As we look toward developing a more effective and seamless system throughout the whole of education (kindergarten through any grade or degree or educational level), this intra-institutional and trans-disciplinary cooperation will have important added benefits for many.

Impact of Resource Policies on the Professorate

Another reality that may affect doctoral preparation is the information age campus, where the number of needed Ph.D.'s could actually go down. In a way, there is a paradox at work here. The knowledge demands of the information age will absolutely go up. However, as networking and technology allow a larger and larger number of campuses to gain access to world-class experts in all areas of knowledge creation and transfer, the need to have top-level faculty on every campus will go down. Also, as resources continue to tighten, this alternative will have greater appeal to department, school, college, and campus administrators as a means of reducing costs while improving the quality of the knowledge resource base (Finnegan, 1993).

Who will fill in the gaps? As a campus reduces its expenses by pooling resources with other campuses to gain access to the best and the brightest knowledge transfer agents, it can fill in the gaps of organization, assessment, and personal interaction with campus learners by using instructors and assistant or associate professors. In those cases in which the department can construct the learning experience to be composed primarily of knowledge interactions between the learners and the networked or electronically connected knowledge experts, the on-campus need for someone with doctoral qualifications could diminish. Although we are not advocating a wholesale reduction in terminally degreed faculty, we are calling attention to the opportunities for improving efficiency and quality, especially if those opportunities assist faculty in advancing the sophistication of what they do and reducing the more menial aspects of their contributions. The savings are undoubtedly going to be appealing to campus administrators and resource providers, especially if the quality of the experience for learners will potentially improve.

Another factor affecting the number of doctorally qualified professors in the future is the overall number of future colleges and universities. Though we do expect the size of institutions in growth states to increase and some new campuses to emerge in states like California, New York, and possibly Texas, that growth may not be able to absorb Ph.D.'s at a rate that will sustain present supply. If that happens, the number of faculty will go down. This will occur because resource providers are likely not to fund colleges and universities at the level the institutions demand because of the cost of improving overall faculty salaries under peer-comparison and market conditions. Many of these campuses are currently economizing by reducing the number of full-time faculty, support staff personnel, and a number of administrative staff. Such cuts are finite and when they are exhausted, it becomes necessary to look at the number, type, and mix of faculty and begin to find ways of economizing there.

Another tactic already in place on some campuses is to induce senior faculty (those who are both tenured and have full professor ranks) to retire early. The hope is to save a significant portion of the salary paid to a full professor and employ a brand new tenure- or non-tenure-track professor instead, thereby realizing a salary savings. This does not always work, however, especially in fields in which market forces command salaries near or above those the campus pays for its full professors. Here, the savings is negligible and over a couple of years of annual salary adjustments might be wiped out altogether. A more substantive answer will be found in eliminating tenure-track positions and replacing them with temporary or instructor-level positions, in effect creating an academic contingent labor force. In reality, such a pool exists on many campuses and is typically used to hire teachers at the last minute as entry classes fill. This practice is threatening to sitting faculty, especially those in faculty unions. The single, critical human resource issue for the information age is the resolution of the conflict between needed savings in a labor-intensive organization and employment rights and guarantees.

If the number of colleges and universities were to increase over the next few decades, the number of new professorial positions would grow, but that growth would not be proportionate. For all of the reasons just outlined, it is unlikely that funding sources are going to support the current level of faculty salaries in growth situations. There will be additional resources made available, but they will be proportionally smaller and will require new campus administrators to seek relatively different mixes of tenure-track and nontenure-track faculties. The net effect will probably be a reduced need for new doctorally qualified campus faculty.

One other situation is worth mentioning. The world's population will continue to grow, and some countries, like China, will not have an educated cadre to meet their educational needs. If current doctoral programs include language training, future Ph.D.'s will have options outside their home country. If current faculty receive language training, they may also be able to consider this option for their careers. The global nature of education is an important consideration in the way higher education should deal with a surplus of qualified faculty.

Character of the Campus Faculty

The character of the overall campus faculty will be altered as changes occur with individual faculty members. Some professors may serve many campuses through networking, resource sharing (locally, nationally, and internationally), distance learning, and the Internet, just a few of the ways to access faculty in the information age. This will broaden such faculty's focus to include more than one campus setting, thereby changing the perspective each of them has of what is going on throughout the academy and on their home campuses. The involvement of such faculty in local campuses will necessarily decline, reversing a common trend of faculty wanting to have a greater say in the administrative activities of their campuses. Technology will permit individual faculty members to act much more like contractors. As contractors, they will negotiate the teaching or research relationship;

the salary and benefits; the library, database, and laboratory rights; as well as the intellectual property rights. These contracts can be negotiated among a number of campuses or different parts of the same campus system.

Faculty who are at the top of their disciplines will be able to use the competitive marketplace to help determine their worth and their salary packages, both within and outside a redefined tenure system. Faculty who are not near the top of their disciplines will have the incentives to improve their academic research and participation in order to better their security and financial packages. Others may have to consider supportive academic positions in which market salaries will be much more competitive. They may well have to settle for less compensation and for less well-recognized academic contributions.

In this scenario, many on-campus faculty will be instructors cast in a supportive role, as select full professors serve the prime, more universal, multicampus needs. This will reduce the number of doctoral faculty but will provide adequate human resources to ensure that the information age learners continue to be well served.

One aspect of the information age campus will be that intercampus networking of faculty and classes will be not only common, but also seamless. Just as learners will be able to choose from a variety of knowledge resource providers, those same knowledge providers will find it easy to move around within the academy to take advantage of a variety of opportunities that will come with the new age. Knowledge experts will find it easy to move from location to location and from campus to campus as the opportunities change. This will become possible as more and more colleges and universities network their resource bases, locally, nationally, and internationally. By developing common compensation bases, institutions within these networks will be able to reduce costs, spread out resources over a wider range of campuses, and be able to rely on a pool of talent to meet temporary and emerging needs.

The world of the professor will indeed be different from what it is today. Yet, it will be a world with increased opportunities for the dedicated and the innovative. Campus participation will change on all levels—from research, to interactions with learners, to working with a variety of campuses and in a variety of settings, to developing a series of network connections that give new meaning to what campuses are supposed to be. This will be an exciting time for an exciting profession. The new campus will be an engaged haven for knowledge creation, distillation, and dissemination.

The most pervasive change that faculty will undergo will be working in teams. Many faculty already work in teams, as the authors of this book have. To use the vernacular, there will be a number of "lone rangers" who work individually in their fields. But the problems of the information age will also be big, complex, and profound. We alluded earlier to the fact that it took more than four hundred scientists twenty years to uncover evidence of the top quark. Problems like these will require many minds. In the classroom, modules that deal with issues of this dimension will require experts from several fields, especially in transdisciplinary subjects and fields. In addition, team dynamics and problem solving will be necessary. Practical experience with this approach as part of learning will be very valuable and in demand.

INFORMATION AGE ADMINISTRATION

The administration of college and university campuses in the information age will have little choice but to be more businesslike in its philosophies and methods for leading, coordinating, and managing college and university campuses around the world. The changes that are occurring in society, among resource providers, within regulatory and legislative bodies, and within the academy itself, all propel administrators to look at current campus structures and find better fits between their campuses and the external environment.

This is no easy task. Not only is external change occurring at an increasing and fast-paced rate, but internal resistance to change also appears to be growing stronger as some faculty perceive their welfare threatened. The job of an administrator on today's campus is increasingly shorter in tenure. As we have emphasized, college and university presidents are under intense fire from a variety of sources and turnover is increasing. We have also argued that governing boards are becoming more intrusive (Gardner, 1995). They are not only questioning the activities of administrators, but in some cases they are starting to make operational decisions.

Yet, although the job of the campus administrator may not be getting any easier, it is still a vital part of the campus structure. What is needed today is a new type of administrator, one who has the business sense to work with business-oriented public and private resource providers and governing boards, and one who has the patience and wisdom to work with a heterogeneous and sometimes troubled faculty and a rapidly changing student body. Aided by a team that places the good of the institution ahead of personal gain, the president must be a diplomat and negotiator who can calm external critics and nudge internal constituents toward change. That leader will need the courage to act in a timely and decisive manner, especially when things move too slowly.

Administrations will be just as subject to the challenges and opportunities generated in the new age as will be the learner and the knowledge expert. In such a world, technology will play an ever increasing role in how campuses will be run and financed. For example, technology will help reduce administrative jobs across the campus. Companies like Datatel of Fairfax, Virginia, SCT out of Pennsylvania, and a brand new company called PeopleSoft are developing administrative systems for every aspect of campus life beyond the classroom. These systems categorize, organize, synthesize, and operationalize every area of administrative activity in ways that allow administrators and other constituents access to information about the workings and well-being of the campus community. Over time, this will cut down on the number of people a campus may require to operate and monitor the complex workings and support systems of a modern campus.

Among other benefits of the electronically controlled campus will be the improvement in communication that can occur at all levels of campus activity. Not only will administrators at all levels be able to find information about campus operation with a keystroke, but they also will be able to share this knowledge readily and directly with other administrators, campus leaders, faculty, students, and off-campus constituents who need to know. The increase in responsiveness will help sharpen the image of campus administrators in the eyes of administrative monitors, faculty, student leaders, and the core of resource providers. It will also allow levels of campus administration to make decisions faster, based on more current and accurate information. This should help cut down criticism and concern over decisions.

The focus of the work of most administrators and the people who support them will change in the information age. Administrators will serve as linchpins connecting the assets and needs of the inner campus with the assets and needs of the external environment. By having better access to current information about the workings of the campus as well as the status of providers, administrators will be in a more credible position to represent the needs of the campus to the resource providers who are most concerned with particular aspects of campus activities. This will help free faculty from many of the reporting and interface activities to which they are subjected by controlling factions of the resource environment (grant providers, corporate sponsors, and so forth) and will allow administrators more latitude in representing campus interests from a more professional perspective. Everyone gains from these types of activities. Faculty have more time to conduct research and interact with learners, providers get more accurate and professionally oriented reports, and administrators become more integral to the campus environment.

The individual who fits well in the administration of the information age college or university will continue to be part academician and part businessperson. Key administrative positions will continue to interface with both elements of the academic environment, but due to the speed and severity of change in the information age, the administrator of the future will be constantly updating and assessing both areas. This means that college and university administrators will also be perpetual learners, finding ways of interacting with emerging knowledge bases and constantly taking advantages of opportunities to learn the changing intricacies of their constantly changing environments. Study time, learning time, and research time will all be necessary parts of the responsibilities of the new age administrators.

INFORMATION AGE FACILITIES

Along with everything else, campus architecture will change to accommodate the information age learner, knowledge expert, and administrative support resources. There will still be some traditional classrooms, but an effective learning environment will mean radically different uses of traditional campus classroom and laboratory spaces. Newer campuses will have fewer and fewer traditional classrooms and more and more group meeting and study spaces, new types of spaces for interfacing with faculty and support staff, and new technological interface sites throughout the campus to aid the learner, knowledge expert, administrator, and support staff function at a higher and more effective level.

Classrooms of the Future

The need for the traditional classroom will remain for certain types of learning activities. For example, many very basic introductory courses can most likely be done in traditional classroom settings for learners who respond well to this type of environment. However, the increased use of technology will make the classroom experience significantly more effective. Lectures will decline to a minimum, as electronic classrooms take an entire class anywhere throughout the world to interact with other knowledge experts, world leaders, industry leaders, field settings, and other classes throughout the world. Learners can be taken through a multimedia showcase of the course material, which will include interactive as well as passive involvement of the learner and the class leader. The key will be developing a connection between the learner and the material that is meaningful to the learner and represents the material in the most accurate and up-to-date manner possible.

Classroom Alternatives

Other learning experiences will be governed by assessment techniques that prescribe programs of study unique to each learner and that allow the learner the time and resources needed to accomplish a given level of proficiency. Smaller meeting rooms or rooms where a learner can interact with a computer in a semiprivate setting will help achieve the highest levels of learning that each individual learner is capable of, or desirous of achieving.

Still other learning experiences will occur through electronic and distance learning, both on and off the campus. For the providers of distance learning, facilities that support the production and transmission of information-sharing programs are essential. For those who take advantage of distance learning opportunities on the campus, special facilities for individuals and groups to meet, receive the transmission (either passively or interactively), and respond to assessment tools and opportunities will be necessary.

Libraries

Another major difference in the campus of the information age will be found in the institution's library facilities. These libraries will be radically different from what we know and use today. Among other things, it will no longer be necessary to go to the library in order to use it. Digitizing the entire holdings of the library will make its holdings available either as a free or for-fee service to learners and researchers both on and off the campus. Libraries will continue to have paper holdings to accommodate those learners and researchers who wish to use them, but these holdings will most likely shrink over time, allowing the library to utilize its spaces in different ways.

Accommodating the information age researcher and learner will be the primary objective of the campus library. It will use its own digitized holdings and also provide access to the digitized holdings of other connected libraries to provide instant access to researchers and learners from across the campus and from around the world. As discussed earlier, there are already major holdings undergoing digitization, which will help anchor this process. The Libraries of Congress, the University of Michigan, the University of Minnesota, and the University of California at Berkeley are among the most important facilities currently involved. Around the world, other campus libraries are beginning the process of digitization as well. Before long, most of the world's major literature, its journals, and its other periodical literature bases will be on-line, making them available to anyone.

Publishers are already gearing up to accommodate the changing world of the information age library needs. The use of interactive CD-ROM disks that allow students to read, absorb, interact with, study, and be evaluated at their personal computers is already challenging the current use of the classroom. Publishers are finding ways of making their materials available on electronic media for purchase in traditional bookstores as well as over the Internet, charging fees for downloading and use.

All of these innovations help eliminate the traditional library's dependence on paper books and the space they require and open up a world of electronic literature that learners and researchers can easily access and use. Many libraries already have major space devoted to computer use, whether for database searches or surfing the Internet. This is, however, just the beginning and the virtual library is the next step.

Faculty Technology

The campus of the information age will need to accommodate all aspects of traditional, as well as emerging, faculty activities. Faculty interfaces with technology will be standard and will provide major linkages to learners, research bases, colleagues throughout the world, and campus information (including student records and progress tools). As the leaders of the knowledge interchange activities of the campus, the faculty will need to be at least at par with the technologies their learners are using. Like administrators, faculty will also be perpetual learners and will need access to a wide range and variety of information bases to help ensure their ongoing knowledge-gathering activities. Technology will accommodate this.

Beyond having computers at every faculty desk, with connected modems at home, technology also will provide a wide variety of peripherals and software packages. Being able to link to other sites, carry on worldwide conversations instantaneously or at chosen intervals, being able to connect similarly with learners, having the ability to analyze new data immediately, and being able to share new knowledge with others at the stroke of a key are all part of the technology that every faculty member will require to stay connected with the information age. By this, we do not wish to imply that faculty need to be desk bound on campus in order to carry on important interchanges with their academic partners. Interfacing from home, on the road, in the classroom, in group settings, in field settings, and from any other location will all be possible and common in the information age. Being able to use up-to-date technology in all environments will help knowledge experts better accommodate the needs of knowledge workers and their employers. This will be one of the major changes that campus decision makers will need to address as they gear up to be competitive in this new era.

Faculty-Learner Relationship

The focal point of change in the new age is the essential interaction between the knowledge experts within a faculty and the learners who come to a college or university to acquire specific knowledge. Faculty mentoring will be more the norm than the exception and will be made possible through the increased use of technology. When a learner is placed in close proximity to the knowledge expert, the learning experience should be dramatically enhanced. This can now happen electronically and need not even occur at a time that is mutually convenient. By using available technology, the learner and the knowledge expert can interface instantaneously or independently. Questions can be answered directly, and checking back and forth between the expert and the learner can occur at once, helping ensure that the learner is receiving the knowledge being sought.

Assessment need no longer be tightly scheduled, using a common medium and oriented toward group standards. Assessment should take place at least twice—once when the learner first signs up to work with a knowledge expert and at least one other time to determine how much learning has taken place. Doing periodic assessments will provide needed feedback and probably help ensure that both the learner and the knowledge expert are working effectively together. After the initial assessment, faculty and individual learners can decide together when assessments should take place, how they should occur, and what they will do with the results. Because the objective of the knowledge-sharing experience is the increased competency of the learner, the sole focus of the expert who is working with an assessment scheme should be to discover whether or not the learner has achieved the competency level both had agreed on.

There is a rich assessment literature readily available for use in specific circumstances. The American Association for Higher Education has provided real leadership in studying assessment tools—how they match specific learning environments, how they are best used, and what their limitations are. The organization is an excellent source of comprehensive information on learning assessment. The Baldrige program of assessment is in use at a number of sites, including Texas A&M University, where the program has acquired national recognition. In addition, the faculty in many colleges of education are particularly active as researchers and teachers of assessment. They are a campus resource that should be involved in any individual campus assessment program.

Assessment can be expanded to group work or even a whole class. Regardless of the modality used to transfer knowledge, assessment methods can be shaped to meet the needs of the learner and the capabilities of the knowledge expert. Using available technologies to expedite the feedback and interchanges between them will help ensure that both the learner and the knowledge provider work to achieve optimal outcomes.

CONCLUSION

We have described the working infrastructure of the information age campus. We have not provided an exhaustive description of the new institution but have focused instead on the essential elements—faculty in its various forms and modes of contribution, learners and their assessment needs, central resources such as technology and the library, and the administration. These are early sketches of the changes that will take place. We provide them as suggestions, ideas that individual campuses may consider, especially in their cross-impact analyses and brainstorming activities. As we have stated before, we advocate a process of strategic change that is built by each campus or system from the bottom up. We urge that the process begin with solving specific and current issues, such as enrollment management, helping the library face resource constraints, or using technology to improve learning. We have tried to provide a few contextual insights about faculty, students, and other stakeholders, which may serve as catalysts for envisioning the strategic changes appropriate to a particular institution.

CHAPTER ELEVEN

Partnerships to Produce and Transfer Knowledge

A s the information age advances, higher education and other learning institutions will have to innovate their structures and practices strategically. For example, K–12 in the United States has been under severe criticism since 1980. Many schools and school systems are criticized for how poorly they prepare students for life in the workplace and in college. Community colleges have fared better. By being responsive to student demand, community colleges are often inundated by both traditional and new learners. Along with higher education, these two members of the educational community are undergoing major change as education in general faces the information age.

Strategic alliances are one of the options that may help solve common problems that these branches of education face. Because what happens in one segment affects the other two, autonomous change in each segment will not work for the whole society. This chapter looks at the problems faced by other members of the educational community, outside traditional higher education, and proposes some relationships among these educational partners that can help overcome many of the problems each currently faces.

K–12 AND THE CHALLENGES OF A NEW MILLENNIUM

Change will take different forms, if for no other reason than the exclusive dependence on public money by K–12. This dependency demarcates the different paths of change and related outcomes. As the first educator of citizens in all societies, elementary and secondary education set the base for addressing the needs of the information age.

The basic education found in American primary schools, as well as in their counterparts throughout the world, has not changed fundamentally since the days of Horace Mann. As we enter the information age, we find that K–12 is undergoing scrutiny and facing pressure to change and meet the demands of today's society. Currently, this pressure at the lower-grade levels is far greater than it is for higher education. For example, in Denver, Colorado, four schools were earmarked in April 1997 for major staff and structural changes if the performance scores of their students did not dramatically increase. The penalties for nonperformance were the laying off or transfer of the teachers and administrators held responsible.

This is one example among many that reflects a major general concern within society that K–12 is not doing its job properly. Coupled with the presence and growth of drugs, gangs, violence, and sex in our public schools, the apparent inability of current K–12 administrators and faculty to come up with adequate "cures" for the problems besetting school-age children is seriously undermining them in their first responsibility, which is to provide basic education to the next generation.

It is not wise for higher education to ignore these criticisms of K–12, even though many of these criticisms may not be particularly germane to the world of colleges and universities. The academy is not immune from the problems that are challenging their counterparts in K–12. Not only are the students who enter colleges and universities the products of the K–12 system, but the academy produces the teachers for the primary and secondary school systems throughout the world.

Higher Education Connection

Because higher education prepares K–12 teachers and administrators, the connection cannot be overlooked. Further, this is not simply an issue for schools and colleges of education. Because teacher preparation involves all academic disciplines, the entire campus must take responsibility.

Teacher preparation has been undergoing change ever since *A Nation at Risk* (National Commission on Excellence in Education, 1983) called for it in the 1980s. Two new trends emerged. The first was to improve assessment and develop tests to demonstrate performance. This standards-and-performance-based testing would be used to determine how well students performed on basic subjects, such as history, English, mathematics, and geography. Student performance would also provide a basis for comparing schools. This would offer a basis, with other measures, for a review of the efficacy of teaching and management in a given school. Reinforced by research showing that principals made a difference in school performance, administrators and teachers would be part of the performance review process.

The second trend the report suggested was content based. It focused on assuring that teachers were trained in both content and pedagogy. As pedagogy ensured effective techniques, content would ensure subject matter competence. So teachers were required to have subject matter majors in addition to the technique and pedagogy required for certification.

K–12 Initiatives Already Under Way

These trends remind higher education of its obligation to help improve K–12 education. However, given the rather slow response of some in higher education, several legislatures, school boards, and businesses have been moving to put a higher level of cooperation on the public agenda.

Nonetheless, in several quarters, progress is being made. For example, the president of a major Ivy League university resigned to head up a K–12 improvement project known as the Edison Project. Private funds are being raised to support these private alternatives to the public school in curricula that are focused on the basics. Charter schools are emerging as another private option. In states like Colorado, the legislature has passed a statute permitting the use of public funds to support charter schools that have demonstrated improvement in student performance.

Charter schools sprang up in the mid–1990s and have produced mixed results. Some have closed as demand subsided or community interest dwindled. Others struggle on, with marginal funding and special foci that offer few real lessons for improving mainstream K–12 education.

In Texas, tests are required of all teachers before they can continue on contract. Some teachers have failed these exams and have been refused continuance. This is an interesting practice, though studies have shown that improved teacher competency has not always led to improved student performance. So the debate of what is best continues.

Elsewhere, others simply ignored the debate and made changes they thought fit local circumstances. In Moundsville, West Virginia, a junior high French instructor used technology to improve foreign language learning by linking learning circles of students in his classroom to others throughout the world. This technology came from AT&T. At Peters Township in McMurray, Pennsylvania, students produce a television show, writing the content, news scripts, editorials, and book reviews. These activities improve their written and oral communications skills. Projects like this occur in many schools across the United States. In a St. Paul, Minnesota, magnet school, students develop their own study growth plans with faculty. Part of this involves doing individual projects in the community, using community resources, and learning from real-world problems. At the University Laboratory School in Greeley, Colorado, students pursue self-paced learning, using jointly set goals and courses that address basic discipline knowledge and also are cast within a broad topic of current interest.

In many cases, these modules require research. Projects co-located at an external site, such as an elementary school and a university, allow the university's library and information resources to be available. University faculty from the College of Education work with the faculty and students on curricular matters. In California, the California State University at Los Angeles helps operate a math and science school in an effort to improve central city programs for youth. Examples like these are in place in every state across the land and show that locally responsive strategies and strategic alliances are essential to long-term reform.

Perhaps we can put the future of education in perspective for everyone: the idea of learning in forty-to-fifty-minute snippets in twelve grades has little to do with how we learn and everything to do with the bureaucratic organization of learning. The current school day and school year are artifacts of another time, when crops and factories dictated when children were available and what they should learn. Even the support services, such as parental activities, all assumed a certain lifestyle and certain priorities that no longer exclusively apply. Single parents have a hard time attending teacher conferences, which are often scheduled for the convenience of the teachers and in many places are part of a union contract. In the growing web of rules and roles, children are lost, as the professionals argue among themselves over their own benefit. This may be a harsh portrayal, but its elements are all part of the fog of blame and angry discourse that has clouded how schools reform in fact rather than in theory.

Mehlinger (1995) proposes the following as essential for the new school of the information age: providing year-round schooling; using a longer school day; using new forums and sensoriums that are virtual reality laboratories for learning; dissolving the schoolwork-homework dichotomy by offering on-line courses, which allow students to study continually with access to the teacher or teacher aide; replacing many textbooks with digital libraries, databases, and CD-ROMs; providing more substantive learning content that is tied to real-world and interdisciplinary problems as the basis for appositive learning; replacing report cards with "case notes," which chronicle the successes and shortcomings of each student, include portfolios and exhibits of work performed, and assist in customizing study plans and learning; and using interactive video for ongoing faculty development and skills improvement.

To these, we would add on-line e-mail connections with parents, for a more ongoing and timely review of student accomplishments and areas that require improvement; the availability of teacher aides around the clock, so students can get assistance while doing their assignments, whether in the school or in the home; and the location of the school near other service providers such as personal counselors, child-care providers, and software and technology rooms, which would displace mindless arcades with educational paraphernalia. Other suggestions include ongoing and supervised recreation activities, which turn the school yard into a supportive neighborhood; individualized learning projects, through which students are exposed to experimentation and discovery as early as interest permits; regular performance testing designed to focus on individual growth rather than on peer comparison; the linking of minimally educated parents to learning by including them as partners in some of the studies, products, and outcomes of their child's activities; and regular programs with recognition and compensation for teacher development and intellectual growth. Still other suggestions include bringing university and community college faculty into the primary and secondary schools as resource guides and individual project mentors to keep the levels experientially connected; regularly using retired citizens as mentors and tutors; encouraging employers to recognize the work of their employees who are involved parents in their child's education when evaluating the employee's workload, performance, and salary assessments; and inviting businesses and service clubs to modernize and equip rooms and laboratories as part of their community relations efforts and as an investment in the future workforce. As the community college becomes an information commons, we envision the new primary and secondary schools as learning commons, intertwined with all of the resources in a community for the benefit of basic learners.

Forging a Better Partnership Between the Academy and K–12

It is important for decision makers in the academy and in K–12 to consider that from kindergarten to postdoctoral study, education is one piece. The burgeoning linguistic and cultural heterogeneity of America's population, the growing distances between income groups, and the explosion of information combine to present a problem in education that no one level can singularly address. In the examples above, one element is clear—partnership. Partnership, in the form of a strategic alliance, is needed in framing the problems and providing the research knowledge to guide action. It is essential for building the content and providing the delivery of solutions. It is needed in bringing interested constituencies together to share ownership in action, both in success and in failure.

Research partnerships are already growing. Further, they are providing clues for effective change and the establishment of meaningful cooperation. Leadership is seen as key. Effective change occurs when a broad sense of community is cultivated, and when it leads families, businesses, professionals, schoolteachers, and administrators to cooperate; when good research and relevant information provide guidance in taking risks as well as minimizing failures; when there is knowledge of how the system works and a willingness to take the criticism that is attendant to change; and when the stakeholders have the personal courage and outlook that lets common sense and patience ameliorate the urgency to find a quick cure (Office of Educational Research and Improvement, 1996). Principals supported by school boards, superintendents, and teachers can overcome the political interference and bureaucratic obstructions that hinder change and dampen innovation. The Principals Academy at the University of Northern Colorado provides one example of the opportunities available across the country for principals to be exposed to innovative ideas and practices and then receive year-round support from faculty as they apply change at the building level.

The National Center for Research on Cultural Diversity and Second Language has sponsored research on dealing with the at-risk. Understanding the mechanics of high-quality schooling; having a plan for students to learn at high levels; supporting innovations in scheduling, teaching format, and pedagogy; and having a community of adult learners who value effective student learning are all conditions associated with high-level language competency and skill.

Standards with teeth and the teaching to meet them are an integral part of reform that sticks. The Mathematical Association of America has developed a large bank of questions for several different levels of readiness. These can be put together in various versions for use in a given locale. The Baylor College of Medicine partners with the Houston Elementary Schools Alliance of three universities and a museum to improve the content of science courses. Teachers are tested after the program, and most have shown clear improvement in their science comprehension and skills in teaching science.

In North Carolina, college faculty inexperienced in elementary instruction work with elementary foreign language teachers to develop a model language instruction curriculum. In New York, Queens College and the New York Hall of Science collaborate. Queens students work as paid docents, take a seminar connecting the job to their academic study, and receive a tuition waiver in exchange for an agreement to teach science for two years in area schools. Pace University uses case studies as a means of improving teaching. Following the case method used in business and public administration education, Pace develops cases to fit the instructional needs of teachers in education courses. The University of Oregon focuses on elementary and secondary administrators. Practicing and aspiring administrators identify problems and skills they need to develop via school-based internships. Faculty engage administrators as co-teachers and work with them in their school environment for a year, developing needed skills. The University of California Lawrence Hall of Science, community colleges, and preschool professionals work together to introduce preschoolers to science. The Lawrence Hall staff design projects for early childhood teachers and day-care providers. Three one-credit community college courses plus eight Saturday workshops are used to familiarize the early childhood professionals with useful materials, to engage them in science and mathematics content, and to develop ways to introduce preschoolers to these subjects.

CREATING STRATEGIC ALLIANCES WITH COMMUNITY COLLEGES

Students do not come spontaneously and without background to the university. They are all products of the K–12 system, and more and more are products of the community college system as well. In the past, community colleges have developed a reputation for being places that provide tracks to a job or that repair poor preparation by high schools. Because the community college is much more community bound, it appears to have adapted more readily to the need for educational reform than has its senior partner. Today, the senior colleges and universities can look to the community colleges for several innovative ideas, as well as the potential of greater levels of cooperation, which could alleviate the problems both face, particularly those of resources.

Travis (1995) tells us that community colleges and their leaders have been addressing the issues that will face them in the future, and they have done so as a matter of national concern. Already, they are redefining courses, forms of instruction, and delivery methods. They are giving more attention to the groups and communities that are their stakeholders, reshaping the community college to be a focal point for the community network necessary to help communities improve economically and socially. They are developing learning communities for traditional and nontraditional students.

Because community colleges are not lavishly funded, most have learned that progress requires partnership. Linking with universities and businesses to amplify library resources, develop articulation agreements that strengthen the curriculum, and forge business partnerships to support internships or provide technology not readily available all reflect the acquisitiveness of community colleges in their pursuit of excellence and effective services. Business and government emphasis on workforce training has turned community colleges toward retraining and lifelong learning, far in advance of colleges and universities. This head start has moved community colleges toward seeing themselves as focal points for community revival and socio-economic improvement.

Cooperative ventures, partnerships, pooled resources, and seamless relationships with high schools are already a part of the everyday vocabulary of reform. Community colleges are especially anxious to support business incubators, industrial parks, school improvement initiatives, high school completion efforts, consortia that deal with high school retention, and programs that address the needs of at-risk students. Distance learning is part of the portfolio for change and includes providing instruction in housing projects, prisons, and juvenile centers.

The new community college that is evolving from these practices is a coordinated community education center, which uses learning as a means of tying community services together in a supportive package for learners. A mix of "campus without walls" and "educational mall" seem to guide thinking. The college as community education center becomes an information commons with satellite library, laboratory, youth and adult activities, and social service providers easily accessible. Buttressed by outreach activities and courses, the new community college will rely increasingly on technology and electronic instruction, especially to link the classroom to the workplace as required by workforce and other career-related training.

Many community college learners move on to the senior colleges to complete their educational experiences. As a result, many colleges and universities are already forging transfer cooperative relationships as a means to ensure a steady stream of transfer students onto their campuses. Although the missions of the two types of institutions may differ in some areas—senior colleges generally do not engage in specific job training in the way community colleges do, and community colleges seldom engage in original research—other mission areas are the same. Both have common general educational requirements and both engage in preprofessional preparation in business, medicine, law, and other fields.

The potential to complement, cooperate, and collaborate is considerable. Why would these two institutions want to? Simply, they would want to because partnership allows both to spread resources more effectively by eliminating duplication of efforts, improving access, and reducing the costs of competition. They should also want to investigate more partnership relationships, because this will end up serving the information learner in a much better fashion. In several examples throughout the country, such cooperative arrangements and other types of strategic alliances are already being tested, and the early results are encouraging.

SEAMLESS EDUCATION

As partnering develops interlinking mechanisms that help provide greater interaction and interdependence between K–12, community colleges, and colleges and universities, one major benefit could be in the development of a *seamless* interface between them. As we have described (Rowley, Lujan, and Dolence, 1997), the linkage between K–12, community colleges, and senior institutions needs to be more seamless, in order to help the learner maximize individual learning and competency. Without this ability to seek out new competencies fluidly, the information age learner will not have the capacity to keep pace with society's expanding skills and rapidly changing knowledge.

The traditional gateways between K–12 and higher education have been qualifying exams, class standing, and earned grade point average (GPA). With the exception of accessing the open universities around the world (where open admission allows students to take classes regardless of high school performance), a graduating senior from a high school system always has had numerous hurdles to leap in order to get into college. The choice of who went to college and who did not was never entirely the purview of the student. Ordinarily, the choice was the institution's to make.

We argue that in the information age, these gateways to the academy are often dysfunctional and perhaps even irrelevant. First, the growth of proprietary institutions of higher education will make higher education available to everyone, regardless of performance in K–12, including the reality that many learners may not have even completed a traditional K–12 program. The open university, as it defines and restructures its role in the information age, will continue to be a popular way of accessing knowledge regardless of previous academic experience and performance. The eventual impact on colleges and universities that continue to impose admissions standards will be that they will become less competitive. They may even begin to lose a significant number of students who are qualified to attend their schools. Some of these students may choose a less-restrictive institution, whether non-profit or for-profit, simply because it is easier to get into that institution's competitive programs of comparable quality.

High demand will ensure that some institutions will be able to maintain high admissions standards. These will likely be Harvard, Stanford, Oxford, Cambridge, the Sorbonne, the University of Heidelberg, the University of Michigan, Ohio State University, the University of California at Berkeley, and other first-tier public and private institutions. The second- and third-tier colleges and universities are going to find themselves in a major competitive race among one another and with the alternative, particularly for-profit, institutions whose accessibility is so much more apparent. To counter this trend, alliances between colleges and universities and their K–12 partners will help create a seamless system of movement between institutions. This is a viable strategy for dealing with likely patterns of intensive competition.

The information explosion and the demand for access to the primary sources of that information will force many colleges and universities to find new ways of increasing their availability to non-degree-seeking learners. These learners will want access to the knowledge that these institutions have developed or that they maintain. Because not all K–12 students go on to degree-seeking programs, offering anyone who wants access to knowledge a means of accessing that knowledge will provide a major service to learners of the information age.

Admissions gateways are an artificial measure of an educational monopoly that no longer prevails. Higher education is no longer provided solely by standard colleges and universities. The Internet, for-profit providers, and the open universities all provide access to the same information that has traditionally been the exclusive franchise of the academy. Qualifying people to access this information no longer prevents people who need and want information from getting it.

The call for a seamless system of accumulating knowledge from K–12 through postdoctoral study in higher education is an essential canto for the future. The current gateways and qualifiers that separate one branch of education from another have little relevance to the extensive educational needs of the information age. If education is seen as a continuum without breaks, it will provide a source of knowledge from which individuals may partake according to their needs. Enabling learners to meet their needs most effectively by allowing them to choose a pathway that goes from kindergarten through higher education should be the goal of the overall educational process. In adopting this philosophy, both K–12 and higher education will form a new series of strategic alliances with each other that will benefit all, by opening up opportunities for learning and creating new knowledge.

Creating a K–*n* System

As a logical extension of this argument, we suggest that education be considered holistic. As there should be no barriers between the various components of the educational system, there should be no limits on the completion of that education either. To assist the needs of the lifelong learner, to accommodate the needs of the people associated with emerging fields of knowledge, to ensure that as many people as possible are educated, and to provide society with a constant and totally involved educational resource, the educational system should be open. It should reflect the reality of lifelong educational needs of the information age worker. Hence, the "K–*n*" designation, or kindergarten through whatever *number* of years of education a person needs or wants.

We are aware that seamless open-ended education is a challenging idea. It challenges our traditional thinking about what levels of education a person within a given society ought to have in order to be a fully functioning, value-producing member of that society. But the thinking that supports this view is from the industrial age, when the need for differential educational levels among managers, workers, service personnel, and societal leaders was fairly well defined. The educational system mirrored those expectations. In the information age, the need for a highly educated workforce that continually refreshes itself with emerging knowledge requires something else. As a result, the educational system should rethink itself in terms of how it can best serve society as a whole as well as serving the individuals within the society, by fulfilling their educational needs on a lifelong basis.

Partnering with Proprietary Schools and Business Corporations

Even more radical than removing the barriers and gateways that separate K–12 from the institutions of higher education is the idea of linking higher education with both proprietary providers of educational services and business corporations. There are few if any connections between colleges and universities and proprietary providers. There has been little incentive on the part of either of these groups to establish them. Nonetheless, some partnering is going on. For example, Davies (1997) reports a strategic alliance between the University of California and the Walt Disney Company. The purpose of the alliance is to create a system for delivering college-level courses electronically in the home or office at prices that will be below that of on-campus programs.

Connections between institutions of higher education and businesses are more common, but one could hardly call them widespread. As the central driving force of colleges and universities is the business of knowledge, a commonality with proprietary providers and business segments that engage in education is increasingly real. It is a matter of cooperation on the one hand versus duplication and cutthroat competition on the other. As noted in Chapter Nine, several corporate universities are already providing programs that seem to be duplicates of what the traditional colleges and universities have always considered to be "their" programs.

In weighing the position of businesses and their involvement in education, it is clear that many of these businesses are developing their own educational resources because they cannot find the types of educational and training resources they need, or because the appropriate resources are not convenient, or because the cost of using external resources is far greater than a company's cost of providing such resources internally. Businesses are not in the business of education as their primary activity. Most develop educational techniques as an adjunct activity to help prepare or update employees in specific areas that will help drive primary business activities. Becoming involved in education is not their preferred course of action. Besides, developing educational activities is costly and uses resources that could otherwise be used to help build and expand the enterprise's primary line of business. Nevertheless, businesses become involved in providing education because they need a workforce that is well versed and possesses the skills and knowledge that will help the business succeed.

This is certainly one area in which colleges and universities could benefit by establishing more direct partnerships with businesses. Through these partnerships, the colleges and universities could work to supply the required educational services that are a first priority for the business enterprise. The benefits for both parties are significant. The business can take advantage of the expertise in knowledge creation and dissemination of a local college or university. The institution could contract for services over a short or long period of time, thereby helping develop new sources of independent revenue or capital support. The company does not have to go through the expense of developing facilities or programs that detract from its bottom line. The college or university can improve its enrollments and revenue base. Everybody wins. Community colleges, including the Los Angeles Community College District, have recognized this and have developed extensive partnerships with area businesses. Others, including traditional colleges, need to explore these opportunities to assess how they strategically fit the institution's niche.

Some universities have already done that. NYNEX partners with twenty-three New England universities. Eaton Department Stores of Canada links with community colleges for a degree in retail selling. But several businesses have state-of-the-art facilities that exceed the best educational facilities found on most campuses. The extensive research and development that occurs in such companies is often the springboard from which the technologies of the new information age are born. Cognizant of this, Arizona State University has located one such center on its campus. Through interconnections between the academy and leading businesses, both can benefit by interfacing in the classroom and the laboratory and by adding to the capacity of both entities. Developing seamless connections in all of these areas would greatly facilitate learning and would cut down on the time-constraining red tape that impedes high levels of cooperation and mutual benefit.

The proprietary providers of education are expanding. Through their presence on facilities such as the Internet, they are easily becoming a viable alternative to traditional higher education. Colleges and universities should be concerned about the potential debilitating effects of the cutthroat competition that will come as these proprietaries become stronger financially, more adept at responding to the demands of professional and lifelong learning, and more closely identified with high-quality education and user-friendliness. Whatever one thinks of the quality of proprietary providers' services, there are areas in which proprietary providers and colleges and universities can and should cooperate.

Cooperation is not an unknown to the proprietary providers. Already, companies such as Sylvan Learning Centers are linking with universities as partners. Sylvan has a partnership with Johns Hopkins University, which allows Sylvan to provide learning assistance, conduct testing assessments, and contract educational services. Sylvan's partnership with the National Association of Secondary School Principals gives Sylvan access to assistance, assessment, and contract services at the secondary level, letting Sylvan help students with special problems or special needs.

These cooperative efforts offer interesting alternatives for remediation at the college and university level. Public colleges and universities provide educational opportunities for a wider range of learners, due to cost, than the proprietaries can. The proprietaries have the flexibility and capability of offering highly specialized educational services in both remedial and specialized areas, which can benefit learners in focused or more traditional academic programs. Both could benefit from cooperating with each other. The university would have access to specialized assistance for learners who need remediation. The proprietary schools would further their value and expertise. Most important, the learner's needs could be more easily and effectively served. Seamlessness in using services and programs between these two educational providers would facilitate efficiency, serve the learner at a higher level of effectiveness, and allow all of higher education to meet the ever growing demand for knowledge and information.

Society as an Important Partner

Society is often seen only as the source of demands on higher education. Particularly in a time when the public views education as a cost rather than an investment, it is hard to get past the reluctance and the criticism to perceive the positive aspects of social concern for education. In the information age, society will thrive only if education thrives. The better the quality of education, the better the state of knowledge and the quality of life.

For this reason, society is an essential partner in the information age. As education increases the capacity to process information and compete globally, the needs of education will be seen as investments once more. The value and significance of research will grow especially from this. By pushing forward the frontiers of knowledge through education in the same way science has pushed forward the boundaries of the universe, economic activity will be richly stimulated. But economic growth without social improvement would make that growth unstable. The historical antagonism between haves and have-nots has always produced tension, and sometimes wrenching change. Resolving key social problems through education will help stabilize the new age. It will also build a better understanding of and public support for aspects of education that are seen today as abstract and unconnected to the everyday world. By adapting to lifelong learning needs, using technology to ease access, and engaging in appositive learning, the world will become a rich and challenging laboratory for educators and their students.

Once the value of education to individuals and to society as a whole is realized, the public will again be willing to tax itself for the sake of education. As more people are tied to education and the range of institutions that serve knowledge, the base of support will grow. Because knowledge will be connected with economic well-being and wealth, resources to sustain education will become a necessary part of public and private spending.

Government as an Important Partner

Public spending is integral to the quality of education. Science research, for example, requires costly supercolliders, vehicles for exploring space, and technology to crunch vast databases. It requires costly innovations to link technology to biology, chemistry, and the study of the structure of living beings. In the United States, governments, both state and federal, will have to join with the private sector to provide the very significant investments future science will need.

The remodeling of physical plants to make them electronically capable, the need for network backbones to take technology to students and consumers, the management of large databases such as the Human Genome Project, and the exploration of the sea and space cannot go forward without sustained public investments.

The primary role of government in education, both in the United States and around the world, will be to seed programs and projects and stimulate necessary partnerships. Government must reclaim the basic responsibility for core and essential education and must retard the growing habit of passing costs on to users, without regard for the cumulative effect of this policy on access and on the necessity to improve the intellectual capacity of all citizens, whether they can afford to pay or not. Financial aid must be recast. It cannot be denied or turned solely into loans, which would sentence generations to long-term and sizeable obligations. The only fair route to resolution is to accept students based on ability and then finance them based on need. Repayment of loans should be linked to tax incentives, which help individuals pay off their loans while they are gainfully employed and help increase the competency of society through the exercise of their educational talents and expertise.

Too often, we focus on what governments should do instead of what they should not do. In the urge to reform education at all levels because of cost and questionable results, governments have moved from setting policy to legislating specifics. Governing boards from the school districts to the ivy halls have been turbulent in their actions to take control and to reform. The positions of college and university presidents along with school superintendents are turning over as never before. Boards are moving from setting constraints and boundaries through policy (which is what they should do) to becoming involved in personnel decisions, unit-level budgets, and management of the institutions (which is what they should not do). Government should never manage knowledge. History shows that when government manages, knowledge suffers. Romania is a recent case in point. Government held the universities under tight control. Political favors determined which scholars would have the access and resources to research and teach. Romania's universities were decimated by the experience. Boards must return to the principle of hiring leaders, making expectations clear, setting policies, and holding people accountable.

Business as an Important Partner

Business can partner with higher education, as well as with education in general, in two ways—by providing research opportunities and support and by helping link the world of work to the world of scholarship. The support of research through grants, equipment, laboratories, and physical facilities is a traditional role that businesses already understand and play well. But linking work to the classroom in an ongoing manner, providing real-world situations and opportunities for problem solving and learning, offering contract learning, and providing settings where appositive learning can take place will all call for new alliances and new ways of interaction. Business, for example, can provide the computers, the software, and the learning expectations. Allowing employees to perform their jobs as they study and learn will also be valuable. Rather than investing heavily in running their own schools, businesses would gain long-term results from using every level of a more seamless system of education that is relevant to work-related learning. This would help build the necessary infrastructure to induce excellence at that level.

Major information businesses such as Microsoft can help revolutionize education by making their expertise available in the digitizing, storing, and retrieving of the essential basic information that underpins education. It is quite conceivable that the capacity of a company like Microsoft, with its sophistication and resources, could fundamentally displace much of high school and lower-division college education, which essentially involves the transfer of information. Software packages, CD-ROMs, and diskettes could easily store and transmit the information that survey courses now require students to labor through. Proprietary and jurisdictional interests aside, an alliance between schools and sophisticated providers can do much to heighten the quality of education and reduce some of its costs. Higher education would gain significantly from a national seminar on these matters involving top information providers, university leaders, librarians, technology managers, student representatives, and faculty of renown. The ideas from this open discussion could guide thinking about how each sector could improve the quality of education from its vantage point.

Higher Education as an Important Partner

Rather than protecting turf, higher education needs to shed some of it. The traditional lines between levels have resulted in a segmented system. These boundaries have permitted each level to blame the other for the shifts we have seen in education from kindergarten to postdoctoral study. Because quality and education are synonymous, many have turned to raising the bar as the solution to a better education. Exclusivity may have worked in the industrial age, but it will not work in the information age. Higher education must reform itself and take the lead in convening the best minds to guide in the new Renaissance. Rather than being a crutch, technology must be a major resource in reconfiguring the educational delivery system.

To keep quality, institutions will have to focus on their strengths and specialize in them. The hard-and-fast rules of the past, which were designed to ensure competence, will have to give way to flexible, learner-centered, and transdisciplinary appositive learning.

To remain competent, faculty will have to learn continually like everyone else. The Ph.D. will not serve for life. Knowledge will change too fast. Competency will need to accompany tenure. Faculty will become mobile via technology, will be able to teach in a number of settings simultaneously, and will see tenure in a given institution as less essential. Technology will put the best faculty in a given subject or problem area in great demand. Faculty without these competencies will be in less demand or in supportive roles. Some of the latter may move elsewhere in the seamless system to improve competency in the areas in which their individual talents lie.

None of this is intended to deride or scare, but the stakes in the information age are high: the society that educates everyone will thrive.

CHAPTER TWELVE

The Academy of the Future: Scenarios and Models

———◦◦◦◦———

Throughout this book, we have argued that the society that educates all of its people will thrive in the new age. Others, Dill and Sporn, for example, urge a new perspective, one that shifts from higher education, the provider, to higher education, the server, in a "new knowledge industry" (1995, p. 149). They see a more proactive business community, government agencies, social groups, telematics firms, and midcareer learners as competitors and collaborators in redesigning how society creates and uses knowledge effectively.

This will stimulate a shift in the emphases that guide our thinking about higher education from faculty, curricula, teaching, and instructional development to learners, learning needs, and learning development. Dill and Sporn reason, and we agree, that the new university will become society's learning commons for the future. In previous chapters, we have charted the trends and environmental forces that are forging change in higher education. In this chapter, we discuss what all of these trends and forces indicate, as we begin to sketch what learning will be like in the new age. We also develop several models that individual colleges and universities might adopt, as they seek to fit effectively into the new millennium.

NEW FACES OF LEARNING

We have suggested throughout that colleges and universities in the United States and around the world face quantum change. We have also supported the view that higher education must take the initiative to address the knowledge needs of the information age. Virtual universities are evolving outside the circle of current university practice and excellence. The Western Governors University (WGU), a virtual university, reflects this, having been designed by education bureaucrats and politicians without major contribution from the present academy. For-profit institutions of learning are thriving, reaching out especially to midcareer and work-bound adults. This struggle for the soul of the university is being won on the innovative side by those outside the academy. Magrath's argument, outlined earlier, is that if the academy does not change from within, change will be imposed from without (1997a, 1997b, and interview with authors, 1996). To this we add, change will be effected not only by regulation but also and especially by competing institutions.

Change in institutional structures alone will not suffice. Change in the curriculum is also essential. Courses and discipline-based degrees are likely not to serve a cross-disciplinary world as well as a disciplinary one. Learning modules that can be combined to meet both the learners' needs and the faculty's sense of excellence and competency are likely to be the new basic units of education. Modules can be delivered by any knowledge or information provider, much as software is now made available. The critical element will be how these modules are combined in the learning plan of an individual student to satisfy appropriate standards of competency and mastery.

This is not a new idea. Already, graduate education exhibits these characteristics, characteristics that have contributed to the world primacy of American higher education. As noted before, Kerr was especially insightful when he spoke of "constructive chaos" (Perkins, 1965, pp. 25–27). Constructive chaos involves internal excellence coping with external criticism. The external criticisms of higher education have continued over a significant period of time, likely evidence of their realness and persistence. Higher education must respond from its base of excellence and genuinely change if it is to preserve excellence and serve society well.

The isolation of the campus is a large part of current dissatisfaction. Universities are still designed to serve resident, traditional learners better than they are able to serve new learners. Continuing education and extension education are used, but they still hold second-class status in the overall university. The long-term solution to this problem is a new pattern of connectivity, one that links the classroom to the workplace. This will allow not only ongoing learning but also will create a real-world context for appositive learning.

NEW INSTITUTIONAL SHAPES

As discussed earlier, the kind of transformation that new learning will require comes in waves or phases, parts of which are already occurring in some institutions. The squeeze of reduced funding and increased expectations is nearly a decade old. Digital learning is rapidly expanding as a means to contain the information explosion in manageable proportions and as a method of effectively reaching learners. Virtual universities exist worldwide, offering modular learning. The typical flow in using modules is from enhanced module to delivered module, from enhanced course to delivered course (where courses persist), and from enhanced program to delivered program. Yet, even the virtual universities vary in the models they are currently creating. Some have core faculty with digital programs; others have core faculty and clusters of digital programs; and the full-blown virtual university is a desktop university with no core faculty, only digital programs.

Global universities are growing in number. The most recent is the Duke University Research University being set up near Bangkok, Thailand. Campuses abroad have a mixed history, but most existed before the world became a global village. Commercial providers thrive, today filling the niches of absence by the academy, tomorrow building those niches into substantive programs of transdisciplinary learning. Personal learning is on the increase as people with their personal computers get on the web, use information channels, and search software to acquire information. Soon, when learners can demonstrate and be certified on what they have learned through accredited institutions, personal learning will become recognized knowledge.

Of the several phases of transformation discussed in Chapter Five, the last three waves (commercialization wave, personally directed learning wave, and wireless education wave) are the most ephemeral. In particular, groupware educational programs will involve learning by interactive sessions connected by computer. Asynchronous conferencing and chat spaces are but primitive predecessors of this means of group learning and group problem solving. Wireless education via satellite is not new, but it is growing. It is largely one-topic intensive learning. But its extension to a series of modules and from modules to programs is only a matter of time. As each form of learning becomes more widely accepted and its use becomes more widespread, newer innovations will be driven by new unanswered questions, incomplete information, academic inquiry, efforts at verification, and new discoveries, which have traditionally come from the academy.

Delivery systems alone cannot sustain education in the new age. The systematic effort to shape an open learning process that advances knowledge at the rate and pace required will provide that sustenance. As we argued in Chapter Three, the real revolution will be in how we learn. Current learning is academic and rooted in basic research; it is discipline and profession based; it is homogeneous and institutionally specialized. It is academically accountable, with its quality determined by peers. New learning is, by contrast, knowledge produced in the context of application, transdisciplinary, heterogeneous, and institutionally diverse. It is socially accountable, with its quality determined by intellectual acceptance and the durability of the knowledge or solution involved. The university designs and structures that overlay this core of new learning will be pluralistic and not dominated by a single model. We see future models evolving from differentiation rather than from cloning, and we urge institutions to focus strategically on areas of distinction as the basis for interacting with their environments. We have urged that strategic planning be specific to an institution's character and involve a careful analysis and setting of priorities that distinguish the institution. This process will help universities turn into learning commons, where unique strengths and programs of excellence are connected distinctively to research and the scholarship of appositive learning.

UNIVERSITIES AS
LEARNING ORGANIZATIONS

In the business world, new organizational forms are redefining organizations. Business managers and chief executive officers speak of flexible, flat organizations that combine, close, and recombine at a rhythm and pace that stays one step ahead of the competition and the rapid cycles of change in the global economy. We have argued that the new metaphor for higher education in this way of thinking is the space capsule. "Thinking as you go" is required as the space capsule adapts to its environment and sheds its parts to keep the shell and central equipment of the spacecraft intact and on mission. In the case of the university, the core activity is how we create and process information to extract new knowledge—learning as we go, and adapting how we are organized to inculcate what we have learned. In this scenario, the university is a connective enterprise, a kind of fractal, shell, or home page that can connect necessary elements of excellence anywhere at any time necessary to enable discovery and learning.

In Chapter Six, we summarized how others have described the connective aspect of a university—as a conglomerate, a general contractor, a network, and a culture. We prefer to think of the university as a composite—a learning commons in which specialties of excellence connect in varying ways to form an open living system in which ideas thrive or diminish and eventually evolve into modules of discovery and learning that are customized to fit the needs of individual and institutional learners.

The challenge to attain excellence requires an enabling shell or commons that attracts innovative faculty and thinkers to join the enterprise. After all, faculty are entrepreneurs par excellence. Their talent and knowledge will make or break an institution. For this reason alone, we need to include them in the design and challenge of building the connectivity for the new college or university. We must especially question the tendency exemplified by the WGU of not inviting faculty involvement at the beginning of design and change. We see the first rule of the new university as bringing together the best talent on a topic (one that already distinguishes a campus) and through the learning commons connecting and enabling their related research and learning. In this way, excellence will drive the knowledge core and ensure that learning is not simply driven by the popular issues or those for which sponsors, and their funding, abound.

Students will link with these faculty in learning modules, in which learning is active and students are contributing partners. Curricula will lead toward demonstrations of competency, for which capstone projects, examinations, demonstrations, and other related outcomes of learning are clear. Students in a module will be connected by technology—chat spaces, e-mail, simulated software experiments, laboratory assignments, and an electronic classroom—that is, a learning situation in which the student is connected with the professor around the clock by keyboard or by voice or by other new technology that comes along. Faculty mentors will use promising student-assistants to respond to e-mail and other queries at odd hours or when the professor is not available. In this way, help will be available twenty-four hours a day, whenever students need it. Lectures will be on CD-ROM. Problems and complementary materials will be on diskette. Students can play and replay these until they comprehend them. Even on the road, faculty will be accessible by e-mail or cellular phone. Faculty will also be free to teach or research at any number of institutions, because they will be less place bound. Students will be able to design a learning program by packaging modules from a variety of institutions, for a fee and with faculty guidance. Learning will be by contract and study plan.

Cooperative ventures and strategic alliances will provide internships and learning laboratories for students. Research will also involve composite funding and plural sponsors, as the cost of equipment and the tools of learning in science and medicine, among others, become considerable. Every physicist cannot have a supercollider. Some problems of the new age will require massive talent to resolve. Although individual scientists and scholars will still contribute, groups will become increasingly useful. After all, the top quark took over four hundred scientists twenty years to uncover, and fractal geometry is the product of a number of mathematical minds. As we venture further into the universe, these problems will only get more complex and profound. Businesses, driven by the hypercompetition of the global marketplace and the information age, will see research as a tool for staying at the cutting edge and setting the benchmark for competitors. Because knowledge drives the information age, businesses will invest more than they ever have in pushing the frontiers of knowledge forward.

In information age learning, faculty-learner connections will go beyond the degree and may well extend over a lifetime. As is sometimes the case in graduate education, the partnership in learning will continue when the intellectual ties once established are nurtured by common interests and common long-term problems. Complex problems will stimulate group linkages to resolve what single minds may struggle over.

Colleges and schools within larger universities will become more self-directed, as self-directed teams become the core of the new flexible and flat organization. Autonomy and resources will devolve to these knowledge units, as will requirements to raise much of their own revenue. Variable fees and tuition will become more commonplace, and colleges of arts and sciences will no longer subsidize the rest of the institution. Programs that use their modules will have to find ways to pay for them or to exchange learning modules of comparable value.

The central administration will provide the essential utilities required by the learning commons, including the digital library, the central computer ports, the backbones and servers. They will coordinate fundraising, assisting colleges and schools and sorting out donors to match donor interest with unit needs. Research will also be centrally coordinated, with development of intellectual property rights and policies as the centerpieces of coordination. The central administration will manage government funds to ensure that the university's research and teaching activities are appropriately seeded. Development funds in the form of incubator projects, project proposals, and other venture funding will also be managed centrally. In this way, the learning commons platform will connect the essential lifelines of each of its units to ensure excellence and market responsiveness for the university.

SCENARIOS OF FUTURE UNIVERSITIES

We have talked throughout about examples and trends of forces that are beginning to shape higher education. In this section, we "prognosticate" how these forces may translate into a variety of specific models. Certainly, individual colleges and universities will take a variety of shapes. Some may be like the pure models we describe here, and others will be hybrids or mixes. In any event, as change is certain, the following presents a variety of future forms that we believe will become more and more prevalent in the academy over the next several years.

Composite Universities

The Association of Governing Boards provides our first scenario of the future (Association of Governing Boards, 1996). Based on activities at the University of Southern California, Indiana University, and the University of Michigan, Responsibility Center Management (RCM) offers a version of the central core of a learning commons. RCM combines mission, accountability, effective use of resources, and restructuring. It allocates earned revenues and indirect costs to units, vests unit deans and faculties with fiscal responsibility commensurate with their authority, requires units to develop budgets by relating expected earned revenue to focused expenditures required for bottom-line targets in the units, rewards effective performance with permission to carry forward surpluses and sanctions nonperformance by requiring deficits be paid, and earns sufficient revenues centrally to complement unit revenues in implementing university-wide priorities or to recognize unit or program differences.

At the University of Florida, the university has created a "bank" as a method of allocating all costs to the two major functions of teaching and research (Lombardi and Capaldi, 1997). Here, the intent is to eliminate the traditional method of allocation, in which budgets are subject to across-the-board increases or decreases. Instead, actual positive performance is rewarded and loss of performance is penalized. So one department that sees a shrinkage of enrollment and scholarly activity will have its budget reduced while another department that sees increases in enrollments and research will see its budget increased. Overall, new resources may not be needed as much as in the past because internal reallocation takes resources from where they are not needed and applies them where they are needed.

In these scenarios, the university is the resource connector. It devolves learning to the schools and colleges; it moderates research projects and related revenues needed to fund the core of buildings, labs, equipment, and management; and it ensures balance in line with mission and related priorities. This central type of management addresses such problems as undergraduate education subsidizing graduate education or sustaining arts and sciences programs, such as the fine arts. Because resources are shifted toward excellence or toward balance, promising programs can be supported until they can generate revenue to sustain themselves. Core programs, which balance learning in areas of excellence, can receive sustaining support.

The composite university is an easy model to implement, for it is an overlay: it connects existing resources and programs to foster change. It will fit any existing university that has multiple revenue and expenditure streams, especially the research university. This approach allows for incremental change. It will succeed in the long run if the changes being funded are genuinely tied to excellence and areas of distinction. A world requiring high performance will settle for no less.

Student-Centered Colleges and Universities

In its simplest form, the composite university is the brainchild of administrators. It says little about the curriculum and how we must teach in the future. To see a contrasting picture, take the case of an undergraduate seminar about the future university taught by one of the authors. Self-directed teams of students were asked to design their model university, after they had conducted focus groups with university stakeholders, both internal and external. The contrast between the student design and the administrator-centered model just described is instructive. The student-designed universities are focused, the programs are specific and purposeful, and the education is aimed at developing job-related skills.

INTERNATIONAL BUSINESS TECHNOLOGY UNIVERSITY. An interesting example of the student-centered model is the International Business Technology University, which was designed to offer direct instruction, distance learning, and optional placements in international locations. The curriculum provides analytical and problem-solving skills acquired individually and in groups. The learning that results is expected to link the student to the university after graduation in a lifelong learning relationship. Learning modules are offered in a flexible trimester schedule that meets students' needs and provides a modern and forward-looking education.

The university is organized around an international board of governors. The international board includes regional chancellors, the chair of the alumni association, the chair of a staff organization, the strategic planner, an academic board representative, and a nonvoting legal counsel. Board chairs are elected for two-year terms. A two-thirds vote is required for major policies and regulations. Regional boards govern regional campuses. They include but are not limited to the chair of the state senate education committee, the presidents of regional campuses, the regional alumni representative, and the university chancellor, who chairs the regional board. The regional board directly oversees the regional chancellors.

The academic board is hired by the international board. It oversees instruction and provides academic materials to the few faculty needed for accreditation and to the educational consultants. Educational consultants are term instructors in a given field of expertise. They must have a minimum of three years experience in the field and must have undergone a three-month course in teaching techniques. Educational consultants do not teach out of the book but reconfirm what students have learned from traditional instruction and through technology. There is no large or tenured faculty. The equivalent faculty role is played by the academic board.

Learning modules lead to master's degrees in international trade; professional accountancy; information systems; international banking; professional investment methods; and analysis and design, which deals with quality management techniques, pricing and public policy, and human resource principles, among other topics. Undergraduate degrees focus on information systems, international trade, computer science, transportation logistics, and management and administration. Students construct their study plans with academic assistance. Students are expected to know English plus one other language.

Tuition and fees are kept modest, to ensure affordability and reflect the lack of the continuing cost of a large core faculty. They cover module costs, testing out of courses, technology, and labs. Educational consultants do the teaching, are paid negotiated stipends, and are annually evaluated. Maintenance and capital construction costs are paid one-third by the state general revenue fund and two-thirds from university sources or gifts. The university is guided by a strategic plan with key performance indicators evaluated annually.

ROCKY MOUNTAIN COLLEGE. Rocky Mountain College (RMC) is another example of the student-centered college. It is an accredited four-year college with a year-round, three-semester program. Learning modules and classes are offered at hours convenient for students with jobs. Day care is available whenever classes are in session. Transfer from community colleges or other institutions is open. Advising is part of a professor's assignment (twenty-five students per faculty member), with central advising serving as a small backup that deals with short-term issues. Classes are kept at forty or fewer to promote interaction with classmates and faculty. For traditional students, housing is in privately owned dormitories.

RMC is organized traditionally, with a board of trustees, a regular teaching faculty, and professionals who oversee field placements and learning. The campus offers a range of majors, with an emphasis on linking the world of work to the world of learning. It is an undergraduate university where research is directly linked to instruction.

Programs are offered in education, business, computer science, and such standard subjects as nursing and allied health, the performing arts, and arts and sciences. Technology is an integral part of all instruction, to link study and work, particularly for the nontraditional learner. A general education core module provides opportunities for analytical reasoning and problem solving. Field study and active learning are central to all degrees. Placement involves partnerships with public and private employers. By linking the problems of the workplace to the theory and analysis of the learning module, appositive learning occurs and provides comprehension of real-world issues, both pragmatically and intellectually. To ensure exposure to quality thinking, one-third of the one hundred credits for graduation are general education modules. More than one field placement is required for graduation. For example, education majors must complete two practicums plus one full semester of student teaching.

A graduation rate of 60 to 65 percent of a beginning class is a campus goal. It is complemented by a goal of placing 85 percent of graduates in their chosen fields of study. Students pay 45 percent of the cost of their education. Scholarships complement this, especially for the academically excellent. The state funds 40 percent of the cost of education. The remainder is covered through auxiliary for-profit enterprises, which contribute annually to academic costs as a part of their contracts. To reduce costs, one-half of texts are digitized and available on-line or on CD-ROM.

The physical plant is centered on a single, large parking lot. A multistory central building houses offices and classrooms, with offices adjacent to the teaching areas. This allows easy access to faculty and offers occasion to include students conveniently in faculty projects and research. A main courtyard serves as a university commons. Adjacent buildings include a dining hall, gymnasium, traditional resident halls, and nontraditional family residence complexes. Computer labs are distributed across the campus and are open twenty-four hours a day. The library is linked to regional libraries and to digitized library consortia. Given the state-of-the-art technology on the campus, students can access these resources from twenty-four hour labs, from their rooms or at any modem for those with dockable computers. Because the campus has been designed both physically and technologically for easy information access, active learning is encouraged, and the field experiences and placements are easily linked to residence or classroom. As a consequence, learning is active and can occur at any time.

EPIPHANY STATE UNIVERSITY. Still another example of the student-centered university is Epiphany State University (ESU), where the theme is, "we bring the old and new together for the best possible results." This university focuses its efforts on students achieving a well-rounded experience that is anchored by a comprehensive career-counseling program, which extends from entry to exit. General education requirements are kept to a minimum so that students can begin work in their major fields of emphasis early in their studies.

The organizing idea of ESU is an affordable tuition, small classes, job placement, and a nurturing experience. That experience is overseen by a board of regents, which includes a member of the legislature, a student representative, a community member, a donor, a parent, and the university vice president. The administration is small, with a president, a vice president, and three deans. The university has three colleges—arts and sciences, business, and technology. This flat, flexible, and self-directing administrative team reflects the lean management structure of twenty-first century organizations.

An undergraduate institution, ESU emphasizes counseling throughout a student's enrollment. Each student must have a study plan built at entry. The plan constitutes a contract between the student and ESU to encourage timely completion of the degree.

Geared for the traditional student, ESU's students are a select group and come from the upper third of the college bound. The college links residency to learning in a twenty-four hour experience. Study halls are located on each dormitory floor, housing a wide range of technology and related equipment. Laptop computers are available to all students, and labs are coordinated by student mentors.

General education involves two history classes (one in multicultural studies) and one class each in English, laboratory science, and mathematics. Required are four years of world affairs modules and technology modules specifically related to one's major field. A January term in which students enroll during the winter break permits the study of special subjects, and a progressive internship is required, in which a student interns in his or her chosen field for four years, moving from an entry-level experience progressively and annually to an advanced one in the same business or professional field.

Faculty have three-year renewable contracts. Evaluations are triennial, coinciding with the decision over renewal. Prized professors may have contracts for as long as seven years, in which case their evaluation occurs in the seventh year. In this particular institution, there is no tenure.

ESU links its admissions and modules of study to national standards of performance and demonstrated competency required of high school graduates by federal mandate. To this base competency, ESU adds the knowledge that students will need to compete in a global society. Technology plays a vital role in this preparation. Digitized databases, libraries, the World Wide Web, and related intranets are accessible to all students. This access must be demonstrably linked to each student's learning by teacher and student alike, through evidence of its use in the classroom, the research lab, science labs, and the workplace or internship site.

The university budget is that which is traditional to the public college or small university. The state funds 50 percent of the cost of education. Tuition and fees fund 34 percent. Sales and auxiliaries provide an additional 3 percent of revenue, and annual gifts provide the remaining 13 percent. A capital budget standard for a state college is used, including current means for calculating maintenance and depreciation. The institution uses a strategic plan to guide its annual decisions, as we have proposed in an earlier book (Rowley, Lujan, and Dolence, 1997). Within this plan, key performance indicators are few. They include tuition at 34 percent of cost, small class sizes as permitted by the 34 percent of cost indicator, annual job placement rates in the preferred field, and evidence of currency in technology.

Student-centered universities like these three are undergirded by several key themes—excellence in teaching, access for students, effective and active learning that can be demonstrated, good advising, and learning linked to society's needs. These students are also unabashed about the need to link theory and practice better. They see the workplace as a source of problems that a good education can help resolve. They also see those problems as part of an ongoing flow of learning issues. These issues lead them to look at education as continuing through life by helping build ways to shape and deal with change. As a group, these ideas are not far removed from the Cornerstones Principles Project of the California State University, discussed earlier. The cornerstones are excellence in teaching, access, effectiveness and accountability, and linking learning to society's needs.

PERPETUAL LEARNING COLLEGES AND UNIVERSITIES

Perpetual learning is based on the premise that individuals will want continuous learning opportunities throughout their lifetimes in order to keep abreast of change. It involves a shift in thinking about education from being discontinuous to continuous. People want to acquire ongoing knowledge and skills that are relevant to changing events and that permit an intellectual independence. This allows them to piece together the ideas and information they need to be informed and competitive with other acquisitive people and societies. Gone is the tolerance for seat time learning, course-based instruction, and place-bound resources, such as libraries or laboratories. Instead of accepting learning that is facility and institution centered, tomorrow's students want learning to center on them, and they want the means for making learning portable.

Portable learning requires a holistic curriculum. This holistic framework links the learner's goal to the learning mode, the method of delivery, and the content of the learning outcome. The learner's goal drives this process.

If the traditional degree is desired, then the classroom mode and the lecture method will lead to the requisite skill or knowledge. If skills are desired, then laboratory work or an internship mode will apply, along with experimentation to produce the requisite skill. For each learner goal, there is a corresponding mode and method to yield the desired content. The significance of this lies in the open and portable system of learning that technology has unlocked. The problem facing a learner shapes the learning goal and the desired content outcome. To achieve this outcome, the learner now has a myriad of tools, modes, and methods from which to choose in piecing together a learning strategy. This focuses learning on the learner. It transforms learning into a continuous stream that the learner can access. It also lets the learner reach out to any provider to customize the learning strategy. This process is the basis of our perpetual learning curriculum framework, as outlined in the following lists:

Learner's Goal

Degree

Skill

Trade

Enrichment

Technical capability

Certification

Professional development

Vocational
Self-discovery
Job
Personal development
Tools
Other goals

Modes of Learning

Classroom
Laboratory
Seminar
Home
Dormitory
Library
Workplace
Network
Shop floor
Factory floor
Other modes

Methods of Learning

Lecture
Experimentation
Simulation
Personalized systems of instruction
Computer-based learning
Collaboratories
Research papers
Learner projects
Learning styles
Other learning methods

Content

    Knowledge

    Skills

    Outcomes

    Other content

One major example of the perpetual learning university can be found on the World Lecture Hall web site (www.utexas.edu/world/lecture/index.html), which lists hundreds of disciplines and thousands of courses, readily available for perusal by anyone who is interested. A veritable smorgasbord of information and knowledge is just a keyboard away from any learner. Another example is the Global Network Academy (www.gnacademy.org:8001/uu-gna/index.html), which lists over ten thousand courses located on the web. These are just two of a large number of sources of information packages available to the individual learner.

Modes of delivery also vary. Ford Motor Company has designed and redesigned learning around the garage bay. These systems are satellite linked, computer driven, interactive directly with the vehicle, flexible, and connected to powerful databases that determine probability, use sophisticated diagnostics to pinpoint problems, and provide diagrams and other information sources to guide in a remedy. If all of this can be done to change a spark plug, imagine what can be done with the operating room, the war decision room, or the strategic management room, and for those who wish to study and understand them. What may be lacking in traditional higher education is not the capacity to provide information relevantly and differently but rather the will to design new modes to address new problems and link them to the curriculum.

Methods of educational delivery are also evolving rapidly. Methods are a conduit for knowledge. Research shows that different learning methods have different effects on learner performance. Pascarella and Terenzini (1991) note that the audio-tutorial approach is built around independent study sessions, in which students work independently on learning tasks in a laboratory properly equipped with sources and access tools, such as tapes, televisions, and video recorders, among others. Using this approach, learners gain an average of 8 percentile points over learning in the traditional format. Packaging information for use in this method would noticeably increase performance and the quality of learning. Computer-based learning is interactive, and it results in a 10 percentile point increase by using simulation, programmed instruction, and drill and tutorial exercises. Developing modes and methods like these will be an essential task for the perpetual university.

The perpetual learning university would specialize in a library of tools and information units like those just described, along with a personalized system of instruction, which would guide their combination into modules a learner could master. Self-paced learning complemented by immediate feedback through on-line assessment would be a part of this and would also shape learning. A new software engine called Microcosm already exists, which can help faculty build personalized systems for any discipline. Such learning packages, according to Pascarella and Terenzini, add an average of 10 percentile points to learning and comprehension.

Virtual Universities

Virtual universities are already in existence and are growing steadily, as described in Chapter Five. They offer the learner an increasing array of options that come with and without traditional college credit and degrees. The growth of this type of information age institution is phenomenal and worldwide.

WESTERN GOVERNORS UNIVERSITY. The most notable among the virtual universities is the WGU. It depends on asynchronous learning networks and other approaches that provide on-demand learning over a computer network. The WGU is presently designing an Internet-based catalogue navigator, which students will use to find and select courses and to assess their comprehension and skills. The WGU offers a competency-based associate of arts degree; workplace certifications via industry-selected competencies; a mechanism to broker traditional and nontraditional course work; assistance in accessing financial aid, libraries, counseling, books, and learning materials; and regional centers. The WGU's web address is www.concerto.com/smart/vu/vu.html.

The idea is simple. Students use a personal computer and surf the learning network for courses of study. If interested in what they find, they apply electronically, have their records reviewed, and are admitted. They establish a study plan and begin work on courses that are self-paced and provide immediate feedback to ensure that they master prior steps before they advance to the next unit of work. The system tracks success, provides instantaneous feedback, and the mastery a student achieves is demonstrated at each step along the way. Resources from digital libraries, databases, and information units on the web are a keyboard away. Completion of the study plan leads to an associate degree, with other degrees in the planning stages as of this writing.

WGU deals with entry-level instruction, which predominantly involves the transfer of information. For virtual learning, this is the easy part. More complex are virtual approaches to upper-division and graduate education. At these more advanced levels, a relevant model is the one underlying graduate education right now. In effect, it is learning through partnership.

The graduate student typically has a knowledge-based research relationship with faculty. Joint problem solving is the mortar of advanced learning. In the more complex virtual university, technology will allow students to work with faculty who serve as mentors and guides, using computerized learning modules to develop mastery of theories and concepts. Research will provide the occasion for sharpening and making learning more sophisticated. More and more, the problems of interest in the real world and the theoretical world will be linked. Examples lie in the exploration of the universe, cloning, the structure of matter, the resolution of cultural conflict, global economic competition, and cures for AIDS and cancer.

As information age problems evolve, their complexity will grow. Increasingly, teams of people will be needed to resolve them, as was the case in discovering the top quark. This need for supportive assistance will help make students potential partners in learning, as literally more heads become better than one. The advanced WGU will provide the on-line options necessary for such analytical study.

VIRTUAL ONLINE UNIVERSITY. Virtual Online University Inc. is another example of a virtual university. It is a nonprofit institution that offers learning from kindergarten through college (athena.edu/vou.html). Its Athena Preparatory Academy provides resources and information for primary education and for home schooling. Its sister, Athena University, offers college level learning that extends beyond the transfer-of-information level. Its courses are on the Internet, and Athena University exists only on the Internet. Athena has eight schools, each with a dean, and all under the vice president for academic affairs. The eight schools are humanities, sciences, mathematics, business, information technology, education, human science and behavior, and fine arts. The university is built around a multiuser dimension object-oriented program known as MOO. A student who logs on to the MOO encounters other users. They talk by typing, listen by reading, and manipulate objects that describe themselves, or anything else, with words.

The curriculum follows an Eidos model, which is described as a reintegration of modern disciplines appropriate for the medium of hypertext, which is the central programming language used on the Internet. It links five broad conceptual categories into a three-dimensional construction. The categories are dialectics, history, poetics, science, and ethics. Together, these categories make up a contextual framework within which discipline-specific information may be integrated.

OPEN UNIVERSITY OF CATALONIA. The Open University of Catalonia (OUC) is an example of still another type of virtual university, which has developed a program designed solely around the delivery of digital learning. Begun in 1995, OUC combines multimedia applications, electronic mail, videos, tapes, and pencil-and-paper units of learning, all of which facilitate distance learning. It is one of the first universities to be built entirely around communications technology. Two hundred students are taking degrees in business studies or educational psychology. Law, engineering, English, Catalan, and statistics are on the way. By the year 2000, OUC expects to enroll eleven thousand students.

This new cyber-student uses a personal computer, a modem, and a telephone as essential deliverers of learning information. Although basic course materials are available on paper via the mail, students across the region hand in essays, receive corrections, and communicate with each other and the teacher via e-mail. Students use the Internet, a virtual library, and a virtual chat cafeteria to stay in touch and relieve isolation. Face-to-face contacts occur twice a semester. Otherwise, students work and carry on their lives, studying as time and interest permit.

The rapid growth of OUC is interesting. It was set up in only twelve months and is continually expanding in order to have a center in every region of Catalonia. Leading academics have been commissioned to provide academic content for learning modules and to convert learning materials into interactive multimedia packages. OUC uses a variety of multimedia to provide a calendar of on-line events, lectures, video conferences, and cultural and sporting events. In this way, cyber-students are linked together into learning and social communities.

Market-Driven Colleges and Universities

The market-driven college or university resides in a digital universe. It is sensitive to learner demand regardless of geopolitical boundaries or regulations. It can cross borders and boundaries without restriction. It is an open system of information with learning modules accessible anywhere by computer. Some current interesting examples of such a college or university already exist.

IBM GLOBAL CAMPUS. This digital campus is organized around the IBM Digital Library (ike.engr.washington.edu.igc). The library is a combination of software and hardware that enables academic institutions to digitize assorted media, distribute multimedia content across public and private networks, search information, manage multimedia databases, and protect intellectual property. One of its features, the Lotus Learning Space, involves a set of modular applications that create a virtual learning environment off the shelf. IBM provides consulting and on-demand learning servers to facilitate use. Lotus Notes is an industry standard in groupware used to provide the communications infrastructure for the IBM Global Campus. Lotus Notes makes possible messaging, World Wide Web access, and learner collaboration, by way of the Internet.

Learners in this institution can use a tool called IBM Global Network (InterConnect), which is an IBM network used to access Lotus Notes instructional material. IBM provides a full range of network services in more than 850 cities around the world. IBM Internet Connection, an Internet service provider, permits local dial-up Internet connectivity in more than 800 cities and nearly 50 countries. An additional tool is the ThinkPad University, a program that lets students with an IBM ThinkPad portable computer bundle software and access resources for a fixed fee per term of study.

GLOBAL NETWORK ACADEMY. Another example is the Global Network Academy (GNA), which is a nonprofit organization incorporated in the state of Texas (www.gnacademy.org:8001/uu-gna/index.html). GNA's mission is to create a competitive market for distance educators. All of GNA's corporate activities occur on-line. GNA maintains a web site that houses a course catalogue with over ten thousand distance and virtual learning programs and courses. Their web site also includes discussion forums and "help wanted" databases for educators involved in virtual and distance learning.

GNA does not assign credit for completed courses. Rather, it carries out credit work through host institutions, which utilize its resources. Faculty compensation for courses taken through GNA is governed by the host institution, not GNA.

WORLD SPACE, INC. Still another example is World Space, Inc. (WSI), a Washington-based company that provides learning material to audiences in developing countries via a satellite-digital radio network. The first of the three satellites will launch in 1998 to cover Africa and the Middle East. WSI has received a license from the government of Trinidad and Tobago to operate a satellite to cover Latin America and the Caribbean. Australia has approved a license for South and Southeast Asia. Each satellite sheds three beams and each beam offers eighty stations. The fee for use will be $150 per unit for a special receiver.

The digital signals will carry print, audio, and visual data. A printer and video screen are needed for maximum use. But simple radio will work for basic information and related learning units. Because radios are cheaper and available to everyone, even in the remotest village, this is an approach to learning especially useful in the less developed and poorer regions of the world. It is a way to connect those otherwise ignored to the technology revolution and to the new age.

Specialty Colleges and Universities

There are a growing variety of specialty colleges and universities that are coming onto the scene. Most of these are the result of individuals or groups of other colleges and universities creating a specialized institution. That institution may or may not remain allied with the founding institution or institutions. As its main concern is to fill a demonstrated need in the marketplace, market forces determine whether it remains linked or becomes autonomous.

Theme Seven is one example of a specialty university. It is a Canadian consortium of universities and other organizations brought together to help teach teachers how to use tele-learning. The focus is on teacher education and professional development and on using tele-learning technologies in classrooms. This particular project centers on a series of Tele-learning Professional Development Schools that are actually virtual learning communities linking learners and educators. There are three Tele-learning Professional Development Schools in Quebec City and Montreal, with a fourth under way in British Columbia.

The University of Laval leads this project in establishing the Professional Development Schools. Laval assists in the practices, tools, and approaches that stimulate collaboration and inquiry among teachers, university professors, and the public. Researchers at McGill University, University of British Columbia, University of Laval, York University, University of Montreal, and Tele-university are all partners in Theme Seven.

The University of British Columbia in Vancouver, along with university colleagues in Toronto, Quebec City, and Montreal, has established an information-technology management program. The program has had assistance from Knowledge Architecture and others in the knowledge-technology business. This program trains students in the skills necessary to qualify for jobs in the field of technological support while they are receiving credits toward their high school diplomas.

Another Theme Seven module is Computer Supported Intentional Learning Environments. It is a computer-based system, designed at the University of Toronto's Ontario Institute for Studies in Education. It makes collaborative knowledge building an integral part of everyday schooling. Simon Fraser University's VIRTUAL-U is another supportive tool. It is an on-line learning environment for design, delivery, and enhancement of courses over the Internet.

Theme Seven also works on the value of electronic conferencing in professional development. The Education Network of Ontario (ENO) was set up by the Ontario Teachers Federation in 1992. It serves over fifty thousand Ontario teachers. Through ENO, teachers get advice on real issues or problems as well as ideas about new ways to do things. They share and receive advice and solutions from fellow teachers or knowledgeable experts, all through on-line interaction and conversations. This constructive use of chat spaces provides an ongoing ready reference system for teachers and those interested in improving teacher skills and performance.

Self-Directed Teams Within Colleges and Universities

Another potential model comes from the world of business. Magsaysay (1997) provides a useful summary of new and innovative ideas in the private sector, ideas associated with restructuring and reengineering organizations. Among the most insightful of these ideas is the notion of reorganizing a firm around self-directed teams. The usefulness of this concept is that if timely and substantive response is the key to success, then a flat, flexible organization that can combine relevant expertise is the most adept at focusing resources to meet the need. Structurally, the organization's vertical hierarchy of departments is displaced by functionally organized teams, which are responsible for either the completion of the whole project or for specific parts of it, reflective of the expertise of the team.

This has become more than an idea in the private sector. For example, Saturn Electronics and Engineering, an auto supply firm, reorganized itself around the concept of self-directed teams. Saturn created eight units, each run by a general manager as an independent unit of about three hundred persons. General managers have autonomy over resources and processes necessary for their product. Although there is a central purchasing unit, it exists to satisfy the eight teams. When needed, a team may purchase directly from a supplier.

The central organization is lean, with human resources, accounting, purchasing, and legal affairs under the CEO. These functional areas serve as consulting services to general managers. Units provide top management with daily briefing reports, and once a month, management meets with business units and team heads to discuss progress and problems. These meetings focus on team and business unit needs and rotate among Saturn's eight units. All meetings end with discussion of a "best practice," which allows Saturn to discover innovations and suggestions for improvement that can improve the output of the company. These meetings become forums for sharing ideas and uncovering leading-edge concepts.

The Saturn experience offers some interesting potential practices for higher education, especially in light of the tradition of collegiality and the relative autonomy of many schools, colleges, and departments. One interesting approach that is adaptable to higher education is to treat each college or school as a self-directed team—allowing these units the flexibility to develop around their areas of distinction and the financial flexibility both to generate revenues through tuition and fees and to spend or purchase according to a strategic plan in which central administration is a concurring partner. In this arrangement, central administration would serve as the enabling shell of central consulting services, much like the top management of Saturn. For example, central human resource functions, such as payroll, collective bargaining, and staff development, would assist and serve units. Faculty and staff would be unit based and tenured, where tenure exists. Fundraising could be centrally coordinated, but with broad autonomy for units to raise their own funds. Research would occur in units, with access to centrally managed technology, intellectual property, and seed funding. The precise mix of central services would vary locally.

The bureaucracy of institution-wide teaching loads, seat time, student ratios, and the like could give way to mixes of teaching and research that generate easier progress and stimulate new areas of innovation in subject fields. In such a system, mixes could vary from one self-directed unit to another, and measures of productivity could be team derived to fit the culture of scholarship in a given unit. In a collegial and supportive manner, academic managers could obtain these reports on regular intervals and use them to monitor progress and suggest adjustments if necessary. To help ensure better understanding by overall campus leadership, governing-board meetings could move from unit to unit, focusing on unit needs, especially in the prebudget phase of decision making. Also, in such a system, central administration could be placed in a position where it could negotiate conflicts across units and monitor how units meet their self-directed goals and strategic objectives. In all of this, the strategic plan would be the social contract that ties the institution together and clarifies unit goals and contributions to the broader institution.

Within colleges and schools, departments could be similarly organized but most likely within a sunset framework, in which units exist for a specific time period and then are evaluated for continuation or termination. This is especially important if the emphasis is on building self-directed teams for rapidly evolving information age issues. This entire idea is not all that far-fetched. Already, some colleges organize across disciplinary lines, which are typically more permanent. At the Evergreen State College, transdisciplinary teams are functionally organized to act in lieu of departments. The key is flexibility and the ability to organize functionally around problems, research interests, or evolving new fields of knowledge.

Other colleges have replaced departments with divisions, grouping disciplinary or profession-based departments around a common element. For example, some colleges of education have replaced many departments with a few key divisions, such as educational leadership, educational technology and statistics, teacher education, and special education. As there need be no common preferred structure in a strategic academic world that is built around an institution's strengths, the groupings could vary widely according to local strategic preferences. They would have to organize according to function and do so in ways that would nourish the culture of self-directed teams.

The entrepreneurship and innovative ideas of faculty should drive any such reorganization if it is to succeed. At Evergreen, faculty created most of the academic units by sharing common interests. Although adjustments have been made over the years in structure, the driving theme of scholars gathered around transdisciplinary common interests that have relevance outside the academy has remained.

Self-directed teams would seem most useful in comprehensive colleges and universities serving a polytechnic role. Their size, their need to relate their role to real-world problems, their limited resources, and their need to build from distinction all serve as a fertile context for developing transdisciplinary self-directed teams organized around ideas of distinction that have potential for generating financial support.

Self-directed teams might also offer a way to deal with the arts and sciences issue on a number of campuses. Arts and sciences often serve a general education role, which is supportive. Their preferred function is to offer disciplinary education. Often, arts and sciences are a sprawl of courses and programs, sometimes without a strong common bond. The division between letters or humanities and science is symptomatic of this. The division of resources, which reflects this, often widens the breach. In some places, the sciences are simply separated from the humanities. In other places, sciences, social sciences, and humanities are separated, but all of this is done along the lines of grouping vertically integrated existing disciplinary units. Such a practice separates disciplines rather than encouraging their interaction. As new fields of knowledge emerge in the new age and as lifelong learners increase in number and varied academic needs, recombining into self-directed units may offer an attractive means for reconsidering how to enhance excellence and distinction in this important core of the university.

The central issue in forming self-directed units is not to isolate scholars into vertically integrated and insulated learning units but to provide a structural means of combining those with expertise and mutual interest into units, which reflect distinction and excellence and will endure sufficiently to serve the strategic purposes of the university. As such, this is a model that might become more widely popular as the academy changes more and more to meet the needs of the new millennium.

Assessment and Competency-Based Colleges and Universities

As colleges and universities begin to pay more and more attention to the time constraints of the information age learner, one potentially effective response will be that of a system of education that seeks to know where the learner begins the interface with the institution and where that learner needs to go to achieve competency. Many learners not only resent a variety of prerequisites that they must take prior to immersing themselves in the heart of the knowledge base they want or need, but many do not need them. Just as modularization may prove a good replacement for seat time, demonstrated competency should prove to be a good replacement for prerequisites. As challenges to the current structure of the course, seat time, the degree, and other staples of today's colleges and universities come under greater scrutiny, assessment will begin to take on more and more importance.

In such a system, a learner will come to a college or university that offers the knowledge base in which the learner wishes to (or needs to) become competent. The learner will undergo a battery of assessments that will tell the learner what areas of the knowledge base are adequate, what areas need strengthening, and what areas need to be learned completely. Assessment tools will be available in a wide variety of forms, from currently familiar standardized tests, to oral examinations, electronic-inventorying techniques, and competency-based simulations. Not all learners will demonstrate their levels of competency through the same assessment methods. Each individual will be evaluated uniquely, based on the type of assessment that provides optimal measurements of that particular learner's ability. In other words, some learners will be able to demonstrate their current knowledge level with standardized testing, whereas others will be able to demonstrate their abilities through some other method that they respond better to.

Once both the learner and the institution determine the learner's initial level of understanding, they can engage in a contracting session to determine what needs to be learned, how it is to be learned, when competency should be measured, and what the outcomes of the experience should be. All of this would be done taking into account the most effective learning styles to apply to each learner. No surprises here: both parties know exactly what they are dealing with and what both expect the results of the learning experience to be. Further, such a process not only can be applied to a single module of learning but also can be applied to an entire degree program.

The effectiveness of such a learning process should be obvious. By tailoring education to fit the specific needs of each learner, the learner will be satisfied, the institution will be able to show its own effectiveness, and a lifelong relationship between the two could be well on the way. Although this model may appear cumbersome on the surface— particularly in those universities whose student-learner population might be fifty thousand or greater—the advances of technology will make such a complex process not only feasible but preferable for any college or institution whose stated mission is to deliver superior knowledge optimally to the learner. Also, there is no danger of reducing that same institution's commitment to research by adopting the learning system this model suggests. On the contrary, by peaking the knowledge transfer experience, knowledge generation should also be expanded and the college or university should also see that the bases and vitality of research will increase.

Co-op Colleges and Universities

One college or university cooperating with other institutions of higher education on the educational and research activities that benefit both of them and their learners is not a new idea; it is just a rare one. As noted earlier, most of today's colleges and universities (at least in the United States) pursue parochial interests in a competitive environment, seeking to expand campus programs, degree bases, and discipline offerings regardless of the existence of such programs at other institutions in the same service area. The excessive costs of such duplication simply do not support such practices being allowed to continue or expand in the future. Also, when many colleges or universities in the same area offer the same programs, it becomes more and more difficult for each of these institutions to provide the highest levels of excellence in the education and research experiences. Instead, by specializing in strength areas, individual campuses can more easily develop excellence and become known for those areas.

These conditions will make cooperation among colleges and universities more and more desirable, as everyone responds to the general reductions in available resources while facing the need to serve a growing demand from information age learners. The nature of this cooperation will be interesting in that some institutions will cooperate on a very formal basis, perhaps even creating still another level of bureau-cracy to oversee cooperative efforts, whereas others will find seamless ways of working directly with other educational institutions on a worldwide basis. Most models will fall somewhere in between the two extremes.

There will be two keys to success—one, the ability to create centers of knowledge excellence in high-demand disciplines and program areas; two, the ability to create seamless interfaces with other centers of educational excellence, which will provide the optimal benefits for both the learners and the institutions. For the first area, individual col-leges and universities will define for themselves where their major strengths lie and concentrate on building these into truly excellent knowledge centers. This will mean reducing duplication across their service areas and centering more and more in particular niches, in which opportunities exist and in which the college or university will be able to develop a dominating presence. For the second area, sys-tems of interchange will be enhanced by emerging technology (much of which is already available), making it possible for worldwide inter-actions and knowledge sharing, backed up with an academic admin-istrative system that tracks and credits the knowledge exchange experience without the gatekeeping that characterizes most interor-ganizational programs today. Such a seamless system will allow the learner to move from one center of excellence to another, physically or electronically, without disruption of a chosen program of study and with full credit toward the individual's learning goals. Such a system will allow the educator and the researcher to pass easily from one envi-ronment into another, achieving optimal opportunities to complete research agendas or intellectual linkages.

Again, effectiveness will be enhanced for both the learner and the college or university. The learner will be able to take advantage of the brightest minds in the world and will be able to easily keep on the lead-ing edge of a knowledge base. The college or university will be able more effectively and efficiently to redirect its resources, establish itself as a niche leader in appropriate disciplines, and increase its population of learners through the greater access of which it has become a part.

This model, along with several others developed in this chapter, will be adopted by those colleges and universities that believe they will help their campuses create a better fit between themselves and their environments. The specific application of these models will tend to reflect the resource base and strategic direction each campus has chosen for itself, and some campuses may well have a variety of different models in place at the same time to help them achieve their strategic goals. This is an exciting prospect, one in which both the learner and the campus can better maximize their objectives and goals in the evolving world of the new millennium.

MODELS FOR TRADITIONAL COLLEGES AND UNIVERSITIES

How do we make any sense out of this plethora of ideas, and what do they tell us about how colleges and universities might look in the future? Is the campus to go away completely and be replaced by the Internet? Definitely not. The various models identified up to this point, however, contain elements that suggest that the campus of the future will be different in a number of ways. In this section, we summarize the various forces for change identified in the first part of this chapter and in the preceding chapters. We project what they will mean for colleges and universities as they respond to the information age. It is important to note again that there will be no single dominant model of how a college or university will be structured or staffed in universities of the future.

Research Colleges and Universities

The model for the research university is already changing. During the twentieth century, research advanced at the expense of good undergraduate teaching. The public has made it quite clear that it is reticent to pay for this particular mix anymore.

The crucial need of society in the information age for the benefits of the research institution will help preserve it. We believe that in the twenty-first century, research universities will continue to thrive, because research drives the knowledge that drives the information age. However, the research university will not be as comprehensive or as free from restraint as it has been in the past. Like the large businesses of the economic world, the large businesses of the educational world will restructure and downsize as public funding diminishes. The research universities of the future will spin off interesting specialties. Highly specialized programs—such as those in uncommon languages—will exist in those few places where it fits the institution's role. Needed but costly support services from hazardous waste disposal to residence halls, food services, maintenance, laboratory management, computer support, and possibly entry-level instruction will be outsourced.

New Undergraduate Studies

Undergraduate education will improve, simply because the public and society's needs demand it. The new ingredient will be the pedagogy of active scholarship. It will drive more participative learning, which means linking in some reasonable way to research at the research schools. This will lead to smaller classes, leaving the retailing of the bulk of undergraduate learning, as has always been the case, to the middle-tier universities with help from the community colleges. At the research campuses, undergraduates who did not learn the basics in high school will likely find courses that transfer basic information on-line or at community colleges, where they will co-enroll. Research universities may be among those that turn undergraduate education into a three-year experience, while providing assistance to community colleges and high schools to improve the quality of introductory instruction.

When one remembers that most of the basic information needed for advanced studies will be digitally available in one format or another, it is not impossible to argue that the quality of K–12 education will improve as a digitally dexterous population of youth grow up and are exposed earlier in life to many of the basic topics essential for an informed mind in the information age. High school teachers, aided by institutes and universities through teleconferencing and on-line assistance, may silence the critics of precollege learning in the not-too-distant future, with improved skills and better learning in their classrooms.

New Graduate Studies

Graduate education, in its current apprentice and shared-learning format, will likely occur earlier in a learner's studies, at least at the senior level of study, as capstone courses, senior theses and projects, and other forms of demonstrated learning. Rather than forsaking research for simply teaching what others discover, the faculty of research universities will extend their research to their undergraduates. Better grounded in basic skills through technology and improved precollege education, these undergraduates will perform at levels that now characterize master's level study, inviting their involvement in the work of their faculty. This mentoring will enrich the research university undergraduate experience greatly.

The resulting displacement will be essential if master's and doctoral studies are to keep pace with unfolding knowledge. The volume, sophisticated nature, and rapid expansion of this new knowledge will require a reinventory of graduate offerings. Existing disciplines will be displaced by emerging ones, calling for advanced students to expand these fields. New fields of knowledge will typically be cross-disciplinary, further reshaping the specialties of graduate study. Moreover, research is increasingly a team effort, as problems become very complex. Research, especially in the sciences, will also be expensive, in terms of equipment, the costs of physical observation and discovery in the universe, the constantly increased sophistication of equipment, and the profound complexity of new problems. These typify why the enterprises of discovery and processing new knowledge will lead institutions to specialize and collaborate. It is worth noting that as the issues of the global marketplace and the universe become intricate and complex, government will find itself investing more, not less, in solving these concerns for the good of the society. These challenges will lead government to form a new partnership with higher education to face the challenges of a new age. This will occur simply because the time is at hand when no one sector of the society can singlehandedly resolve the "quarklike" issues raised by the joint events of the information explosion and the rise of a global society.

In all of this, the research university will be a shell that attracts, connects, spins off, consolidates, and eliminates programs and fields of study in the continuing effort to adapt to the knowledge explosion. The university will serve as the hub and commons where specialties connect and where university-wide resources keep the whole of the institution as a definable priority. In this sense, universities will be the learning commons that guide how new knowledge evolves.

Comprehensive Colleges and Universities

As we have argued earlier, the middle tier of colleges and universities will undergo the most significant change. Most of these campuses have for half a century aspired to become like their research relatives. Many, especially the former teachers colleges, have really turned into teaching mini-universities. Research occurs but not at the level of sophistication of the research campuses. Teaching is recognized in tenure and so it has survived by tagging along. Now, these institutions face the hard fact that they must educate the bulk of undergraduates in an age when information is exploding, rapidly evolving technology is changing how research and teaching both occur and interact, and the central utilities of a campus response such as libraries and technology are stressed or out-of-date. The lament is widespread over inadequate libraries, lack of fiber optics, too few or too old computers, outdated labs, asbestos in the hallowed halls, and no water for the ivy. Add to this the typically heavier teaching load at this level, and you have campuses in distress.

The psychological issue is as complicated as the resource issue. Trained in research universities to do the work of research faculties, middle-tier faculties have their hearts and skills in tier one and their realities and challenges in the middle tier. The inertia that results is a major element for restructuring. The challenge is to find areas of distinction and quality and then place them at the core of the new mission. These campuses cannot stay as they are, because they are underfunded for current needs. Students will go where education is current and forward looking, where faculty have an attractive reputation, and where the price is within reach. Students will do this, no matter how well grounded faculty are in the good and valuable aspects of the hallowed past to which many of them cling. Knowledge is not frozen in place. The canon is not complete. And tradition does not buy currency in the new knowledge.

Although a common set of knowledge that everyone should have will emerge and will be part of the new undergraduate experience, by itself, it will not bring the enrollments and revenues these underfunded and overcommitted campuses need. By specializing—finding a niche in the competitive market for traditional and nontraditional students and linking to professions and advanced programs that hire or admit undergraduates—middle-tier schools will begin to fashion the distinctive character that will build both reputation and support for their programs of study.

To teach effectively and with lower labor costs, these campuses will have to rely heavily on technology, especially to augment their libraries and the databases essential to twenty-first century knowledge. They would be wise to link to community colleges, farming out introductory education and shortening the time to degree. They would be prudent to require their students to be technology literate and able to use English plus a second language, so their graduates can compete effectively for jobs or advanced study. Their professional schools would gain by significantly linking with related businesses or professions— for internships; for needed equipment for labs and classrooms; for better ties to the workplace; and for improved partnerships with other entities, such as elementary, middle, and high schools (through activities such as mentoring by professors and college students, technology sharing, mutual fundraising projects, and contractual agreements that reduce admission requirements). Some of these institutions may choose to join the ranks of those universities that reach out to transfer students and the lifelong learner and focus on the upper-division and master's level studies they require.

The middle tier will become a niched tier of teaching campuses, where undergraduate education flows into professional study and placement per Kerr's idea of the polytechnic. Some general education will be essential at this level, but preparation for very advanced graduate study will occur primarily at the research institutions. We are speaking here of focus, emphasis, and distinction. As institutions do what they do best, not all will have the resources to prepare students for advanced study, especially at the doctoral level and particularly in big science and other highly specialized and evolving fields of study. Although some undergraduates will go to select private or public research universities, it is primarily the middle-tier institutions that will initiate the process of making learning a lifelong pursuit for the bulk of future undergraduates. This is the role of the educational backbone that links knowledge to real-world problems. That connection will forge lifelong relationships between middle-tier faculty and their students, support the financial health of the university, and infuse teaching with unique capacities to serve continuously the needs of tomorrow's workers and their leaders.

Small Colleges and Universities

The small colleges, public or private, are the third tier. These schools will be especially valuable as repositories of tradition, face-to-face learning, analytical thinking, and customized education. Of course, they will cost more and those who value them will have to find the means.

We are not assuming that these institutions will exist in some nostalgic time warp of the past. We see these campuses playing a significant and lead role in accruing human knowledge, sorting it for its deeper meaning, and challenging the knowledge that is unfolding rapidly from other segments of society. Detachment from the harried pace of creating knowledge will give these institutions and their students the opportunity to challenge the longer-term aspects of human knowledge, the world of values, and the epistemology so central to extracting human meaning from the world of discovery and experience.

This role will not except these institutions from technology, the problems of big science, multiculturalism, world languages, or any of the other conundrums that accompany the unfolding of human knowledge. Because of their values role, these institutions will continue to be feeders to the tier-one schools and will contribute especially to the variety of thinking and learning those other institutions will require.

The institutions in this tier that are not research universities, but that have graduate programs, will continue to play an important role by offering alternative fields of study covered neither by the tier-one nor the tier-two schools. Examples of such alternative offerings include the study of religion, the study of small or disappearing cultures, the study of tribal music, and the study of naturopathic medicine, among others. Each of these specialized subjects help keep the breadth and scope of education open and enriching.

The select liberal arts colleges will keep their traditional role, but they will have to tie that role to real-world professions and fields of practiced knowledge. Otherwise, their costs will continue to escalate, further diminishing demand for what they offer. In addition, their reliance on private giving requires a responsiveness to society's needs. They will have to ensure that technology is current and state-of-the-art, so their students can keep apace of what is happening outside the safe harbor of the campus and be successful after graduation.

As society increasingly becomes a global village, these institutions will bear a special responsibility to broaden the cultural, ideational, and linguistic bases of the liberal arts beyond the confines of the western world. This will no doubt lead to frothy debates about what deserves inclusion and what does not. But the reality that seven-ninths of the world is not western will clash sooner rather than later with any efforts to ignore the ideas, values, practices, and beliefs of such a large portion of humankind. Select liberal arts colleges can contribute significantly to the capacity of the American society to adapt to life in a global society.

CONCLUSION

In this chapter, we have argued that the colleges and universities of the future will be as pluralistic and varied as their roles and areas of distinction and quality permit. Some of them will be desktop institutions, without faculty and where learning is fully digitized. Others will look like they have in the past but play a more focused role. Many will fundamentally change, downsizing and finding specialized niches. All will be more learner centered than they are today, and all will be more decentralized and flexible in how they are organized.

Research universities will have to restructure and downsize, focusing on specialties in which they excel and can go beyond setting the benchmark to creating new knowledge continuously. Middle-tier universities, the comprehensive universities, will become more focused and less comprehensive. They will specialize in upper-division and master's education, becoming polytechnic universities where learning is linked to work in a lifelong relationship between student and institution. They will educate the bulk of undergraduates and be the backbone of workplace competitiveness. The liberal arts colleges will continue as the living archives of human values, but they must broaden their perspective to include nonwestern cultures and face the reality of global living. They will also have to link liberal studies to careers and professions, if they are to remain connected to the businesses and other groups that support them.

Regardless of the tier, organizations will become focused, flexible, less hierarchical, open to virtual integration and disintegration as events shift. They will be as encouraging of intuition and creativity as they are respectful of rationality and probability, open to discontinuous change, and mindful of the need to find the seam of opportunity in events, no matter how daunting or challenging that may be. The university will be a learning commons and resource shell where self-directed teams develop and deliver programs of instruction and carry out research. The university will devolve responsibility, resources, revenue raising, and acquiring the essentials to these self-directed programs, institutes, departments, and schools. Cross-subsidies will likely diminish as units buy needed services from other units. Central resources will be used to encourage and seed excellence and to provide a balance necessary for the homeostatic equilibrium of the institution.

Technology will be central to the continuous evolution and change that will surround programs, units, and the institution. Desktop programs of study and degrees will be common and flexible. Students will shape their programs of study with faculty help. These programs of study will displace many degrees as we know them today. The lifelong link between student, faculty, and institution will render degrees less valuable than the linkage of ongoing knowledge that makes the student more valuable in the workplace, profession, and social role. In a world where analytical skills, intuition, creativity, and problem solving are valued, the increasing intellectual demands of the lifelong learner will guarantee the role and value of the university and will give substance to the ponderous riddle of what is true and good in the course of rapidly changing human events.

CHAPTER THIRTEEN

Achieving Strategic Transformation

T hroughout this book, we have developed a variety of
scenarios about the present and future of higher education here and
abroad. We have attempted to describe a new age under way and a
world different from the one we grew up in and became accustomed
to in the twentieth century. We are already in the information age and
the imperative to change is here. For growth and survival, this imperative will require transforming the campus and the activities associated with it to meet the needs of the new era. In this chapter, we
examine practical options for change available to colleges and universities and offer some ideas about best practices so that institutions
can choose a scenario and a strategy that build on their distinctions
and on the strategic planning model we presented in our earlier book
(Rowley, Lujan, and Dolence, 1997).

STRATEGIC CHOICES ABOUT THE FUTURE

As we have stressed throughout, the information age is an age of opportunity. It encourages institutions to help shape change. There are
no long-term benefits to resisting or reacting to new expectations

(Rowley, Lujan, and Dolence, 1997). In either case, the institution loses control over its fate. The economic system will favor those entities that lead the change. Because the major business of colleges and universities is information and knowledge, they should play a lead role in paradigm development. One of the major motivations in writing this book has been to develop an understanding of new environmental forces, to identify how and in what ways colleges and universities should respond, and to provide some catalytic models of how academic institutions might want to change in order to fit the needs of the information age. Our perspective in all of this is proactive, enabling, and initiating. It is designed to help institutions sculpt their own futures.

By acting constructively to fit the needs and demands of the information age, colleges and universities can be strategic about the choices they make and the futures they design for themselves. The environments of the new information age are rich with opportunities that will allow those institutions who build a strong relationship with the working public, information age companies, agencies, learners, and emerging phenomena to shape the future.

The obvious benefits of the strategic planning process we support come into play here. The central constructs of strategic planning are those essential and distinctive activities of a college or university that will help them achieve a fit based on excellence with the most important forces in their environments. These external forces seek ways of coping with new definitions and ways of conducting commerce, discovery, communication, and regulation. By involving themselves in these efforts through alliances and partnerships, colleges and universities can contribute to the new age and help others define and understand it. As the age advances, those same colleges and universities can continue their strategic relationships and become assets in the pursuit of knowledge and understanding.

Defining the Environment

To begin this process, each college and university should develop a coherent understanding of just what the emerging environmental forces are in their sphere of distinction. These forces are not simply technological. They are also rooted in the evolving international commerce, the communication media, and the explosion of new information, ideas, and techniques. As the economic and competitive segments of the environment have attempted to harness these new forces, new industries with entirely new needs have also emerged. Examples of this include the explosive growth in digital communications, microcircuitry, microelectronics, and of course the Internet. These forces encompass a rich set of opportunities for learning, knowledge sharing, and creating new knowledge bases.

These have traditionally been the central concerns of the academy. But the slowness of some to recognize changes occurring within their relevant environments put those colleges and universities outside the loop in the development of information bases leading the new age.

Implementing New Ideas

Each institution can address change by scanning the new environments, then seeking ways of meeting environmental needs from its base of distinction, including its particular heritage, character, strengths, capabilities, and programs of excellence. Mediocrity and attempting to be all things to all situations will not work in the information age. The institutions that will grow and prosper will be those that can meld their greatest strengths with the opportunities in their environment. Niching is an important choice, and colleges and universities should identify the set of niches that their strengths and character match. They can do this through a typical Strengths, Weaknesses, Opportunities, and Threats (SWOT) analysis, followed by cross-impact analyses to identify areas of convergence, and brainstorming to develop a central set of key strategies that they determine will achieve the relationships they desire. By determining a strong set of strategic partnerships for their niche set, the participating colleges and universities will help strengthen their foundations, provide the sought-after knowledge base, and position themselves as effective partners. There is no need to compromise academic integrity or central mission in all of this, because strategies flow from an institution's strengths and sense of purpose.

Strategic planning and the strategic management of resources provide pathways to change. Strategic management tools such as matching budgets to strategies, developing position control systems to monitor how resources flow into salaries and into support dollars for strategic activities, providing program accomplishments to policymakers, and using results to raise new money all help ensure that the day-to-day use of resources reflects the strategic purpose of the institution. These management tools have proven their value in helping organizations of all types better understand their environments, discover ways of meshing with emerging needs, and develop successful competitive strategies to take advantage of the opportunities that exist. We firmly believe that the most successful colleges and universities of the information age will be those that take up the challenges of defining themselves and their environments and then successfully responding to those environments, sometimes by forging alliances within their new environments that benefit both optimally.

TRANSITION MODEL FOR STRATEGIC CHANGE

How can a campus decide what deserves response and what the character of that response should be? What questions should it consider, what processes should it examine, what should be preserved at all costs, and what is it willing to risk in order to position itself in its environment? These are not easy questions to answer. To assist in answering them, we present a four-stage model, represented in the four lists below, which builds on the Strategic Planning Engine we developed in our earlier book (Rowley, Lujan, and Dolence, 1997). Added to the institution's strategic planning process, this model identifies that part of a college's or university's environment that is central to the institution's character and programs of distinction. The model is sequential and includes specific steps within each phase, which help clarify questions like the ones just posed and identify activities a campus strategic management team would need to undertake.

Stage One: Cognitive Phase

1. Recognize that the future is different from the past.

2. Recognize that others are carving out their niches.

3. Recognize that already established niches are hard to break into.

4. Recognize that time for learning is the primary design function of the process.

5. Recognize that the future must contain a broader context for learning.

Stage Two: Preparatory Phase

1. Recognize that transformation is a formal process.

2. Engage all constituents in the process.

3. Evaluate the current strategic position of the college or university.

4. Understand how these steps affect the institutional key performance indicators (KPIs).

Stage Three: Introspective Phase

1. Determine how current strategies hurt or advance the institution's KPIs.

2. Determine how current goals hurt or advance the institution's KPIs.

3. Determine how current objectives hurt or advance the institution's KPIs.

4. Determine how current policies hurt or advance the institution's ability to change.

5. Determine how current institutional processes have been engineered (if at all).

6. Determine how current procedures hurt or advance change in the institution.

7. Determine how current infrastructures hurt or advance change in the institution.

8. Determine how the current curriculum hurts or advances learner needs.

9. Determine how the current culture hurts or advances the institution's ability to change.

10. Develop an understanding of the modern learner.

11. Determine society's learning needs and expectations.

Stage Four: Action-Process Phase

1. Brainstorm ideas with all constituencies about the issues developed thus far.

2. Evaluate all ideas as objectively as possible.

3. Synthesize the best ideas into new goals, objectives, and strategies.

4. Test the new goals, objectives, and strategies against the mission.

5. Translate the new goals, objectives, and strategies into implementable work plans.

6. Establish an implementation calendar, concurrent with the academic calendar.

7. Establish a quarterly review cycle.

8. Evaluate new goals, objectives, and strategies against institutional KPIs.

9. Evaluate what went right and what went wrong and determine needed modifications.

10. Extend the process into long-term strategic management.

Stage One: Cognitive Phase

The purpose of this phase is to allow campus strategic planners the opportunity to identify specifically and to inventory both the internal and external forces related to the information age that they must take into account before they begin to look at options.

Step One—Identify how the future will be different from the past. It is essential that strategic decision makers understand and can describe how the future is *significantly different* from the factory model of the industrial age. Some on campus may see no differences, and others do. Regardless, ages *differ* and all decision makers should generally agree on what those differences are and how they may impact campus activities and programs, both primary and support programs.

Step Two—Realize that others are already carving out their niches. Other colleges and universities and other educational entities, such as the proprietary and virtual universities (among others), are already identifying that portion of the educational environment they will serve. It is a competitive world, and each institution needs to understand with whom it is competing and the extent of that competition.

Step Three—Recognize that occupied niches are harder to serve for late entrants. Just because a campus may believe that its strengths lie in particular areas is no guarantee that those strengths secure a niche. Timing is crucial for effective strategic competitive activities. As business has learned, once a competitor occupies a niche, it is difficult to enter that same niche, and the cost of doing so can be extremely high for the new entrant. The *first-mover strategy* in a demonstrated area is always superior to the *late-mover strategy*. This means that college and university strategic decision makers must seek currently unoccupied niches to exploit, create a niche, or compete in an already-occupied niche.

Step Four—Remember that timeliness is a primary design function. Education is time-consuming. As we have pointed out many times, information age learners seek knowledge but cannot always conform to a particular college's or university's timetable and schedule. This means that the delivery of learning should provide choices to learners and whenever possible link to their places of work or study. Making learning accessible through modules, personalized study plans, on-line chat sessions, and e-mail help provide the flexibility many learners need.

Step Five—Recognize the need to broaden the ways we learn. The lists below identify a typology of learning objectives, venues, methods, and content types, which demonstrate the variety of learning options that are available. As campus decision makers begin to think about their academic programs and how to transfer their knowledge to learners, these learning options provide a set of choices, which broaden the possibilities of how specific academic objectives might be achieved. Together these lists make up the Strategic Curriculum Management Model.

Learning-Objective Options

- Degree
- Knowledge transfer
- Skill
- Certificate
- Enrichment
- Technical
- Professional
- Trade
- Development
- Training

Learning-Venue Options

- Classroom
- Laboratory
- Library
- Workplace

- Home
- On assignment
- Network
- Hotel
- On-site
- Anywhere

Learning-Method Options
- Lecture
- Recitation
- Simulation
- Experimentation
- Seminar
- Audio tutorial
- Projects
- Thesis
- Computer-based instruction
- Personalized systems instruction

Learning-Content Options
- Course
- Module
- Assessment
- Choice
- Knowledge
- Skills
- Competencies
- Values

Stage Two: Preparatory Phase

With the knowledge gained from the first stage as a background, strategic planners and campus leaders can begin to solidify the elements of a SWOT analysis, which forms the basis of the strategic plan.

(See Rowley, Lujan, and Dolence, 1997, for details on how to prepare for strategic planning.)

Step One—Understand that transformation requires a formal process. Whenever an individual or a group begins to contemplate changing an organization's prevailing structure, culture, or direction, it does so at a risk. Anything that changes an organization in some significant way must be thoroughly thought out and analyzed. Those affected should be included, and it is important that they take planning seriously. This implies that as a campus or system puts together a strategic plan, the process must be formal and legitimate. The process must also be consistent with campus rules, and it is important that all constituencies know about the process and are given the chance to participate or share their ideas. Finally, the process must be formalized with scheduled events and clear, anticipated outcomes.

Step Two—Have the process engage all constituents in discovery and analysis. Strategic planning affects the entire campus. To ensure inclusion, all connected constituencies *must* be involved in some way. Without this collaboration, negative politics can easily form to discredit the process, undermine it, or stop it.

Step Three—Evaluate the strategic position of the institution in the learning environment. Understanding where a particular campus stands relative to the learning and knowledge environment is essential. This requires leaders of the process to inventory and analyze environmental trends and events and to identify competitors as well as collaborators.

Step Four—Clarify the impacts of the previous step on each KPI. As part of the Strategic Planning Engine, planners and participants should analyze the impact of environmental factors against institutional KPIs, such as enrollments, revenues, and other key performance measures. In *Working Toward Strategic Change* (Dolence, Rowley, and Lujan, 1997), we developed a discussion of the cross-impact analysis tool that we believe makes this type of analysis much easier to understand.

Stage Three: Introspective Phase

This is the point at which specific knowledge areas from the internal environment are specified and analyzed. Within the framework of strategic planning, this is also the place to identify internal strengths and knowledge bases and to match them with the opportunities of the external environment. This helps strategic planners and campus decision makers choose among the options available to them.

Step One—Know how current strategies advance or hinder the institution. Strategic decision makers should inventory and assess what the college or university is currently doing in all areas of its operation— academic, administrative, and other services—and then establish how these practices help or hinder its ability to develop a strategic fit with its most important environmental factors. Part of this analysis involves a review of how the campus already is addressing competitor initiatives as well as the requirements and objectives of collaborators.

Step Two—Review the effect of current goals. Review current campus goals and ask the hard questions about how the goals of campus constituencies, especially the academic component, the campus administration, and the governing board, influence the institution's ability to accomplish its leading expectations successfully. Analyze the relevant KPIs, and determine if they are being met and if the learning environment is adequate. Part of this analysis is a consideration of how campus goals compare with competitor initiatives and collaborator requirements and objectives.

Step Three—Review the effect of current objectives. Determine if the important objectives that are the prerequisite to achieving goals are being met. Consider if objectives are aids or impediments in goal achievement. Modify tactics according to this analysis, revising affected strategies to improve goal achievement.

Step Four—Determine if the institution has the capacity to implement its strategic policies. Policies are the guiding principles that decision makers use to choose among alternatives on a given set of related issues. These guidelines for action determine the courses of action any campus undertakes to accomplish its strategic ends. The institutional capacity in terms of resources and intellectual capital should be assessed in terms of how they help or hinder strategic accomplishments. Such an analysis may highlight, for example, the curriculum development and approval process, budget development, spending practices such as vacancy savings and year-end balances, recruiting and retention methods, and campus communication. All of these substantially affect the ability of the campus to behave strategically.

Step Five—Clarify how decisions in one major area affect those in another area. The cross-impact of decisions outside their segment of the institution is a complicating factor, which should be understood. For example, an administrative decision to intensify recruiting efforts to increase enrollments by 10 percent in three years will have an impact on all of the academic programs, housing, student services, and even the community. We have found that it is a real mistake not to discover these relationships or not to take them into consideration when developing the strategic plan. If improved enrollments cause the quality of the resident experience to decline because of overcrowding, the long-term effect could be further enrollment decline. Effects like this must be addressed if the strategic plan is to be effective.

Step Six—Consider how current procedures enable or hinder initiatives. Discovering how current rules work and affect initiatives for innovation is a critical step in this phase. Are certain procedures and regulations impediments to growth, innovation, and building on areas of distinction? To what extent do procedures or regulations foster territoriality rather than facilitate cooperation? How do they hinder areas of excellence? If well-paid, high-quality faculty in educational leadership experience low enrollments, while lower-paid, less-qualified faculty in student personnel administration face burgeoning enrollments and unrealistic dissertation workloads, how do procedures permit a resolution like, for example, their merger or sharing dissertation responsibilities?

Step Seven—Determine whether the current infrastructure can support strategic change. This analysis looks at a different sort of question. How capable is the current campus infrastructure of supporting change initiatives? This includes assessing the physical, communications, organizational, financial, and general campus infrastructures and determining how they can actually work together. This analysis should also take into account the transformational goals emerging from all of the previous steps.

Step Eight—Look at how the current curriculum fits learner-centered and market-driven learning. This is a difficult and controversial analytical step. There is good reason to object to learning being market oriented. Education that meets market needs is typically skills training. Colleges and universities educate for the longer term, and the content is not job specific. At the same time, pressure is great to improve the general analytical skills of college graduates. Campus academics and planners should ask the hard question: Does the current curriculum meet educational requirements in ways that also address public and employer concerns about better thinking and analytical skills? The answers to this question should provide the basis for formulating strategies about how the campus can better fit its environment.

Step Nine—Weigh the effects of current institutional culture and politics. Campus culture is the result of a variety of forces, including tradition, orientation, mission, student makeup, academic mix, the campus professorate, the accepted way things get done, and the current balance among campus special interests. Campus politics reflects this culture and has a vested interest in its continuance. Although these forces of culture do not easily come together to initiate or define change, through campus politics, they can blend to stop the changes they do not like or on whose development they have not shared. This veto power is an important constraint that planners and decision makers must always consider.

Step Ten—Focus on the learner. As a final step, we suggest that campus leaders come to understand the new learner. Apart from the descriptions of them as users, their intellectual interests, proclivities for learning, learning styles, and capacity to contribute actively to learning are important ingredients for curricular change. We refer the reader again to the lists in the Strategic Curriculum Management Model as a beginning point for determining the variety of mixes that may promote effective learning. Learning is potentially lifelong, and if learners are satisfied with their educations, they can have a long-term stabilizing effect on enrollments, curriculum, and support for higher education.

Step Eleven—Find the mix of traditional and innovative programs. Understanding the ongoing educational needs of new learners will help a campus achieve an effective fit with the expectations in its environment. In this analysis, a sense of the appropriate mix between the *time-out for learning model* and the *perpetual learning model* should emerge. This will help strategic decision makers better determine how to mix their traditional programs with newer, innovative programs to serve the information age learners adequately in their niche.

Stage Four: Action-Process Phase

The three initial stages set the framework for effective strategies and plans. The key steps among them are: define the difference between the past and the future, find a realistic niche, broaden learning methods, review the curriculum to enrich offerings, spell out a process for building strategies and plans, evaluate the infrastructure for the capacity to innovate, consider goals and strategies, recognize the effects of campus politics on the capacity to innovate, and find a strategic mix of programs. This preparation done carefully by using sound facts and reflective judgment will lay the groundwork for effective planning.

The Strategic Planning Engine can now take the information that the group (or groups) have generated and organize it into an initial plan. This is an iterative, not a one-time process. Because strategic planning is a process for fundamental change, many programs, operations, and procedures of a campus will alter but will be monitored for interface with the changing external and internal environments. This change-and-scan process means that innovations are continuous, and elements that have run their course are dropped along the way. This requires that campus decision makers constantly update and renew the plan and its strategies. This ongoing measurement of KPI progress and strategic evaluation is anchored in the areas of distinction that identify the institution's niche.

Step One—Brainstorm. With all of the essential data gathered, preliminary analyses conducted, and constituents consulted, it is time to plan formally. The first step is to brainstorm about what the best alternatives for the campus might be and to discuss initial ideas about the niche, areas of distinction, the current mission, and initial versions of goals, objectives, and strategies. Implementation requirements should also be considered and a clear determination should be made of the capacity of the infrastructure, with requisite changes, to foster effective implementation. The kind of brainstorming we are speaking of should build on critical analysis—a classic strength of the academy—and should be designed to solicit the best ideas from all constituencies. We especially recommend using a Decision Support Laboratory, found in many Colleges of Business and used as a process for encouraging frankness and objectivity. The use of these computer network centers allows anonymous input, immediate feedback of group ideas, analysis tools, and electronic summation. This brainstorming will help align the institution with its external environment and will identify ways both to enhance campus infrastructure for strategic accomplishments and to assist the knowledge age learner in achieving excellence. The process should also be used to develop ideas about increasing campus strengths, reducing weaknesses, overcoming threats, and taking advantage of opportunities.

Step Two—Evaluate objectively. Good planning is frank and focused. It concentrates on the good of the institution rather than on special interests. It is important to be as objective as possible in discussions, to recognize but not be guided by campus politics, and to focus on the impact each idea will have on the institution's KPIs. One good way of doing this is to use cross-impact analysis in a Decision Support

Laboratory facility. (For a complete discussion of the process, see Dolence, Rowley, and Lujan, 1997.)

Step Three—Synthesize the best ideas into new goals, objectives, and strategies. Brainstorming and cross-impact analysis should serve to help prioritize strategic ideas. This prioritization should lead to a session in which participants and decision makers can look at everything they have done and draw conclusions regarding the most important, effective, and reasonable alternatives they have developed.

Step Four—Test and revise the mission. The goals, objectives, and strategies that emerge from this filtration process provide an excellent referent for participants in conducting a thorough mission review. If the process thus far has been open and reasonably objective, then comparing initial goals, objectives, and strategies with the current mission will legitimately identify areas of congruence and areas in which change is necessary. In areas of dissonance, the campus must choose either to adapt the mission or to retain the current mission. If the decision is made to retain the current mission, this incongruence will have to be resolved. Resistance usually occurs if the groundwork outlined in stages one to three has not been well laid, which results in the lack of a working consensus. It could also reflect resistance that has been reticent or has "gone along" until a fundamental decision with long-term effects was required. In either case, it is time to stop, get a blue ribbon committee whose credentials are not easily challenged in place, review the preplanning process (stages one to three), and fill in what was not effectively accomplished. Then repeat the brainstorming process. If consensus is impossible, these are governance issues that only the existing governance structures can resolve. Ultimately, regents can decide if others are not ready.

Step Five—Translate the new goals, objectives, and strategies into work plans. Goals, objectives, and strategies are not very useful if they do not become the responsibilities of individuals, offices, departments, and groups to carry them out. The need for supporters and implementers is the most important reason for including a large number of people in developing the strategic plan. It is difficult to ask people to take responsibility for a goal, objective, or strategy if they did not share in its formulation. Shared ownership is lacking. On the other hand, if the people who will be affected by the policy changes that result from the new goals, objectives, and strategies are responsible for their implementation, they are more likely to accept responsibility and may even be eager to do so.

Step Six—Link implementation with current academic calendar. We suggest that as implementation begins, review should be tied to the academic calendar. This is not a major matter, but we believe that the more strategic planning becomes part of the campus routine, the more it blends with the infrastructure. Then, its effects and responses to them become a natural part of doing business. For example, the end of the traditional school year (May or June graduation dates) is a good time to look at the overall strategic performance of the campus. This way, a natural ending point serves the strategic planning and management processes as naturally as it does the academic activities of the college or university.

Step Seven—Periodically review and check performance. The efforts of individuals, officers, and groups involved in the process help achieve goals and objectives that formalize planning. The emerging strategies that flow from this base should be regularly and periodically reviewed. The intervals between reviews should fit campus practices and the seriousness of the changes involved. Periodic review of performance helps everyone involved with the process understand just how well things are going forward and which obstacles need attention. Review helps discover problems early and permits intervening with new strategies or revising goals and objectives to be more practical and achievable. Most important, it does not let the process stall.

Step Eight—Use KPIs to test effectiveness. During both the quarterly and year-end reviews, the strategic decision makers should use the organizational KPIs as the measures and outcomes for assessing progress and changes in goals, objectives, and strategies. KPIs should meet the standards that the strategic decision makers have set for them during the planning phase. If not, then it is appropriate to revisit the plan and make changes in it or in responsible units, in order to facilitate accomplishment and a working plan.

Step Nine—Identify causes, then modify. Rather than just accept outcomes and treat measures as mere facts, strategic decision makers should analyze *what caused* things to go right or go wrong. Although the tendency of many groups is to go through such an analysis only when things do not work out properly, it is also important to understand what caused things to go right. These are instructive lessons that help decision makers and those responsible for implementing strategies be more successful.

Step Ten—Extend planning into management. Strategic planning should evolve into strategic management. A strategic plan is a format for change that extends through iteration into the future. Its logic helps array the strategic issues before decision makers, highlight the cross-impacts within an organization, clarify effects on the environment, note opportunities and threats, and focus on distinction and strengths as the backbone for change. Because the environment consistently changes, a strategic plan of the campus must change right along with it, assuring that leadership is making future choices from current best practices. This is how the college or university can go beyond survival to shaping its own future.

WHAT IT WILL TAKE TO SURVIVE

Excellence, productivity, relevance, flexibility, cost-effectiveness, and being valued are all hallmarks of survival. This was true in the industrial age and will apply to the information age. Achieving these hallmarks takes resources, which is the most perplexing problem facing colleges and universities today. The model we have described should help each campus understand where it is in relation to these values and what it needs to do to capitalize on its strengths, reduce its weaknesses, adequately confront its threats, take full advantage of its relevant opportunities, and enhance excellence.

The following anecdote may demonstrate the point. One of the authors conducted an interview with a vice president of Harvard University. The discussion focused on the importance of strategic planning. The vice president confided that Harvard was involved in doing strategic planning around its resources. The comment was made that Harvard was having problems around its (at the time) approximately $8 billion endowment. When sharing this story with others, the common response has been, "I would like to have Harvard's problems!" But in fact, there *was* a problem. Endowments are seldom given to colleges or universities as blanket gifts that the institution can use however it prefers. Normally, an endowment is given for a specific purpose to a specific program. Though Harvard has more endowment money than any other college or university in the world, the endowments are not spread evenly across the campus. Some programs have very rich endowments (a significant percentage is held in the business school, for example), whereas other programs may have no endowments at all. Under the terms of the endowment, the Harvard University administration does not have the right or the power to move monies from one area to another, so in Harvard terms, certain programs are consigned to relative poverty. Some of these programs are excellent, but without the ability to properly support them, Harvard faces the unpleasant task of reducing institutional support. In some cases, this could mean significant downsizing or even elimination. Now, that is a problem that Harvard faces, and a problem every other institution *also faces,* in one version or another.

We believe this is an important reason for the colleges and universities to think strategically about the future and to use strategic planning as a guiding tool. The old beliefs are becoming less true. One belief in particular, often held by state-supported institutions both here and abroad, is that the importance of higher education to society is so great that they need not be concerned in the long run about funding, because the resources will always be there to support salaries, research expenses, teaching expenses, capital needs, and administrative costs. That is no longer the case. Not only has funding diminished, so too has broad public support for higher education. Accountability has displaced the informal trust forged by higher education in earlier times.

On the other hand, those same resource providers are still in a position to provide support and new resources. The growth of the American and global private sector is significant and more robust than at any previous time. Wealth exists and can support higher education at higher levels, if colleges and universities can reestablish their value to society as the generators of knowledge and as essential resources in addressing the most difficult problems and issues of our time.

The issues for such providers are excellence, productivity, relevance, flexibility, and cost-effectiveness—the same issues that mark success in any enterprise in the public or private sector. There is a clear and strong connection between the things that a college and university can do to survive and grow and the needs and wants of the environment that can supply the necessary resources.

AT THE THRESHOLD

Today's colleges and universities are at a threshold. Continuing industrial age research and teaching will not be as rewarded in the information age. The companies and knowledge workers of the new age need information and knowledge that will come from new paradigms. For higher education to advance, it too must maintain currency with these new paradigms and must reclaim its role as the major source of significant discoveries and new knowledge that benefit society. To succeed in the new age, colleges and universities must transform themselves and resume their leadership in generating knowledge that allows society to better cope with its emergent major social and economic problems.

Although the ultimate challenge of transformation is great, the elements of requisite change are incremental. The first steps in transformation are not profound. Most are unobtrusive. Many are practices we already use. When new endowments are suggested, the institution can direct them toward the development of information age resource centers and programs. When capital expenditures come due, new buildings or remodeling can occur to facilitate information age programs and methods. When determining how to use funds to improve a library collection, the funds can be used to help support digitizing the collection or connecting to larger library networks on-line. When retirements occur, the institution can purposely hire a new brand of faculty to meet program priorities that address the needs of information age learners. When seeking alliances, institutions can look toward developing contractual relationships in which both partners can work to benefit the other. These and other similar tactics help phase in significant changes over a period of time. The result is no discernible disruption to the campus and its students, faculty, administration, support staff, and other stakeholders.

The key is deciding what should happen and then developing the strategic plan—and the strategic thinking that this type of planning encourages—to ensure that it will happen. Time and process are important. The transition from the modes and methods of industrial age education to the modes and methods of information age education can be smooth or rough—fraught with denial, struggle, and disruption. A practical plan for the transition through the paradigm shift will ensure that a campus shapes its future and adapts in ways that improve its excellence and distinction.

FINAL THOUGHTS

It is most encouraging that all of these issues are matters of choice. We know that some campuses in the United States and around the world are choosing not to move forward or not to grow and manage their futures. But, in general, the future is bright. Wars of annihilation are contained, the world is less divided, the economy expands, and cures for diseases may even keep pace with the emergence of new ones. As we have said many times, the information age holds a wide variety of opportunities for growth, exciting discoveries, and prosperity. The key to sharing in this excitement lies in matching the strengths and distinctions of the institution with the opportunities in the environment, then shaping them to the betterment of the human mind and humankind. It is exciting and risky. Perhaps a Scottish proverb puts it best: danger and delight grow on one stalk.

~~~ References

Acherman, H. A. "Selective Retrenchment and Growth in the Netherlands." *International Journal of Institutional Management in Higher Education,* 1988, *12*(1), 41–48.

Altbach, P. G. "Students: Interests, Culture and Activism." In A. Levine (ed.), *Higher Learning in America: 1980–2000.* Baltimore: Johns Hopkins University Press, 1993.

American Association for Higher Education. "What Research Says About Improving Undergraduate Education." *American Association for Higher Education Bulletin,* Apr. 1996, *48*(8), 5–8.

American Association of State Colleges and Universities. "UA Link with Local Schools Provides Range of Educational Needs." *Memo,* 1997, *37*(2), 7.

Appleberry, J. A. "Re-engineering Higher Education: Changes in Academe." Speech at the University of Central Florida, Orlando, April 6, 1995.

Association of Governing Boards. *Priorities,* Winter 1996, p. 10.

Atwell, R. H. "Higher Education Governance in Despair." *Journal for Higher Education Management,* 1996a, *11*(2), 13–19.

Atwell, R. H. Speech presented at Rollins College commencement, Winter Park, Florida, April 26, 1996b.

Atwell, R. H. "Doctoral Education Must Match the Nation's Needs and the Realities of the Marketplace." *Chronicle of Higher Education,* Nov. 1996c, *43*(14), B4–B5.

Birnbaum, R. "The Latent Organizational Functions of the Academic Senate: Why Senates Do Not Work but Will Not Go Away." In R. Birnbaum (ed.), *Faculty in Governance: The Role of Senates and Joint Committees in Academic Decision Making.* New Directions for Higher Education, no. 75. San Francisco: Jossey-Bass, 1991.

Bollag, B. "Italy's Minister of Education Pushes to Break Up Overcrowded Universities." *Chronicle of Higher Education,* Feb. 1997, *43*(22), A45–A47.

Botstein, L. "Structuring Specialization as a Form of General Education." *Liberal Education,* 1991, *77*(2), 10–19.

Brawer, F. "Community Colleges International." *Digest.* Report EDO-JC-96–04. Washington, D.C.: Office of Educational Research and Improvement, 1996.

Breneman, D. W. "The 'Privatization' of Public Universities: A Mistake or a Model for the Future?" *Chronicle of Higher Education,* Mar. 1997, *43*(26), B4–B5.

Bronner, E. "Adults-Only College Races to Top." *Denver Post,* Oct. 15, 1997, pp. 2A, 13A.

Bureau of Statistics. *Education in the Republic of China.* Taipei: Ministry of Education, 1996.

Byrne, G., and Chait, R. "Thawing the Cold War over Tenure." *Chronicle of Higher Education,* Feb. 1997, *43*(22), 4–5.

California Higher Education Policy Center. *Shared Responsibility.* San Jose: California Higher Education Center, 1996.

Carnegie Commission on Higher Education. *The Purposes and Performance of Higher Education in the United States: Approaching the Year 2000.* New York: McGraw-Hill, 1973.

Carnegie Council on Policy Studies in Higher Education. *More Than Survival: Prospects for Higher Education in a Period of Uncertainty.* San Francisco: Jossey-Bass, 1975.

Carnegie Council on Policy Studies in Higher Education. *Three Thousand Futures: The Next Twenty Years for Higher Education.* San Francisco: Jossey-Bass, 1980.

Carnevale, A. P. *America and the New Economy: How the New Competitive Standards Are Radically Changing American Workplaces.* San Francisco: Jossey-Bass, 1991.

Cerf, V. "Networks." *Scientific American,* 1991, *265*(3), 72–81.

Chickering, A. W., and Gamson, Z. F. "Seven Principles for Good Practice in Undergraduate Education." In A. W. Chickering and Z. F. Gamson (eds.), *Applying the Seven Principles for Good Practice in Undergraduate Education.* New Directions for Teaching and Learning, no. 47. San Francisco: Jossey-Bass, 1991.

Chodorow, S. "Educators Must Take the Electronic Revolution Seriously." *Academic Medicine,* 1996, *71*(3), 221–226.

Clark, B. R. "The Insulated Americans: Five Lessons from Abroad." In D. D. Dill and B. Sporn (eds.), *Emerging Patterns of Social Demand and University Reform.* New York: Pergamon Press, 1995.

Cohen, A. M. "Projecting the Future of Community Colleges." *Digest.* Report EDO-JC-96–01. Washington, D.C.: Office of Educational Research and Improvement, 1995.

Cohen, D. W. "The Constitution of International Expertise." *Journal of the International Institute*, 1994, *1*(1), 6.

Cohen, D. W. "Understanding the Globalization of Scholarship." In M. W. Peterson, D. D. Dill, and L. A. Mets (eds.), *Planning and Management for a Changing Environment*. San Francisco: Jossey-Bass, 1997.

Commission for Educational Quality. *Changing States: Higher Education and the Public Good*. Atlanta: Southern Regional Education Board, 1994.

Commission on the Presidency. *Renewing the Academic Presidency*. Washington, D.C.: Association of Governing Boards of Colleges and Universities, 1996.

Cornerstones Principles. Unpublished reports, Task Forces 1–4, California State University System Office, Long Beach, March 1997.

Corson, J. J. *Governance of Colleges and Universities*. New York: McGraw-Hill, 1960.

Davidson, J. L. (ed.). *Counterpoint and Beyond*. Urbana, Ill.: National Council of Teachers of English, 1988.

Davies, G. D. "Higher-Education Systems as Cartels: The End Is Near." *Chronicle of Higher Education*, Oct. 1997, *44*(6), A68.

Dessruisseaux, P. "A Record Number of Foreign Students Enrolled at U.S. Colleges Last Year." *Chronicle of Higher Education*, Dec. 1996, *43*(15), A64.

Dill, D. D., and Sporn, B. *Emerging Patterns of Social Demand and University Reform*. New York: Pergamon Press, 1995.

Dillman, D. A., Christenson, J. A., Salant, P., and Warner, P. D. *What the Public Wants from Higher Education: Workforce Implications from a 1995 National Survey*. Technical Report 95–52. Pullman: Social and Economic Sciences Research Center, Washington State University, 1995.

Division of Undergraduate Education. *Division of Undergraduate Education News 1996*. Washington D.C.: National Science Foundation, 1996.

Dolence, M. G., and Norris, D. M. *Transforming Higher Education*. Ann Arbor, Mich.: Society for College and University Planning, 1995.

Dolence, M. G., Rowley, D. J., and Lujan, H. D. *Working Toward Strategic Change*. San Francisco: Jossey-Bass, 1997.

Dooris, M. J., and Lozier, G. G. "Adapting Formal Planning Approaches: The Pennsylvania State University." In F. A Schmidtlein and T. H. Milton (eds.), *Adapting Strategic Planning to Campus Realities*. New Directions for Institutional Research, no. 67. San Francisco: Jossey-Bass, 1990.

Duderstadt, J. "The Modern University." *Crosstalk,* 1995, *3*(3), 18.

Economist, Jan. 15, 1994, p. 65.

Ehrmann, S. C., Renwick, W. L., and Hebenstreit, J. *The Future of Post-Secondary Education and the Role of Information and Communication Technology.* Report No. CERI/CD(94)11. Paris: Centre for Educational Research and Innovation, 1994.

Ewell, P. "The Neglected Art of Collective Responsibility: Restoring Our Links with Society." Paper presented at the National Center for Higher Education Management Systems, 1995.

Finley, B. "Trends in Overseas Study Change Higher Education." *Denver Post,* Oct. 8, 1997, pp. 1B, 3B.

Finnegan, D. E. "Segmentation in the Academic Labor Market." *Journal of Higher Education,* 1993, *64*(2), 621–656.

Fosnot, C. T. *Enquiring Teachers, Enquiring Learners.* New York: Teachers College Press, 1989.

Gardner, D. P. "Managing Transitions in a Time of Acute Modernity." *Trusteeship,* 1995, *3*(4), 10–15.

Gast, G. "Successful Online Course." Draft of paper on GLOSAS-L Computer Bulletin Board, University of Ottawa, 1991.

Gates, B. *The Road Ahead.* New York: Penguin Books, 1996.

Giudice, B. "Education Reforms in France Get a Skeptical Reception." *Chronicle of Higher Education,* Feb. 1997, *43*(25), A5.

Guskin, A. E. "Restructuring the Role of Faculty." *Change,* Sept./Oct. 1994, *26*(5), 16–25.

Hannan, M. T., and Freeman, J. H. *Organizational Ecology.* Cambridge, Mass.: Harvard University Press, 1989.

Harasim, L. *Online Education.* New York: Praeger, 1990.

Hardy, C. "Configuration and Strategy Making in Universities." *Journal of Higher Education,* July/Aug. 1991, *62*(4), 363–393.

Hartle, T. W. "The Specter of Budget Uncertainty." *Chronicle of Higher Education,* June 1996, *42*(46), B2.

Hayes, A. B. "Shortcomings of the Virtual University." *Trusteeship,* Nov./Dec. 1996, *4*(6), 4.

Hodgkinson, H. L. *A Demographic Look at Tomorrow.* Washington, D.C.: Institute for Educational Leadership, 1992.

Holmberg, B. "Open Universities—Their Rationale, Characteristics and Prospects." *Ziff Papiere,* 1994, *92,* 25–39.

Horne, E. V. "The Diploma: Time Card or Stamp of Approval?" *Trusteeship,* Mar./Apr. 1995, *3*(2), 5.

Immerwahr, J., with Boese, J. *Preserving the Higher Education Legacy.* San

Jose: Public Agenda for the California Higher Education Policy Center, 1995.

Jones, R. T. "The New Workplace and Lifelong Learning." *Community College Journal,* 1996, *67*(2), 1–3.

Kanter, R. M. "Nice Work If You Can Get It." *American Prospect,* 1995, *25,* 92–98.

Kaufman, R. "Beyond Tinkering: Education Restructuring That Will Work." *International Journal of Educational Reform,* Apr. 1993, *2*(2), 154–165.

Kaye, A. *Computer Conferencing and Mass Distance Education.* Report No. 98. Milton Keynes, England: Institute of Educational Technology, Open University, 1990.

Kearsley, G. *Training for Tomorrow.* Reading, Mass.: Addison-Wesley, 1985.

Keegan, D. "Teaching by Satellite in a European Virtual Classroom." *Ziff Papiere,* 1994, *92,* 4–18.

Kellogg Commission on the Future of State and Land Grant Universities. Report to the National Association of State Universities and Land Grant Colleges, Jan. 1996.

Kember, D., and Gow, L. "Orientations to Teaching and Their Effect on the Quality of Student Learning." *Journal of Higher Education,* Jan./Feb. 1994, *65*(1), 58–74.

Kerr, C. "The New Race to Be Harvard or Stanford." *Change,* May/June 1991, pp. 14–15.

Kerr, C. *Preserving the Master Plan.* San Jose: California Higher Education Policy Center, 1994.

Kirschner, P. A., and Valcke, M.M.A. "From Supply Driven to Demand Driven Education: New Conceptions and the Role of Information Technology Therein." *Computers in Human Services,* 1994, *10*(4), 31–53.

Koch, C. "Market-Based Management." *Imprimis,* Aug. 1996, *25*(8), 4–7.

Laudato, N. C., and DeSantis, D. J. "You CAN Teach an Old Dog New Tricks: Extending Legacy Application to the New Enterprise Architecture." *CAUSE/EFFECT,* Winter 1996, *8,* 30–42.

Leslie, D. W., and Fretwell, E. K., Jr. *Wise Moves in Hard Times: Creating and Managing Resilient Colleges and Universities.* San Francisco: Jossey-Bass, 1996.

Levine, A. "Higher Education's New Status as a Mature Industry." *Chronicle of Higher Education,* Jan. 1997, *43*(21), A48.

Levine, A., and Weingart, J. *Reform of Undergraduate Education.* San Francisco: Jossey-Bass, 1973.

Lewington, J. "A Panel Urges Ontario to Adopt a Free-Market Approach to Higher Education." *Chronicle of Higher Education,* Feb. 1997, *43*(23), A44.

Lombardi, J. V., and Capaldi, E. D. *Measuring University Performance: The Bank.* Gainesville: Office of Institutional Research, University of Florida, Sept. 1, 1997. Report.

London, H. L. "The Death of the University." *Futurist,* May/June 1987, *21,* 17–22.

Luhrs, J. "Plugging into the College of the Future." *Hispanic Outlook,* Jan. 1997, *7*(14), 7–9.

Lundin, R. *Communication and Information Technologies in Business and Education.* Brisbane, Australia: College of Advanced Education, 1988. Working paper.

Magner, D. O. "Minnesota Regents Change Tenure Policy for Their Law School." *Chronicle of Higher Education,* Nov. 1996, *43*(12), A13.

Magrath, P. C. Letter to the National Association of State Universities and Land Grant Colleges, Jan. 1997a.

Magrath, P. C. "Eliminating Tenure Without Destroying Academic Freedom." *Chronicle of Higher Education,* Feb. 1997b, *43*(25), A60.

Magsaysay, J. "Managing in the 21st Century." *World Executive's Digest,* Jan. 1997, pp. 18–22.

Marshall, E., and Palca, J. "Cracks in the Ivory Tower." *Science,* Aug. 1992, *257,* 1196–1201.

Maslen, G. "Australian Academics Are Alarmed by Makeup of Panel Studying Higher Education." *Chronicle of Higher Education,* Feb. 1997, *43*(22), A47.

Mason, R., and Kaye, A. *Mindweave.* New York: Pergamon Press, 1989.

Mehlinger, H. D. *School Reform in the Information Age.* Bloomington: Indiana University Center for Excellence in Education, 1995.

Meister, J. C. *Corporate Quality Universities: Lessons in Building a World-Class Workforce.* Alexandria, Va.: American Society for Training and Development, 1994.

Miles, R., and Cameron, K. *Coffin Nails and Corporate Strategies.* Englewood Cliffs, N.J.: Prentice Hall, 1982.

Munitz, B. *Never Make Predictions, Particularly About the Future.* Washington, D.C.: American Association of State Colleges and Universities, 1995.

National Alliance of Business. "Workforce Economics." *Workforce Trends,* 1996, *2*(4), 8.

National Association of State Universities and Land Grant Colleges. *For Every Dollar Invested.* Washington, D.C.: Office of Public Affairs,

National Association of State Universities and Land Grant Colleges, 1996a.

National Association of State Universities and Land Grant Colleges. *National Association of State Universities and Land Grant Colleges Newsline,* 1996b, *5*(9), 4.

National Association of State Universities and Land Grant Colleges. *National Association of State Universities and Land Grant Colleges Newsline,* 1997a, *6*(1), 4.

National Association of State Universities and Land Grant Colleges. *National Association of State Universities and Land Grant Colleges Newsline,* 1997b, 6(4), 6–8.

National Center for Education Statistics, U.S. Department of Education. *The Condition of Education: 1996.* Report 96–304. Washington, D.C.: Government Printing Office, 1996a.

National Center for Education Statistics, U.S. Department of Education. *The Pocket Condition, 1996.* Report 96–305. Washington, D.C.: Government Printing Office, 1996b.

National Commission on Excellence in Education. *A Nation at Risk.* Washington, D.C.:. U.S. Government Printing Office, 1983.

Office of Educational Research and Improvement. *Office of Educational Research and Improvement Bulletin.* Washington, D.C.: U.S. Department of Education, 1996.

Office of Policy Development and Research. *University-Community Partnerships.* Washington, D.C.: U.S. Department of Housing and Urban Development, Oct. 1996.

Oviatt, T. "America the Beautiful." *Hispanic Outlook,* Jan. 1997, *7*(12), 7–9.

Pascarella, E. T., and Terenzini, P. T. *How College Affects Students: Findings and Insights from Twenty Years of Research.* San Francisco: Jossey-Bass, 1991.

Pelton, J. *Future Talk.* Boulder, Colo.: Cross Communications, 1990.

Perkins, J. A. *The University in Transition.* Princeton, N.J.: Princeton University Press, 1965.

Peterson, M. W., and Dill, D. D. "Understanding the Competitive Environment of the Postsecondary Knowledge Industry." In M. W. Peterson, D. D. Dill, L. A. Mets, and Associates, *Planning and Management for a Changing Environment.* San Francisco: Jossey-Bass, 1997.

Peterson, M. W., Dill, D. D., Mets, L. A., and Associates. *Planning and Management for a Changing Environment.* San Francisco: Jossey-Bass, 1997.

Pew Higher Education Research Program. *Policy Perspectives,* Apr. 1996, 6(4), 6.

Pfeffer, J. *Managing with Power.* Boston: Harvard Business School Press, 1992.

Piederit, J. J. "Where Universities Have Gone Wrong." *Wall Street Journal,* July 30, 1996, editorial page.

Ravenche, H. J. "How Trustees Can Firm Up Corporate Alliances." *Trusteeship,* Nov./Dec. 1996, *4*(6), 16–21.

Richardson, W. C. "Coming in from the Cold War." Speech to the National Association of State Universities and Land Grant Colleges, Washington, D.C., Jan. 1996a.

Richardson, W. C. "A New Calling for Higher Education." Oswald Lecture presented at Pennsylvania State University, University Park, Mar. 25, 1996b.

Ringle, M., and Smallen, D. "Can Small Colleges Afford to Be Technology Leaders? Can They Afford Not to Be?" *Proceedings,* CAUSE 95. New Orleans, Nov.–Dec. 1995.

Rivera, J. "Is There a Doctor in the Class?" *Hispanic Outlook,* Dec. 1996, *7*(11), 5–6.

Rost, J. C. *Leadership for the Twenty-First Century.* New York: Praeger, 1993.

Rothblatt, S. "An Historical Perspective on the University's Role in Social Development." In D. Dill and B. Sporn (eds.), *Emerging Patterns of Social Demand and University Reform.* New York: Pergamon Press, 1995.

Rowley, D. J., Lujan, H. D., and Dolence, M. G. *Strategic Change in Colleges and Universities: Planning to Survive and Prosper.* San Francisco: Jossey-Bass, 1997.

Rudenstine, N. L. "The Internet and Education." *Chronicle of Higher Education,* Feb. 1997, *43*(24), A48.

Ruscio, K. P. "The Distinctive Scholarship of the Selective Liberal Arts College." *Journal of Higher Education,* Mar./Apr. 1987, *58*(2), 205–222.

Scott, J. W. "Defending the Tradition of Shared Governance." *Chronicle of Higher Education,* Aug. 1996, *42*(48), 13–14.

Seymour, D. "The Baldrige in Education." *American Association for Higher Education Bulletin,* Apr. 1996, *48*(8), 9–14.

Shane, H. G. "Britain's University of the Air." *Futurist,* July/Aug. 1989.

Smith, P. *Killing the Spirit.* New York: Viking Penguin, 1990.

Stewart, H. M. "OLAP/EIS Tops Off the Data Warehouse." *CAUSE/EFFECT,* 1996, *18*(3), 47–48.

Stinson, D. "An Era of Stability and Economic Growth Leads to a Boom in Peruvian Higher Education." *Chronicle of Higher Education,* Dec. 1996, *43*(17), A37–A38.

TERI (The Education Resources Institute). *Life After Forty.* Washington, D.C.: Institute for Higher Education Policy, 1996.

Terrell, S. "From Teaching to Learning: Transition in Distance Education." Paper presented at Intercom '96, Miami, Fla. 1996.

Thurow, L. C. "The New Economics of High Technology." *Harper's,* Mar. 1992, *284*(1702), 15–19.

Trachtenberg, S. J. "Preparing for 'Baby Boomers.'" *Chronicle of Higher Education,* Mar. 1997, *43*(28), B7.

Trani, E. P. "Creating a Broader Model of Shared Governance." *Chronicle of Higher Education,* Jan. 1997, *43*(18), A72.

Tratjenberg, M., Henderson, R., and Jaffe, A. "Ivory Towers Versus Corporate Lab." Working Paper No. 4146. Cambridge, Mass.: National Bureau of Economic Research, 1992.

Travis, J. "Community Cores: The Future Community College Campus." Paper presented at the annual convention of the American Association of Community Colleges, Minneapolis, Minn., April 1995.

Treisman, U. "A Study of the Mathematical Performance of Black Students at the University of California at Berkeley." Unpublished doctoral dissertation, Department of Mathematics, University of California, Berkeley, 1985.

Trombley, W. "Back to the '60s." *Crosstalk,* Oct. 1996a, *4*(3), 7–8.

Trombley, W. "Florida Gulf Coast University," *Crosstalk,* Oct. 1996b, *4*(3), 1, 5–6.

Tugend, A. "In Britain, Research Assessments Can Make or Break a University's Reputation." *Chronicle of Higher Education,* Feb. 1997, *43*(25), A48.

University of Florida. *Measuring University Performance: Costs.* Issue 2(6). Gainesville: Office of Institutional Research, University of Florida, 1996. Pamphlet.

van Vught, F. "The New Context for Academic Quality." In D. D. Dill and B. Sporn (eds.), *Emerging Patterns of Social Demand and University Reform.* New York: Pergamon Press, 1995.

Virginia Commission on the University of the Twenty-First Century. *The Case for Change.* Richmond: Virginia State Council of Higher Education, 1989.

Walker, D. "U of Cambridge Plans Expansion." *Chronicle of Higher Education,* Feb. 1997, *43*(22), A47.

Wechsler, H. (ed.). *National Education Association (NEA) 1996 Almanac of Higher Education.* Washington, D.C.: National Education Association, 1996.

Weinstein, L. A. *Moving a Battleship with Your Bare Hands.* Madison, Wis.: Magna, 1993.

Western Governors Association. "Governors' Goals for a Western Virtual

University." In *From Vision to Reality.* Denver: Western Governors Association, 1996.

Western Interstate Commission for Higher Education (WICHE). *Exploring the Relationship: A Survey of the Literature on Higher Education and the Economy.* Boulder, Colo.: Western Interstate Commission for Higher Education, 1992a.

Western Interstate Commission for Higher Education (WICHE). *Meeting Economic and Social Challenges: A Strategic Agenda for Higher Education.* Boulder, Colo.: Western Interstate Commission for Higher Education, 1992b.

Western Interstate Commission for Higher Education (WICHE). "Summary of April 8, 1996 Kick–Off Meeting on Virtual University Organization and Governance." [http://wga-internet.west.cov.org/smart/vun/orgmtg.htm]. 1996.

Western Interstate Commission for Higher Education (WICHE). "AT&T Grant Boosts Western Governors' 'Bold' Educational Project." *News, Western Cooperative for Educational Telecommunications.* [http://www.wiche.edu/telecom/news/newswguatt.htm]. 1997.

Wheeler, D. L. "Caltech's Motley Crew." *Chronicle of Higher Education,* Feb. 1997, *43*(24), A12–A13.

Will, G. "Higher Education Takes More, Offers Less." *Rocky Mountain News,* Mar. 24, 1996, editorial page.

Williams, G. "The 'Marketization' of Higher Education." In D. D. Dill and B. Sporn (eds.), *Emerging Patterns of Social Demand and University Reform.* New York: Pergamon Press, 1995.

Wilshire, B. *The Moral Collapse of the University.* Albany: State University of New York Press, 1990.

Wilson, D. L. "At UCLA, Big Plans for Using Technology." *Chronicle of Higher Education,* May 1996, *42*(40), A25, A29.

Young, L. T. "Academic Computing in the Year 2000." *Academic Computing,* 1988, *2*(7), 8–12, 62–65.

⟿ Index